IN SWEET *Company*

CONVERSATIONS
WITH EXTRAORDINARY WOMEN
ABOUT LIVING A SPIRITUAL LIFE

MARGARET WOLFF

D0055128

JOSSEY-BASS
A Wiley Imprint
www.josseybass.com

Published by Jossey-Bass
A Wiley Imprint
989 Market Street, San Francisco, CA 94103–1741   www.josseybass.com

Jossey-Bass books and products are available through most bookstores. To contact Jossey-Bass directly call our Customer Care Department within the U.S. at 800-956-7739, outside the U.S. at 317-572-3986, or fax 317-572-4002.

Jossey-Bass also publishes its books in a variety of electronic formats. Some content that appears in print may not be available in electronic books.

Cover art: "Joyfull Dance," 2001 by Diana Ong, Diana Ong/Superstock
Book design by Carla Green

Library of Congress Cataloging-in-Publication Data
Wolff, Margaret.
    In sweet company: conversations with extraordinary women about living a spiritual life / Margaret Wolff.—1st ed.
        p. cm.
Originally published: San Diego, CA: Margaret Wolff Unlimited, 2002.
Includes index.
ISBN-13: 978-0-7879-8338-3 (alk. paper)
ISBN-10: 0-7879-8338-1 (alk. paper)
1. Women—Religious life.   2. Spiritual biography.   I. Title.
BL625.7.W58 2006
204'.092'2—dc22
2005021212

Printed in the United States of America
FIRST EDITION
PB Printing   10 9 8 7 6 5 4 3 2 1

IN SWEET
Company

CONTENTS

This book is dedicated to four who came before me.
Your lives compelled me to unearth my real Self,
to honor my must needs, to speak and stand in Truth
then lay everything else at the feet of God.
I am grateful beyond words.

PREFACE

Many years ago, I came across a quote that to this day continues to claim me, continues to lift my heart to new understanding whenever I am in the presence of something beautiful. I can no longer recall its exact words, but the marrow of the quote is this: A painting has many lives, those lived by everyone who loves the piece and the life the artist lived as the piece was created. This applies, I believe, to other forms of artistic expression, including books, and certainly to the book you hold in your hands.

The life this book lived when I began writing it was primal and parched. It tottered daily—sometimes moment to moment—on the brink of extinction, dependent on my tenuous ability to navigate the lingering hallmarks of an auto accident that did irreparable damage to my brain. Despite its improbable genesis, *In Sweet Company* ripened into maturity. Though it gave my life meaning and purpose, I often wondered whether something that burned as bright in me as any sun would also live in others.

It had never been my intention to self-publish *In Sweet Company,* but in the wake of 9/11—wanting as everyone did to help—I petitioned for guidance, for a way I might ease the pain. My inner directive to self-publish the book took me through a labyrinth of printers and artists until it was finally birthed in fitful batches of e-mails to a small coterie of colleagues and friends.

It was my habit to pray before I undertook any activity related to *In Sweet Company;* to pray before I wrote, before I made a phone call, before I sent an e-mail, and especially before I got on a plane. As the last cluster of e-mails floated into cyberspace, I suddenly realized I had forgotten to precede this launch with a prayer. I gasped in horror and then listened in awe as my inner conciliator declared, "The book never belonged to you in the first place, Margaret. Now it belongs to the whole world."

Since that night three years ago, *In Sweet Company* has been loved into the world by thousands of women and men. I have met some of its readers in the retreats I now lead based on the book, at conferences where I speak, and in e-mails I receive telling me how the book has prompted readers to nurture their inner lives and inspired them to face their outer challenges. *In Sweet Company* has been passed down through families, through generations of women and their husbands and sons to show them, in the words of one man, "what real women are about." It has been read by women on death row, women in shelters, women in hospices, and by women who, after 9/11, were left to raise their children alone. It is used as a text in women's studies programs, read in book clubs, and has been the subject of articles and workshops created by writers and trainers other than myself. *In Sweet Company* has had many very good lives.

One morning last February, I awoke with the words "Jossey-Bass" pealing in my head. I contacted Margaret Wheatly, one of the women profiled in these pages, thinking Jossey-Bass was her publisher, and asked if she knew of someone there I could talk with. It turned out that Meg published with another company, but her editor had recently worked with Jossey-Bass and was happy to connect me with Sheryl Fullerton, a colleague for whom she had great regard. I queried Sheryl and sent her a book. Six weeks later, she called to say she wanted to publish it.

Midway through our conversation, Sheryl asked what had prompted me to approach Jossey-Bass. I hesitated for a moment, and then Sheryl said, "It's OK, Margaret. You can tell me." So I did.

"Margaret," she said softly, "One of the women profiled in your book is Miriam Polster. Did you know that our spiritual book division was founded by Sarah Polster, Miriam's daughter?" I did not.

Both Miriam and her daughter passed away before *In Sweet Company* was published. Maybe yes, maybe no, but I like to think that somehow, thanks to them and to you, dear reader, this little book will live many more inspired lives.

Margaret Wolff
San Diego, California
January 2006

IN SWEET COMPANY

We sit together and I tell you things,
Silent, unborn, naked things
That only my God has heard me say.
You do not cluck your tongue at me
Or roll your eyes
Or split my heart into a thousand thousand pieces
With words that have little to do with me.
You do not turn away because you cannot bear to see
Your own unclaimed light shining in my eyes.
You stay with me in the dark.
You urge me into being.
You make room in your heart for my voice.
You rejoice in my joy.
And through it all, you stand unbound
By everything but the still, small Voice within you.
I see my future Self in you
Just enough to risk
Moving beyond the familiar,
Just enough to leave
The familiar in the past where it belongs.
I breathe you in and I breathe you out
In one luxurious and contented sigh.
In sweet company
I am home at last.

—Margaret Wolff

INTRODUCTION

For me there is only traveling on the paths that have heart, on any path that may have heart. There I travel, and the only worthwhile challenge is to traverse its full length. And there I travel, looking, looking, breathlessly.
—Carlos Castenada

This book is about what it means to be a spiritual woman in the twenty-first century. It is about connectedness to God by any name, and connectedness to other, including Self. It is about the depth and breadth and height a soul can actually reach even in an age where global technology and Wall Street reign fairly uncontested.

Though *In Sweet Company* is about women's lives, it is not just a book for or about women. Specifically, *In Sweet Company* is an affirmation of what is possible, a demonstration of what individuals and society at large can learn from women, particularly women who are deeply committed to living with meaning and integrity.

Some of the reasons I decided to write *In Sweet Company* were obvious to me from its inception: a fascination with what people think, a desire to learn from other women, and a yearning to know things that would fill my heart with gratitude. I began working on the book sixteen months after a momentary encounter with an oncoming car left me with enough brain damage to definitively blunt the interior processes that had previously ordered my thinking. I lost 80 percent of my peripheral vision and much of my ability to process and communicate information in a linear fashion. When I went out, if I went out, I almost always cupped my hands over my eyes to reduce the input of stimuli into my visual field. I got lost in neighborhoods that I'd once known like the back of my hand. I frequently stuttered. It wasn't pretty. In spite of a diagnosis that I would never again regain my former level of function, I intuitively knew that my healing depended, to a large degree, on my ability to keep my mind focused on something positive, something that inspired me. So along with the help of some very innovative therapies—and though I couldn't string a paragraph together to save my soul—I also wrote this book as a means to carve new pathways in my brain, to restore function and order and meaning to my life.

What I did not know when I cast my net out on these waters was that writing *In Sweet Company* would be, for me, a life-transforming experience. It was not just the richness of these conversations that re-made me, though each conversation took me deeply within myself. Rather, it was that I felt called to conduct the entire project with "spiritual impeccability," to *become* my best work as well as *do* my best work. Once this mandate became clear to me, I strove to respond to anyone having anything to do with the book with kindness and respect. I grappled with and affirmed choices that supported my artistic vision and my own personal boundaries, yet made every effort to remain open to the potential in each suggestion that came my way. I asked hard questions—of myself as well as the women I talked with—about things that were unique to each situation and very specific to life because I *really* wanted answers. I sought guidance at every turn, often proceeded on sheer faith—sometimes boldly, sometimes not. The process so nourished and expanded me that I now see no other option for myself than to conduct my entire life in this manner. In some inexplicable and beautiful way, this book became the mentor I had always hoped to find.

In India, it is the custom to *pronam* when greeting another, to gently touch the palms of the hands together at the level of the heart and slowly, reverently bow the head until fingertips touch forehead. In essence, this ancient gesture means "my soul bows to your soul" or "the God in me bows to the God in you." *In Sweet Company* has also been like a perennial *pronam* for me. Every woman I talked with filled me with awe and confidence at what one individual, no matter what her path or process, can actualize inside herself and accomplish in the world when she connects her life to Something Greater. Even me.

Being with the fourteen women featured in this book—during our initial conversations and then keeping company with them intellectually and emotionally as I edited their words—answered many questions I had about myself, my life, and my own spiritual search. Each woman shared her God with me and, as a result, I moved closer to my own. For that alone, I am immeasurably grateful. The intimate nature of the subject matter and every woman's facility to authentically share her life, at times, shape-shifted our conversations and turned the interview process into a dynamic and reciprocal relationship. Giving these women a forum to talk about their lives also connected me more deeply with my own voice, with my own ability to speak and act from Truth as I know it—both when I was with them and forever afterward. Everything I learned as a result of being with them became part of me and got used again and again and again. I am far, far better for knowing these women. As you read their words, I trust you will be as well. Therein lies the importance of sharing our stories with each other.

Living a spiritual life may look different on the outside, but on the inside there are communal threads that weave us together in majestic tapestry. Gandhi once said, "God has no religion." Neither does a heart filled with Spirit. Faith is a universal, inner experience that is not dependent on one external doctrine. Though I knew this when I began writing *In Sweet Company*, thanks to these women, I now believe it with every fiber of my being.

Unlike any other species on Earth, human beings can transform the circumstances of our lives in profound and meaningful ways by what we choose to think—and then do. Change our thoughts and we change our lives. Change our inner reality and we change our outer reality. Though it is seldom easy to alter one's thoughts or actions, the primary significance of making such a change—and doing it consciously—is that the process makes you aware that your life is a construct that is, in the final reckoning, determined by you alone.

While we will never be able to change everything that happens to us, we can change how we *respond* to what happens to us, just as the women in this book have done. Each of us must claim the power to do this for ourselves. If we are to be fierce about something in our lives, let it be that we do not let fear keep us from manifesting our own greatness, that we do not let God's will for us lie fallow. Wherever you are in your search for God, whatever path you walk, it is my fervent hope that reading *In Sweet Company* will, in some way, expand your thoughts and help you respond to your life in ways that build your confidence, deepen your peace, and bring you joy.

IN SWEET
Company

One
Sister Helen Prejean

Some day, after we have mastered the wind, the waves, the tide, and gravity, we shall harness the energies of love. Then, for the second time in the history of the world, man will have discovered fire.

—Pierre Teilhard de Chardin

ON A COLD day in January of 1982, Sister Helen Prejean had a brief conversation with a colleague from the Louisiana State Prison Coalition about becoming a pen pal to a man on death row, a convicted murderer named Patrick Sonnier. She was teaching high school dropouts at an inner city housing project in New Orleans at the time, with no experience working in prisons and little familiarity with the judicial and political systems that govern the life and death of the inmates. But she took Sonnier's address and sent him a letter. Little did she know that this simple act of kindness would eventually give rise to a personal and spiritual metamorphosis that, along the way, would include a Pulitzer Prize–nominated book, an Academy Award–winning movie, speaking engagements throughout the United States, Europe, and Japan, and the unleashing in her of a passion that is nothing short of inspired.

The root word for inspiration in Greek, *inspiro*, means "to breathe into." Being Sonnier's spiritual advisor and walking with him to his execution, meeting his family and the families of his victims, interacting with the prison officials and politicians who orchestrated his death, all breathed a fire into her that now defines her every thought and action. When her book, *Dead Man Walking*, was released, it hit the *New York Times* bestseller list almost immediately and remained there for eight months. It also catalyzed advocates on both sides of America's system of capital punishment and became an extraordinary example of the power of unconditional love.

I first became aware of Sister Helen's work with death row inmates in 1995, when Tim Robbins's film based on her book was released. I was glad to know she was doing this work. It was important and necessary, I believed. But I kept my distance from the film, even after it won an Academy Award. Though I did not know it then, I came to understand that my reticence was not all that uncommon, that many people keep her work at arm's length for one reason or another. My reserve did not, however, prevent her name from entering my consciousness like a meteor descending to Earth as I sat at my desk one morning four years later musing about women to talk with for this book. Once her name came to me, I intuitively knew she would contribute to the project. I was, however, still eight months away from realizing exactly how she would contribute to my life.

Finding her was relatively easy; as was making a connection with Sister Margaret, her assistant and the guardian of her schedule. I would come to look forward to the sound of Sister Margaret's syrupy Louisiana drawl and self-effacing humor in the months and phone calls ahead. But on the day I first talked with her, she told me only how busy Sister Helen was—and not to get my hopes up.

I faxed Sister Margaret some information about this book as soon as we got off the phone, but it took several months until she could present it to Sister Helen, and several more months until Sister Helen was even able to read it. Once she agreed to talk with me, her presence infused everything I did to prepare for our conversation.

❖ ❖ ❖ ❖ ❖

ON A SUNNY January morning, I drive to Newport Beach, California, an affluent community about fifty miles north of my home outside of San Diego, to meet with Sister Helen. She has flown to California early that morning and will fly out early the next, criss-crossing the country at an unremitting pace to talk with church groups, college students, politicos, and so forth—audiences of varying sizes, backgrounds, and degrees of receptivity. I will meet her at the convent where she is staying, resting I am told, during the few precious hours she has before she will address the parishioners at Our Lady Queen of Angels Roman Catholic Church. I arrive in Newport Beach early, grab a quick lunch, then make my way through the cordons of elegant communities to the address I have been given.

I have not seen the film yet, but I have read her book. I know that she is a member of the Sisters of St. Joseph of Medaille, a community of Catholic women living and working in her native Louisiana. I know that in 1965, after Vatican II, she exchanged her habit and a semi-cloistered life for street clothes and active participation in the social justice movement, and that she worked in the St. Thomas Housing Projects in Baton Rouge for four years before meeting Sonnier. But nothing I've read prepares me for the real thing, for the vital, dynamic woman in her mid-sixties who opens the door and enfolds me in her arms in greeting. She is short and compact; solid like granite. Her embrace opens me, like the man in the parable about the north wind and the sun who bares himself in response to the sun's warmth.

She is easy to be around from the get-go. "Well come on in, Mahgrut," she drawls in her Bayou-laden voice, and escorts me into the living room. "I'll be with you in a minute. I'm on the phone with some folks back East, and as soon as I finish up with them, I'm all yours." From these few moments of greeting, I know that she will be all mine—that every moment she is with you, no matter who you are, she is always all yours.

I sit on a long beige couch, my back to a large picture window that looks out into the front yard, set up my recording equipment, and wait for her to join me. By the end of the day, I will discover that it's easy to forget she's a nun but never that she is a woman who loves God. She laughs easily and frequently throughout our time together and enjoys it when I laugh with her. She's a Southern storyteller—informal, funny, and unpretentious. Gradually, lovingly, she accompanies me, and all her listeners, toward the heart of her message: "What if each of us were judged solely by the worst thing we ever did in our lives?" she asks. "While I do not condone violence, I do advocate compassion. While I cannot imagine the grief of losing a loved one to violent crime, I also could not bear the pain of living with revenge in my heart. And while it is important to feel safe—as a society and as an individual—each of us must decide for ourselves how to translate outrage into mercy."

Sister Helen finishes her phone call and strides into the room. She sits down opposite me on the couch near the microphone. "Let's do it!" she says. I start our conversation by asking her to tell me about her Order. She talks about its beginning in 1650 in France, then tells me about the tenets on which it was founded.

"Our charism is very broad and has to do with connecting people with people and people with God. Inevitably, as part of this process, we come face to face with all sorts of human wounds, all the painful experiences that separate human beings from each other and from God. Reconciliation and healing need to happen in order for people to move beyond their suffering, so this too, is part of our charism.

"Community also plays an important role in our work. Individualism implies that it's up to one person to get the job done. Community means we stand present together. We recognize that none of us have all the gifts necessary to bring about reconciliation on our own."

Is there a Golden Rule that guides you?

"Our Sisters are rooted in the Gospels, but there are two maxims that mean a great deal to us. The first is 'Never leap ahead of grace, but wait for grace and quietly follow with the gentleness of the spirit of God.' This means that I don't ever have to get cerebral and lay out an elaborate blueprint about how events should proceed. Nor do I have to try to coerce things into happening or push for answers. There's no tension or stress, no anxious anticipation or grasping for control, because I have an organic sense that I will know what to do when the time comes to do it. I simply wait and watch for grace to unfold like the petals of a flower. There is an energy, a dynamic, and a passion in doing this that I could never willfully mandate or create intellectually."

Her statement is in direct opposition to the dictum that guides my paternal gene pool, the infamous words "Is everything under control?" It's familial code for finding out if the other is safe—or reliable—but it also became a subliminal directive about how to live in an unpredictable, sometimes chaotic world. I'm on intimate terms with the pitfalls of this approach, having taken up my ancestral banner and waved it for many years from the rafters of my subconscious. I've been actively reprogramming the premature leaping and grasping Sister Helen now describes, learning to be more comfortable with not knowing. Having tasted a modicum of success, I recognize the validity of her words immediately and nod my head in agreement as she speaks. Her eyes warm to my response.

"The merit of this approach became particularly clear to me once I started to visit Patrick Sonnier on death row," she says. "I had no special training for being the spiritual advisor to a man condemned to die, no idea where the relationship would take me, and no plan about how to proceed. But God makes a way out of no way. By remaining present to Pat, I learned what to do to help him. I received everything I needed to know about how to be with him—and more.

"Another maxim our Sisters follow is to be a congregation of the great love of God, to be a group of women who love. This may sound like a cliché, like teddy bears and candy hearts, but there is a warmth and love among our Sisters that I find very appealing and that translates into the ability to work for people's good, to be present to those who are suffering."

When you're *in* Love, I say, in the manifestation of God as Love, it's so full and rich that you don't want to be anywhere else.

"Exactly!" she says, and I see the schoolteacher in her come alive. "Being in Love is beyond trying to make things happen. It's beyond willing or intention, beyond goal-setting and strategizing. None of that is the language of Love.

"This doesn't mean that Love doesn't get itself organized when it needs to or that Love lacks the discipline to do what's required to make things happen—especially when you're dealing with economics and social injustice. Loving is always about being in the presence of a wellspring that carries you. It transcends who you are."

Is this how you would define spirituality?

"I think spirituality means that the way you live, move, and have your being comes forth out of the depth of Spirit, out of the resonant depths of life, instead of from anything compartmentalized—or mechanistic or cerebral. It's not determined from the outside. It's an inner fire and passion.

"For me, spirituality is grounded in the Christian paradigm of Jesus and the way he touched people, the way he loved and included people— especially the most marginalized. It's about the ways in which I am for you. It's very broad and deep. It's challenging. It stretches and beckons you. It's not settled in or domesticated."

Domesticated?

"Yes, living a terrarium existence, one that's defined by specific perimeters you don't go beyond. Being domesticated is about staying in familiar territory because you're afraid of change or afraid that you might get hurt.

"Jesus said, 'Launch into the deep and you'll have the stars and you'll have the currents of the water which you will learn to read.' We have to move beyond our comfort zone and trust we'll be shown the way.

"There's a lot in our society that separates us from each other. We're afraid of the poor, we're afraid of different races, so we live segregated lives. Martin Luther King used to say that the most segregated hour of the week was 11:00 A.M. on Sunday morning when everyone was tucked inside their own church. We must excavate ourselves from our terrariums and be present to others, especially those who are different than we are."

This self-excavation you speak of is a lot of work. How do you stay energized to meet the challenge?

"I renew in quietness, meditation, prayer, and contemplation. Renewal feeds action; it's like the inhalation and exhalation of breathing. Re-energizing and contemplation also happen in the presence of the people I serve. Some of my deepest spiritual moments occurred when I walked with Patrick Sonnier to his execution."

The image her words conjure up in my head is in such stark contrast to what I imagine my own behavior would be in this situation that I gasp. But Sister Helen is not aware of my response—or she lets it pass.

"Suddenly, all life was clear to me," she declares. "Was I going to be for love or for hate? Was I for compassion or was I for vengeance? The words of Jesus that welled up in me when I walked with Pat were, 'And the last shall be the first.' I understood this to mean that all life has value, even the lives that others want to throw away. The experience summoned me to a place of deep spiritual awareness and renewal I will never forget."

It was a defining moment. Your most essential questions were answered. It must have also brought you great peace.

"Absolutely, but it wasn't a quiescence where everything was still and unmoving. This peace was fierce and ever-unfolding, always unfinished. It's a peace born of the harmony of the different parts of ourselves. Surrender has a lot to do with it, saying 'Yes' to the Big Adventure, not acquiescing or giving up—launching the little boat of my life out into the deep, as Jesus said."

The afternoon sun has been blazing through the living room window and the back of my neck is getting sunburned. I rise, reach behind the couch, and tug at the drapery cord until the curtains come together *en masse*. As I go through this process, I think about how open and bold she is, how out-going and unconstrained. Everything about her is vibrant, almost electric—even this peace she now describes. She puts to rest any stereotypical images I have surreptitiously carried around in my head about Catholic nuns since my childhood. I'm curious about what precipitated her decision to become a nun. As I sit back down on the couch, I ask her about this.

"Precipitation probably implies too much of a cause-and-effect relationship," she says reflectively. "I think it was more of a dawning. I grew up in a loving Catholic family. My parents affirmed all their children and provided us with plenty of opportunities for personal growth. Daddy was a lawyer. From him I got the love of books, of articulation and debate. Mama was a nurse. From her I got compassion. We prayed together and said the Rosary every day. By the time I was in the sixth grade, I knew I wanted to be a teacher. The Sisters who taught me were so alive! They were funny and their faith made sense to me. I think it was born in me then that, though I'd seen a wonderful family life, there was also a way of loving where you didn't just marry one man and have one family. I wanted a wider sweep for my love, and religious life seemed to me to be the way to do that.

"When I entered the Order in 1957, nuns wore habits and lived a semi-cloistered life." The habit, she tells me, was a by-product of the repression of women in the Middle Ages. In order to have access to the people they served, nuns were forced to dress like widows, the only women permitted to walk the streets alone.

"The habit, the cloister, the long hours of prayer and silence, were formative years for me," she continues. "I developed an interior life. I learned to listen to my inner voice, to be receptive and at home with silence. When Vatican II occurred in 1965, we came out from behind our habits and the cloister and made ourselves more accessible to the people. For the next eleven years, I taught seventh and eighth grade English and was the director of religious education in a parish school. I loved the kids. It was like being in a room full of Alka Seltzers!"

I laugh out loud at the image her words evoke.

"I still feel that I'm a teacher," she says, "because teaching is about *educarè*, about opening things up, drawing forth or, as they say in Zen Buddhism, always having a beginner's mind. But now my classroom is big; it's the whole world." She smiles at the prospect.

"By 1980, there was a lot of fermentation going on within our community about how our Sisters should be more involved with the poor. I resisted this at first. I thought it was enough to be kind and charitable and pray for others. Some of the sisters had been active in the '60s and '70s, but not me. I wasn't ready to get involved. I just played my guitar," she says strumming the air, "and loved the children, while Martin Luther King and the others were blasted with fire hoses and sent to jail.

"That June, my community went to Terre Haute, Indiana, to discuss the direction of our work. Sister Marie Augusta Neal, a prominent Catholic sociologist and theologian, was the main speaker at the conference. The second day of her talk, she brought about a huge shift in the spiritual axis of my life."

Her eyes begin to dance. "I still remember the exact words she said that transformed me: 'Jesus preached Good News to the poor and integral to the Good News was that they would be poor no longer.' At that moment, I realized that social justice, reaching out to excluded people—the poor and the suffering—was essential to the Gospel of Jesus, and that the life I'd been leading was far removed from this experience. I knew then I had to make a change.

"I didn't have a plan. Once again, I just put my little boat out on the current and trusted I would be led to where I needed to be. I went out among the people, first in homeless shelters and then in the St. Thomas Housing Project in New Orleans. I learned from them and a passion was born in me; their suffering galvanized and transformed my heart. You can't be in the presence of people who are suffering, knowing that their pain is the result of an injustice, and still remain neutral. By the time I got the invitation to write to Pat, there was a readiness in me to do that. I'd been prepared for this by all the experiences that preceded it."

It takes guts to not leap ahead of grace at times like that, I say, to even trust that grace will carry you when order has not yet risen from the chaos. And faith. It also takes faith. Did you always believe in God? Have you always had such a deep faith?

"Oh, I don't know what it would be like not to believe in God. My image of God is always unfolding though."

She pauses for a moment, then asks me a question. "Have you read the Gospels?" She asks because she is curious to know whether or not I have a frame of reference for what she is about to say.

Some, I tell her.

"Well, it was in the Gospels that I began to see who Jesus was and how he loved, to see the wildness in him."

Her statement makes me grin. I frequently use this same word to describe someone who has a genuine and unyielding commitment to live from their true self. Her comment adds another dimension to my definition—that "wildness" can also be a spiritual *tour de force*.

"His wildness was born of a deep passion—one that was inclusive, but at the same time, it pushed all your boundaries. I think cultural Christianity tries to domesticate that wildness out of Jesus. It treats him like a French poodle—clips and paints his nails, puts a rhinestone collar around his neck and only walks him in certain places. It blesses executions and nuclear submarines in his name. It blesses an economic system that allows some people to get rich out of their minds while others live in poverty. Jesus said to forgive seven times seventy, to love even your enemies, to invite not just your friends but also the lame and the poor to your banquet. God is a living, emanating center that is loving, not a controlled or controlling vengeful force that wants pain and separatism."

There is a mixture of reverence and indignation in her voice, a cool burn that both challenges and sustains her. I'm curious if she had any mentors who helped formulate her thinking early on.

"In the beginning, it was my mother. In high school, it was Sister Alice Marie—she was always pushing the edge, reading the latest theology book and challenging us to learn—and Sister Jane Louise. She was more contemplative and gave me books about Saint Therese of Liseaux to read.

"In college, I read Bernard Herring, who took the whole of moral law, so compartmentalized by the Catholic Church, and put it into the context of love, and Gregory Baum, who wrote about the ongoingness of the experience of God, the freshness and continuing revelation of God in our lives. These two theologians had a tremendous impact on me.

"After my meeting with Sister Marie Augusta Neil, she became an important mentor to me. And once she opened me up, I started to devour Martin Luther King, Dorothy Day, Gandhi—all the great proponents of nonviolence and social transformation.

"The new edge for me now is Thomas Berry's new cosmology, his ideas of a self-emerging universe and the importance of loving the Earth. I know my mission is to stop the killing of humans, to stop the death penalty and help victims' families heal. Thanks to Berry, I now see this within a larger context, that nothing on Earth, including the Earth, should be hurt or maimed or killed."

She tells me that she recently spent time with the Northern Cheyenne Indians in Montana to learn more about how to make a connection to the Earth. She talks about being in their Prayer Lodge, about saying her name to the Four Directions to greet the spirits that reside there, and then recalling her name when her visit ends. "It's a new way to experience communion," she says, and a great calm comes over her. "It feels so right."

These new connections seem as if they have deepened your faith. In *Dead Man Walking*, you wrote that the faith of your childhood was about "a personal relationship with God, inner peace, kindness to others, and heaven when this life is done." What characterizes your faith now, the faith of your midlife?

"Making love present in the world and letting love be in my life. What counts now is being with people, especially with those people who are most excluded—death row inmates and their families.

"The word 'love' is so bandied about today, but love is the most powerful energy in the world. It's so important to unleash it. To be present to the dignity of the forgotten, to recognize the beauty of the scarred and maimed, draws forth their goodness and self-respect in a way that nothing else can.

"It isn't just that I lavish love on them," she says. "The deepest gifts are always mutual. I've received so much from the men I've accompanied. It's not an extrinsic reward. Being with them has summoned forth my own dignity and gifts I never knew I had. It's been a tremendous grace in my life." She sighs and rests for a moment in the quiet.

"When I was younger, I prayed for people in the world, but I was praying for people I felt no connection to. It was almost like my dipstick didn't hit the oil!"

I laugh.

"I am *so* grateful to be awake now. I could have gone my whole life and never really known what the power of love can do, how it can enlighten me and others."

Her eyes well up. Mine too. We smile at each other. I wait in the silence for a moment before I ask my next question.

You wrote that witnessing Sonnier's death was like a second baptism for you. Obviously, the direction of your outer work changed. How did the experience affect your interior life?

There is a palpable energy shift in the room, the deepening that happens when a conversation centers around the inner workings of a life. There is no hesitation in her voice, no self-consciousness. She shares herself freely.

"It focused all my energies," she says. "I had become a witness to a story that needed to be told. Though I didn't know how I would do it, I knew I had to play my part in bringing what I'd seen to the world so we could stop the killing. I had a mandate. From that point on, I knew I would not scatter my energies—I would not spend my time doing anything, attend any meetings, that were not about essential things, about solving the problems of those who were suffering.

"Pat's death also taught me about spiritual resistance. I could no longer sit around and wait for things to change. I had a responsibility to act, to take a moral stand. Gandhi said that we have to actively resist what is evil. We have to expose evil. Otherwise people who don't know what's really going on buy into it.

"My experience with Pat also helped me develop compassion for my audiences, for the people who listen to my story. When I share what happened to me, I am very generous in telling my stories because I take my listeners to places they have not been and connect them with people they would not otherwise meet. I don't preach or beat anybody over the head. I trust the audience to reflect on what they've heard and then do with it what they can."

I've noticed this throughout our conversation but it becomes particularly obvious to me at the lecture she delivers later that night at the church. I sit alone near the front of the sanctuary after having spent the day with her, wondering if anyone in the room even realizes they will have an experience they may not soon forget. She jokes with us and tells us about the mistakes she made when she began this work. She tells us about her fear of facing the families of Sonnier's victims and her concerns about her ability to help Sonnier—weaving the light and dark, the warp and weft of her experience, with skill and grace. The audience relaxes, our hearts and minds open, the lids of our individual terrariums lift a little. Her stories make witnesses of the parishioners of Our Lady Queen of Angels Roman Catholic Church. Some day, they too, may have a story to tell. Maybe it won't be about working with death row inmates. Maybe they will feel called to help at a homeless shelter or to stand by a friend in need. Maybe they won't do anything at all.

Sister Helen and I talk about this very thing earlier that afternoon, about how it's not easy for some of us to heed this kind of call because we lack experience with those who are suffering or because we're afraid, for any number of reasons, to act on what we believe. So we accept the status quo. Or we drift. Or we ignore and deny.

"Conformity and obedience," she says. "That's where it comes from. Do what you're told. Never get angry. Don't ruffle any feathers. These are the internal messages that hold us back. We have to learn to form our own opinions and trust our own perceptions. Especially women. Without this, we have no ethical independence."

There's not a trace of judgment in her voice. She knows firsthand about the barriers that keep us each from pushing the lids off of our airtight terrariums.

"It's not that people aren't good or kind. We're all struggling with something. Most of us just operate the best we can within our terrarium. We can, however, blast the top off that terrarium and change. Witnessing the suffering of another human being was for me the transformative experience, the beginning of my passion for justice. I try to give others that experience through my stories so they can have a wider context to operate from, so they too can venture forth."

Venture physically and emotionally?

"Yes. If you're not meeting people who are different than you are, you will believe every stereotypical thing you hear about them."

You write frankly about the appalling conditions in the prisons, the inequities in the criminal justice system, the sorrow and rage of the victims' families, the humiliation of the prisoners' families, and the terror of the men you walk to their death. What sustains you in the face of such violence and despair? How do you keep from getting pulled down by it?

She looks me square in the eyes. "It goes back to the ability to be present with people. When I accompany these inmates to their death, I leave myself—even my fear—behind. I'm totally focused on them. It's the same thing when I sit with the victims' families. I'm not thinking about myself at all.

"Each person I'm with needs something different and I have to be attentive to what that is. Dobie, another man I accompanied to execution, needed me to be his coach. He was very scared. In those last hours of his life, I said things to him like, 'Dobie, you're about to do the bravest thing you've ever done. Jesus is here with you and you will have all you need to get through. I'm here with you, too.' I took him moment by moment to his death, keeping him focused in the present every step along the way.

"After an execution, I thaw out. That's when I get in touch with the horror of it all. But when it's happening, I'm so drawn out of myself that I don't feel my own feelings. Each time, I seem to be moving in a circle of light. God's grace is there. Strength is there. I have what I need to do what I must do."

I start to commend her courage, but she holds her hand up and stops my words in midair. "I never use that word about myself. I'm only doing what love requires. Love dignifies people. Execution is such a shameful, stigmatizing thing. The message these men get is that they are disposable human waste, human trash. It's not a time to be silent. I don't intrude, but I do provide a presence that's there as they need me. Love carries me through. That's what sustains me."

Is this something you consciously think about doing beforehand or is it something you move into when the time is right?

"I move into it. Having walked with five inmates to their execution, I now know what to expect. There's a readiness in me to move into that circle of light. It's unlike anything I experience anywhere else. Time absolutely stops and yet it absolutely races."

As she talks, I feel myself slipping into that rarefied place within that wraps me in stillness like a babe in swaddling clothes. For just a brief moment, I have a sense of what she is talking about—the strength and safety and comfort that fuel her ability to do the work she does. I look at her and smile. She tells me how much she is enjoying our conversation, and I well up. "I'm so glad," I say quietly. I wipe my eyes and ask my next question.

One of the things that so moved me in your book was the way you confronted every criticism hurled at you about your involvement with these men, how you examined yourself with unblinking honesty, how you did not subordinate your conscience or sense of self in the face of the pressure to back down. How were you able to keep from giving in to what others thought you should do? To not feel hurt?

"None of that criticism touched me. It was as if the words just pinged off me. I had been in this white hot crucible of seeing these men executed and their suffering was almost like a shield. I also knew that what my critics were saying was not really about me personally; they were acting out of their own pain. I was sensitive to the comments about not reaching out to the victims' families because there was truth in that. I'd been afraid to confront them in the beginning, afraid I would be overwhelmed by their grief and anger, afraid of their rejection. To be in the presence of people who are in that much pain and know I'd added to their pain, caused me great turmoil. But I knew I would change that, that I would never again be with anyone on death row without first contacting the victims' families. They almost always reject my help. They can't understand how I can be for the person who killed their loved one and also be for them. But I reach out anyway."

She takes a minute to reflect. "You asked me earlier about my definition of spirituality. I think spirituality is also about the reconciliation of opposites. It's about diving deep inside yourself beyond the polarities to a place of unity where everything holds together."

It's holistic.

"It's very holistic. Initially, it seems as if you have to choose one thing or another; if you're against executions you must also be against victims' families. But that's not true. When you operate out of the wounded places within yourself, places that are not your truest, the extremes seem irreconcilable. Life is too deep for cynicism or polarization. It just is. Compassion enables you to transcend these polarities at a place within yourself where you stand for the dignity of every human life."

Her words hit me like a ton of bricks. They are the answer to a paradox I've often wrestled with regarding self and other: When I operate out of the wounded places within myself, care of self and care of other seem irreconcilable. Move beyond my wounds, and beyond either/or, one-or-the-other. Stand for the dignity of every human being—even myself. There is no polarization in that; no decision to make. There is only unity, only Oneness, only Love.

Wow.

Have you ever been in a place where it seemed like there was no way out, no light at the end of the tunnel? Have you ever had a "dark night of the soul"?

"I've been in what St. Ignatius of Loyola calls 'desolation,' where I was confused, searching, agitated, and argumentative. That was after Vatican II, when I didn't yet have a big enough agenda for my soul. A big part of my compassion for my audiences is because I know what it's like to live removed from suffering people and the large issues of our day that call for social justice. I was forty years old before I understood that the Gospel of Jesus meant that getting involved is the way to transform the world.

"There are times when I get tired." She tells me about her schedule, where she's been and where she's yet to go in how many days. It's relentless. "And there were times when I was afraid. Sometimes I have moments when things seem futile. What steadies me though, is that I know my commitment and passion will not waiver—not because I'm willing it, but because I am so carried by it. I don't pull from my own resources. I have a fidelity to the men who looked in my eyes before they died. When you witness what I've witnessed, you don't forget it. Though it's been a struggle to watch them die and see these families suffer, it's also served to stoke my passion and augment my mission." After a pause, she says, "I don't think of darkness as a bad thing, though. We are conceived and swim in darkness until we are born. Darkness is fertile and fecund. It's a womb. It brings interiority."

And it helps you understand that you really can't do anything without the grace of God.

"Yes," she says, "God is everything in this: the power and the life that brings you into the big waters, then dissolves the boundaries quietly, gently, like the unfolding of the petals of a rose. Ego becomes dominant when your personal agenda is small. You become self-conscious and competitive because it's what you think you need to do in order to survive. When your little boat gets caught up on a wave that's bigger than you are, ego drops away."

She tells me about making the movie with Tim Robbins and Susan Sarandon. "Media people always ask me what it was like to have Susan portray me. Of course, it's interesting. But as I watched the filming, I just moved right back into the original event and that holy ground where I met all those suffering people. What I do isn't about me. Being famous just means that more people know about you and can ask you to help them."

Is there anything you would do differently?

She thinks about this for a nanosecond, then shakes her head no. "I think the whole universe is involved with the things that happen within us, so there's a certain wisdom about why something occurs and a certain timing. It's the providence of God. That said, I truly wouldn't know how to redesign my life."

What do you think is your greatest accomplishment?

"I never use this word either. A gift I've been able to share is that I can tell these stories and will continue to do so until we eliminate the death penalty."

Her hands rise and touch her heart. "I've been given so much. I've been loved more than the law allows. Thanks doesn't even cut it. I don't even want anyone to thank me because the experience itself is thanks enough."

Is there a secret to your success?

"When I was on the book tour, my escort in Chicago carried a little card in his wallet that said, 'Seek excellence and avoid success.' Success will kill you! It can give you a false sense of satisfaction and keep you from continuing to grow. I don't think in those terms."

Do you have any advice you would like to give to others?

"Giving advice is something I don't do much of."

I rephrase the question and ask her what she likes to share with others.

"Stories that, hopefully, can be a sounding board for others or can spark their potential, that talk about how life unfolds and that interiority is important. My stories are about stretching our horizons, about being in touch with and listening to all kinds of people, and about how we've got to develop all aspects of ourselves—especially our minds and the poet or artist within us. My stories talk about the significance of friendship and how we must cultivate friendship like a garden. It's so precious and so beautiful, a way of being in relationship that allows us to share our dreams and our love. My stories are also about community and how we don't do anything alone." She smiles at me.

When you leave this Earth and all is said and done, for what or how would you like to be remembered?

Without missing a beat, she answers, "That I rejoiced in love when I met it, and that love flowed out of me into other human beings."

Of this I have no doubt.

To Learn More About the Life and Work of Sister Helen Prejean

Contact:

On the Web: www.prejean.org

www.moratoriumcampaign.org

Read:

- *Dead Man Walking*, Vintage Books
- *The Death of Innocents*, Random House

Listen:

- *Dead Man Walking*, Sony Records
- *Dead Man Walking—The Opera*, www.home.pacbell.net/dstein1/jh/n_dmw.htm

View:

- *Dead Man Walking*, directed by Tim Robbins, Polygram Filmed Entertainment, 1995
- *And Then One Night*, a documentary on the making of the opera *Dead Man Walking*, made by KQED and shown on PBS

Two
Grandmother Twylah Hurd Nitsch

They could not dislodge the garrison which was within—her serene, great heart and spirit, the guards and keepers of her mission.

—Mark Twain

IT WAS THREE days after I met with her that I realized Grandmother Twylah Hurd Nitsch is a small woman. Her fathomless eyes, her great good humor, and the magnitude of the peace that effortlessly flows from her heart convey a physical presence that reaches far beyond her diminutive frame. She is warm beyond measure, mercurial, and deeply connected to the Earth.

Daughter of a Seneca mother and an Oneida/Scots father, Grandmother Twylah is a direct descendent of Chief Red Jacket, a renowned Seneca orator whose discourses are still studied by scholars today. The Seneca are one of the original members of the Five Nation Peace League known as the Iroquois Confederacy and are the acknowledged philosophers of the League. Seneca society is composed of various clans. Grandmother Twylah's clan, the Wolf Clan, teaches the wisdom, philosophy, and prophecy of Earth history, namely that all creatures—all creation—are members of the one family born of Mother Earth, and that our destiny is to reclaim that Oneness. Her family has been teaching the wisdom-traditions of the elders since the 1700s.

Born in 1913 on the Cattaraugus Indian Reservation in upstate New York, Gram, as she is often called, was raised by her grandparents, Medicine Man Moses Shongo and his wife Alice, and trained to become the Lineage Holder of Seneca wisdom and leader of the Wolf Clan Teaching Lodge. This role was prophesied before her birth and assumed after her grandfather's passing—when she was just nine years old.

As a young woman, Gram worked for a time as a jazz musician, singing and playing the drums, and was once invited to sing with Jimmy Dorsey's band. She married and raised five children. When she began to teach, Gram brought students into her home to live with her family and learn the ancient ways firsthand. As her work grew, she formed the Seneca Indian Historical Society, a school without walls, and began disseminating her teachings through a home study correspondence course and holding semi-annual councils and workshops around the world. True to her Seneca name of *Yeh-Weh-Node*—"She Whose Voice Rides on the Four Winds"— she has single-handedly spread her ancestral teachings to Australia, Africa, Holland, Germany, Poland, Canada, Israel, Russia, Japan, the British Isles, Italy, and the United States. In April of 1999, she received the prestigious North American Living Treasures Award in recognition of her life's work.

I first heard about Gram from a friend who is a great admirer of her teachings. I knew little about her then, but something about her beckoned me, stirred pristine images within me of walking barefoot on the loamy trails of an ancient redwood forest. I had a hard time finding her for she had recently moved from her home on the reservation to live with her son Bob, the future Lineage Holder of the Wolf Clan Teaching Lodge and the current President of the Seneca Indian Historical Society. Eventually, I contacted her publisher who forwarded my invitation to participate in this project on to her. Several weeks later, Bob phoned. They were preparing to leave for a European lecture tour, but he offered me one brief window of time to meet with Gram and I jumped at the chance. I made my travel arrangements that day and one month later, met with Gram, Bob, and Lee, Bob's wife and the Society's Program Coordinator, at their home in Jacksonville, Florida.

❖ ❖ ❖ ❖ ❖

DRIVING FROM THE airport to Gram's modest ranch home in the neo-wilds of suburban Jacksonville is no easy task. As a result of my car accident, I have immense difficulty with linear thinking and in perceiving spatial relationships. Though I have written out every step-by-minute-step of the drive, I cannot track even my own directions and must ask for help at least a dozen times en route. I talk to myself as if I am the little engine that could—"I think I can. I think I can. I think I can."—and it helps, but the glue that holds me together, that actually keeps my frustration in check, is my heartfelt longing to be with Gram. This provides me with an important key to managing the impotence I feel whenever my cognitive dissymmetry leaves me geographically or mentally adrift: Now I know that staying in my heart, that connecting to someone or something that fills me with meaning and purpose, can propel me to the other side of oblivion.

I arrive at her front door relatively unscathed, take a deep breath, then climb out of the car. Bob greets me with a firm handshake and ushers me inside, past a desk piled high with educational materials, into the simply furnished living room, a room pulled together by a man who has little interest in material things beyond the practical necessities. He introduces me to Lee who welcomes me warmly, then excuses herself to get Gram. For a moment I blanch, wondering if there's some protocol I must follow when greeting a tribal elder, but my concern evaporates when Gram enters the room. Her long white hair is woven into two braids that sit on top of her head like a crown. Her face is weathered, etched by time. She wears a cardigan over a simple cotton dress and tennis shoes. Lee introduces us and Gram looks squarely at me with crystal-clear gray eyes. She opens her arms in an embrace, and I step inside. I feel as if I am a lost child come home.

We all chat for a few minutes about the tribulations of cross-country travel. Gram is surprised to learn that I came from California to talk with her. "I cannot imagine why anyone would want to come all that way just to talk with me," she says as she sits down on the couch. I settle in on the floor at her feet with my questions and recording equipment fanned out before me. Once I'm situated, I look up at her and smile. She returns my grin. Lee retreats into her office and Bob hunkers down at his desk near-by. Gram and I talk for a few minutes about the fact that we are wearing the same tennis shoes. Then we go from the mundane to the sublime as I ask my first question.

All the great religious teachings presuppose that the everyday world and our individual consciousness are manifestations of an underlying Divine Reality. The Hindus call it *Brahmin*, the Buddhists call it *One Mind*, the Christians call it *The Kingdom of Heaven*. What do you call it?

"The Seneca call it *Swen-i-o*, the 'Great Mystery.' Great Mystery is everywhere. It has no one particular form or manifestation, no criteria or rules that limit or define it. It is present in all creation and is beyond matter. It is spiritual energy, spiritual intelligence, the original source and the creator of all life forms, of all existence. It is the essence of all things."

The word "mystery" intrigues me—the implications of complexity and secrecy—and I ask her to tell me more about this.

"When something is mysterious," she says, "there is an energy, a magnetism about it that draws you to it, that makes you want to know more about it. It propels you to ask questions, to explore and, hopefully, to learn. Eventually you understand that you cannot grasp the totality of Great Mystery, your Creator, with the small mind, with the logical, linear mind. Great Mystery can only be understood and remembered through the experience of Oneness."

You said Great Mystery has no one specific form. Does It manifest to each person in the way that most appeals to them?

"It can. It's very personal. Once Great Mystery nips you, you follow the way you are shown."

What kind of a relationship do you have with Great Mystery?

"It's an energy that lives within me constantly. It calls to me internally and prompts me to develop or expand specific information or insights for myself and for others. It talks to me through my mental processes, through my intuition and feelings, and through inner visions. Great Mystery both sends and receives—it's a two-way street. I talk to Great Mystery all the time and Great Mystery responds."

She is quiet for a moment, then adds, "I once asked Great Mystery for more understanding about this way of communication and the answer I received was, 'We speak the universal language of love.' *Hail-lo-way-an* is the word Great Mystery used to describe it.

"Everyone has experiences of being inwardly guided like this," she says, "but most of us simply don't honor the information we're given. We say, 'Not now,' and let the guidance pass, because we do not want to take the time to enter the silence."

What is "entering the silence"?

"It's communion with your true nature in spirit, mind, and body. When you enter the silence, you go through an inner portal into the unity of all life. The more you go into the silence, the more you learn about your true self and your capacity to function in society. But you can't just say, 'I want to go through the portal,' and off you go. You have to become receptive; your purpose and intention must be pure. That's why most of us don't go there. Initially, it takes work."

It sounds a little like meditation.

"Well, that depends on how you interpret meditation," she replies. "Going into the silence is listening within. I have a feeling that when some people meditate, they are busy concentrating on a process or they are daydreaming. They are doing instead of listening. I sometimes sit in a chair in a comfortable position when I go into the silence, but that's where any similarity to meditation ends.

"When I enter the silence, I have something specific I want to discuss with Great Mystery or with my Band Members, the friends and relatives in the spirit realm who serve as my teachers and guides. To go into the silence, you must first enter what the Seneca call your *Sacred Space*."

What and where is your Sacred Space?

"Imagine a dot in the center of a circle that is located at the solar plexus. This dot represents what we call your *Vibral Core*, the home of your inner wisdom, balance, and stability. A vertical line that starts just above the head and ends just below the feet dissects the Vibral Core. This is your *Truth Line*. Another line extends horizontally as far as the arms can reach on either side of the body and intersects the Truth Line also at the Vibral Core. This line represents your *Earthpath*. The endpoints of the Truth Line and the Earthpath rest on the circumference of a circle. Inside that circle is your Sacred Space."

I close my eyes and visualize what Gram has just described. When I open my eyes again, she is smiling at me.

"In the North, at the twelve o'clock position of the circle, rests your wisdom; in the East, at the three o'clock position, rests your integrity; in the South, at the six o'clock position, rests your stability; and in the West, at the nine o'clock position, rests your dignity. When anything negative enters your Sacred Space—such as an inharmonious thought or a disagreeable person—it disrupts your peace and harmony. You become unbalanced and things begin to get difficult. The only way to restore harmony is to act with wisdom, integrity, stability, and dignity."

Wisdom. Integrity. Stability. Dignity. I take these words in each time I edit this piece, breathe them into me so that I can move them beyond the ideational realm and make them part of how I operate in the world. I ask myself: What do these qualities actually look like in my life? How can I develop them more fully? How do they relate to each other? To my needs and my desires? I see this questioning as integral to living my life with more effectiveness and meaning. Gram explains why this is so.

"If you continue to avoid Truth Within, your difficulty lasts longer and hurts more because it also affects Love Within and Peace Within. Eventually, your pain compels you to grab hold of the Truth you tossed aside so you can integrate it into your life and remember the experience of Oneness with all creation that is locked inside your Vibral Core at birth. Hopefully, this experience provides you with the understanding that prevents you from making the same mistake over again. But you will continue to learn through opposites until you remember that you are a part of the unity of all life."

Learn through opposites?

"Yes. You confront the opposite of Truth so that you can learn Truth."

24

Oh, yes, I say, and roll my eyes, for I have ample experience of my opposites. I have learned to be more honest with myself, to be proactive, to take time for personal renewal—the list is endless—as a result of being in intimate communion with the silver-tongued converse of each of these behaviors.

Gram looks at me with a twinkle in her eye as I tell her this and chuckles.

In your book, *Other Council Fires Were Here Before Ours*, you wrote about the fallout that occurs when we lose that deeper connection to Truth and have to learn through opposites, how we "unconsciously project our sense of separation from the unity of all life out onto the world and see it as broken." In the heat of battle, most of us rail against the opposition—whomever or whatever is outside of us—rather than try to reconnect with our inner Truth.

"Yes. Once the bonds of Love Within are broken and you begin to operate outside of your Sacred Space, you forget that you and all of life are a part of Great Mystery and that Great Mystery loves all creatures equally and unconditionally. When you are no longer aware of your true nature, you feel threatened by anyone or anything that is different from you; so, in an attempt to restore your own balance, you make others wrong or the world broken.

"When something inside us needs work, most people generally don't take the time to look at it honestly or deeply enough because, initially, it can be a painful exploration. So we hang onto false beliefs, false patterns of self-knowledge because they keep us from making important inner changes or we try to 'fix' others rather than make things right within ourselves.

"Truth Within is sacred. It's whole. It's a positive energy that unifies and feeds the body and the mind. It helps you digest your food, digest your lessons, and move through your Earthwalk in a focused and positive manner."

Truth Within is like soul food.

"That's right. And when you live Truth Within, your challenges do not affect you as deeply."

Is Truth Within the same for everyone?

"We each have an individual truth that relates to our gifts, to our willingness to develop our gifts, to the time and environment we're born into, and so on. There's also a *Uniworld Truth*, a Whole Truth, derived from our oneness with Great Mystery that is the same for everyone. We have to live in accordance with both aspects of Truth to maintain our inner balance. If we don't, that imbalance becomes the part of you others will notice most."

It's also the part of myself *I* notice most. And, if I'm not living my Truth, I can't be of real service to myself or to others.

"If you really want to help others, be an example," she counsels. "A good example is the best teacher. Others admire you and want to be like you. They sense your inner comfort and want that for themselves."

She leans toward me and says, "It's like this: If you wear a sharp outfit that makes you feel good, yet you can't maintain that comfort and wholeness when you take off the outfit—or no matter what else you put on—you've got a problem. Your outside image doesn't ring true. Unfortunately, there are not a lot of people today who feel whole."

I think, these days, more people are working at it though. Sometimes we get it together, and sometimes we don't.

"That's part of the growth process. We learn in increments because we can take in and hold just so much at one time. Attempting to remain in your truth is better than not trying at all. The main thing is to be open to learning and to learn with a humble attitude. Seek more than immediate or exterior comfort. Be true to yourself. When it's time for you to learn more, Truth is there for the asking. It's always with you. Unity is always with you. All you have to do is recognize it."

What blocks our recognition of Truth and Unity?

"Not knowing Who you really are and not understanding your connection to Great Mystery. Not knowing limits you; it compels you to look to the small mind to sort things out. We know there's 'something more,' we hunger for it, but we haven't the remotest idea what 'more' really is! In our ignorance, we create exhaustion, fear, or intentional busyness, or we passively let others tell us what to do just so we can have something to use as an excuse for why we're not happy. Once you get distracted and pulled off-center like this, you see only the periphery of Truth. The energy required to navigate through this illusion is immense, often more than we can muster. But the process can be simplified through prayer and willingness to follow Great Mystery's guidance."

She smiles at me and I get the sense that she knows that I am both fierce about my own growth and looking for answers to questions I have not yet named. I am not at all intimidated by this. She is so comfortable to be around, so safe, that I'm happy to let her in. She may see parts of me that aren't particularly attractive, but I intuitively know this doesn't matter to her. She looks out at me, out at the world, from some cavernous core not molded by theory or opinion—or judgment. I notice how internally quiet I have become just by being with her, and I rest for a moment in the silence.

Something else I read in her book floats up to the surface of my mind—her belief that all creatures are *Relations*, members of one planetary family. Humans, she wrote, are the only Relation unaware of this familial association. The animals, the trees, the stones, and so on, have all chosen to endure the harshness of mankind's delusion of separate existence until we remember our unity with all life and can then all return to Great Mystery together. I tell her how moved I am by the compassion, the patience, of creatures we consider to be "less than."

"The sun and moon, the Earth and sky are our family," she says. "The Earth is our Mother, the sky is our Father. It's Grandfather Sun, Grandmother Moon. White society doesn't feel this connection the way Native people do. They walk the Earth, they eat Her food and drink Her water, they even love Her trees and mountains, but they don't feel their natural bond with the Earth.

"Humans have become pushy and egocentric. We do not know that all life is interdependent. Our other Relations can wait until we remember this Truth because they know that within the challenge of separation lies the promise of equality and unity."

As I begin to grab hold of these words, Lee emerges from the inner sanctum of her office and suggests we break for lunch. I look at my watch and am surprised to see that three hours have passed. Ten minutes later, the four of us are sitting on stools around the breakfast counter holding hands, each offering Great Mystery our gratitude for something the day has brought. I listen to their effortless words of thanksgiving and when my turn comes, I give thanks for being able to share this day with them. I do not feel as if I am a guest in their home; rather I am a Relation, a member of the family.

The salad Lee prepares is delicious and we laugh and talk as we eat. Lee and Bob giggle as they try to piece together a wonderful story about Gram's visit from the Dali Lama. I get the full report several months later from a student of Gram's who witnessed the event.

It goes like this: During the winter months of 1991, the Dali Lama and an entourage of Buddhist monks visited Gram for two days at her home on the reservation. She often received guests, people from all walks of life, who came to learn more about her teachings and enjoy her warm hospitality. The two spiritual leaders spent many hours in deep conversation about the state of international affairs and exchanged thoughts on their shared desire for world peace. As was her custom, Gram invited the Dali Lama to visit the twelve-sided Wolf Clan Lodge located a short distance from her home.

The two elders walked slowly, arm-in-arm, along the ice and snow-covered path to the Lodge, with members of the Dali Lama's party and the Wolf Clan Teaching Lodge following at a respectful distance. Then, without warning, Gram and the Dali Lama slid on a patch of ice, lost their balance and fell, in Gram's words, "butt over tea kettle" on their backs into the snow. For a few brief moments, no one breathed. Horrified monks and Wolf Clan members engaged in a mad scramble to assist their leaders, but Gram and the Dali Lama just turned to each other and burst out laughing. Then, like two mischievous school children, they each gathered a lump of snow in their hands and initiated a snowball fight. From the little I know of Gram, it is not at all difficult to picture this in my head.

After lunch, Gram meanders back to the couch and I resume my place on the floor. The tape starts to roll as I ask her if there's one precept, a Golden Rule she follows, that guides or inspires her.

"My Grandfather taught me to follow the Twelve Cycles of Truth and the Pathways of Peace to preserve my wholeness and help me walk in balance and fulfill my life's mission. They are: learn the Truth, honor the Truth, know the Truth, see the Truth, hear the Truth, speak the Truth, love the Truth, serve the Truth, live the Truth, work the Truth, share the Truth, and be thankful for the Truth. The Pathway of Peace is living in harmony with this ancient philosophy."

So, if you live in harmony with these cycles, you fulfill your life's mission?

"You fulfill your Earthwalk, your Pathway to Peace, the personal pattern that guides you toward wholeness. Each person must develop their dreams and discipline themselves to achieve what they desire for their life in a way that satisfies Truth Within."

What is your Earthwalk?

Gram looks over at Bob, who is back at his desk, and chuckles. "Well, my Earthwalk is just about over," she says. "At this time in my life, I'm happy to sit back and take it easy. But when I was a young girl, my elders told me I would carry on the work of my Grandfather Moses Shongo to spread our teachings and help others understand their connection to the Earth. My grandparents also told me I would experience certain disabilities when I grew older that would help me learn how to carry out the work and better understand others. This too, has been part of my Earthwalk. I was crippled to teach me about perseverance, positive thinking, and faith in Great Mystery's plan. I was blind to learn to perceive more than what my outer eyes could see and be more sensitive to the energy of others. And I was deaf so I could become aware of a deeper vibration and rhythm of life that extends beyond my sense of hearing."

I make a presumption and say, "Those must have been difficult times." But Gram is on a totally different wave length.

"Actually, they were wonderful times! My elders also told me I would fully recover from these challenges, but I had to do my part and be willing to grow through them. I never lapsed into 'Poor me.'"

Did you ever have periods of doubt?

"Never."

Lack of faith?

"Never."

No "dark night of the soul"?

"No. Never."

That's amazing! What do you attribute this to?

"To these teachings. Everything that happened to me was just like going to school. Even when I couldn't hear or see, I didn't feel disappointed. I felt like I was being gifted because of what I was learning through the experience.

"When I was a child my elders taught me it was up to me to make myself happy each day, and when I go to bed each night, I should thank Great Mystery for my happiness. Most people don't take responsibility for their own happiness—it doesn't even enter their heads to do this! And at the end of the day, they're not grateful for the good things that happen to them."

Were your grandparents your mentors?

"They were my examples. My grandparents raised me before I went off to boarding school. My grandfather was a Seneca Indian Medicine Man. He was always in the woods looking for herbs, and I learned from him how to live in harmony with Nature. Our kitchen constantly smelled like a 'medicine factory,' as he called it. He was a brilliant man. All the doctors in the community were his friends. Sometimes they would send him patients who didn't respond to their medicine. My grandmother was a very quiet person, but when she spoke, her words were packed with meaning.

"Our house was always full of people. My grandparents knew how to make everyone feel comfortable with who they were. I often heard them tell people, 'You were born with these gifts so use them.' They showed me how to listen and pay attention to others and to be aware of what was going on around me. They also taught me that I was worthy of having my own ideas and that the answers to my problems lay inside me."

After your grandfather died, you assumed the responsibility for carrying on his teachings. You were just a young girl at that time. Did you feel prepared for this?

"His passing was a devastating loss to me, but he had been preparing me for this role all my life—by his example, in everything we did together, and in the ancient stories he told me. In our tradition, wisdom is passed on orally. Those who tell the stories are called the Wisdom Keepers or the Storytellers. They are chosen for their ability to listen and speak, so that the people can be sure our wisdom is passed on correctly. That role, like the stories themselves, is passed on from generation to generation. When I die, my son Bob will become the Wisdom Keeper. I have prepared him in the same way my grandfather prepared me."

What advice would you give to others seeking to live a more spiritual life?

"Be kind. Do nice things for others; speak kindly about others. If someone does something nice for you, be grateful. Say 'Thank you.' Be grateful for every day. Be grateful for waking up. Be grateful for being able to breathe.

"You know," she says, after a moment's pause, "gratitude is actually based on love, and nothing is more powerful than love. It's lack of love, or the misuse of love, that causes many of the problems we have today. People don't appreciate what they have. They don't love and respect themselves or each other. They take without giving anything back. They hide their elders—the ones who have the most life experience and can be most helpful in guiding them—in old folks' homes to get them out of the way. No wonder people today are so confused! No wonder people are not happy!

"In order to be happy, you need to develop and share your inner love. That's how it grows. If you're not sharing what you have with others— your gifts and abilities as well as your material possessions—if you're not helping others to grow, if you're not a teacher or an example, you're a *user*. Users don't honor what they have. They don't know how to take care of things so they can be perpetuated. Madison Avenue steps in and tells us to 'Have it your way,' so we push for more. Once we get what we want, we devour it until it's gone. There's no happiness in that," Gram declares and shakes her head.

"Happiness—inner happiness—is the goal of life. Most people can't even look at themselves in the mirror and smile! If someone comes to me and tells me they're unhappy, I tell them to examine their feelings and figure out what their limitations are and deal with them! You may have a nice house, a nice car, a good job, and make $100,000 a year, but if you have all that stuff and you're still unhappy, you have to ask yourself, 'What's wrong with this picture?'"

She doesn't mince words. The real question then, I say to her, is how do you foster self-love?

"You have to nourish self-love all the time. If your parents or husband didn't give you the love you wanted, you have to give it to yourself. If something throws you into a slump, look at it right in the eye. Figure out what you didn't see about yourself that allowed that slump to happen, then change it. After all, we live in a do-it-yourself world!" She chuckles once again.

Looking back over your lifetime, what do you think is your greatest accomplishment?

"I really don't know how to answer that. If you were to ask me about my greatest experience, I would say being married and raising my five children. But 'accomplishment' . . . I don't know."

She looks at Bob for a way into the question. They talk about this for a while and then she realizes why the question is so difficult for her to answer. "You see, Seneca people gauge accomplishment by where we are on our Earthwalk, how we've developed our natural potentials and shared our gifts. Our elders know we're ready to move forward by the questions we ask. There is no criticism or praise, there is only movement through the labyrinth of experience until we remember Who we really are. A bear wakes up in the morning knowing who he is and what he must do each day. He doesn't 'accomplish,' he just lives in harmony with Great Mystery. This is true for us as well."

OK, I think to myself. Be bear-like: know who I am—part of the Oneness of all life—and live in harmony with Great Mystery. It's a good thought to hold on to when I get sucked into the vortex of my To Do list.

When your Earthwalk ends, how would you like to be remembered?

"For greeting people with a smile and for spreading the Seneca Peacemakers' message of 'All for One and One for All.' When you feel your Oneness with all life, you carry that with you everywhere you go. You feel centered. Then whatever you do helps others; it unifies life. I believe in these words and honor them by how I live my life. It's really as simple as that."

I look at Gram and smile. Is there anything we didn't cover? Anything else you want to add?

"No," she says. "It's been nice."

It's been nice for me, too. More than nice. I try to thank her but I cannot find the words.

Bob tells me, with an impish smile on his face, how someone once told him that when you don't know what to say, you can always ask the other person if their shoes fit right. We all laugh.

Gram, do your shoes fit right?

"When my stockings don't get all bunched up," she says, and we howl. As I pack up my gear, Bob suggests I listen to the tapes I made of my conversation with Gram to see if anything needs clarification. He invites me to come back the next day to pull together any loose ends. I've so enjoyed being with them, it's an offer I can't refuse. Before I leave, Gram takes me into her room and gives me a "wish pouch" she knitted, a small apple-green sack she tells me to fill with wishes for my life. She walks with me to the door. Gram and Lee hug me good-bye and I drive to a nearby hotel to spend the night.

That evening, I listen to the tapes and come up with a few questions to ask Gram—not really enough to warrant another visit, but I'm so glad to have the opportunity to sit at their table again, to hold hands and express my gratitude for being a part of their sweet family, that I return for a few hours the next morning. At noon, I pack up my gear, and Gram and Lee hug me good-bye for the last time. Though I know I can call up the comfort I have felt here whenever I think of her, I am reluctant to leave. Gram smiles at me and gives me one last gentle word of counsel: "Remember the Peacemakers' message: All for One and One for All." I nod and return her smile. My voice catches in my throat as I say good-bye, then I turn and walk out the door.

To Learn More About the Life and Work of
Grandmother Twylah Hurd Nitsch

Contact:
The Seneca Indian Historical Society, Inc.
Wolf Clan Teaching Lodge
P.O. Box 2313
Orange Park, Florida 32067-2313
Voice: (904) 276-2735
On the Web: www.wolfclanteachinglodge.org
E-mail: sihs@worldnet.att.net

Read:
A complete catalog of Gram's books are available from the Seneca
Indian Historical Society upon request.
- *Creature Teachers: A Guide to the Spirit Animals of the Native American Tradition*
- *Other Council Fires Were Here Before Ours*, Grandmother Twylah Nitsch and Jamie Sams
- *Entering the Silence*
- *Handbook of Prophecy*
- *Language of Trees*
- *Mythological Philosophy*
- *Native Voice*
- *Nature Chants and Dances*
- *The Rope*

Listen:
- "Nature Chants and Dances"
- "Life Changes as Earth Changes"
- "Interview with a Gramma"
- "Mother Earth"
- "Native Voice"
- "*Nyah We Oh:* How It Has Happened"

View:
- *Prophecy Video: Grandmother Twylah with Sam Abbott*

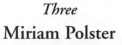

Three
Miriam Polster

Surely goodness and mercy shall follow me all the days of my life.
—Psalm 23:6

I FIRST HEARD Miriam Polster's voice on a warm summer's evening in 1992 gilding the air waves of my local PBS radio station with unspoken kindness. I had turned on the radio, weary from four tedious hours of the last lecture of my last graduate school course, hoping to find something that would keep me conscious during my drive home. And there she was. A Gestalt psychotherapist of international renown, she was talking about her latest book, *Eve's Daughters: The Forbidden Heroism of Women*, describing the ways a woman's inner development progresses from listening to the opinions of others to finally trusting her own inner voice. "Each woman needs to redefine the heroic spirit for herself in a way that is relevant to her everyday actions as well as to the epic moments of her life," she said. Though her words immediately struck a chord in me, something in her voice—the compassion and the promise of the possible—opened my heart. Though she made no references to her spiritual beliefs, her spirit lit my drive home.

Miriam Polster earned a Ph.D. in clinical psychology at Case Western Reserve University in 1967, returning to school when her children were just five and seven years old. The demanding life of a full-time doctoral student and mother of small children is hardly effortless, yet Miriam carried out her academic and familial responsibilities with aplomb. Trained by Fritz Perls, Paul Goodman, Isadore Fromm, and Paul Weitz, the legendary architects of Gestalt Therapy, she went on to nurture the development of this method and the province of psychotherapy in her private practice and in the thousands of mental health professionals she trained throughout the United States and Europe. Her brilliance and insight as a clinician and teacher earned her the respect of the psychoanalytic community, but it was, in the words of a former student, "the authenticity, emotional availability, and sense of humor she brings to her life and work" that made patients, students, and friends feel supported by her presence.

An associate clinical professor of psychiatry at the University of California at San Diego School of Medicine for many years, Miriam also cofounded and codirected the Gestalt Training Center in San Diego with Erving Polster, her husband and partner of fifty years. Their individual and joint service to psychotherapy has been so extensive that they were honored by an international gathering of their peers for their lifelong commitment to the practice and teaching of Gestalt Therapy. Miriam also received numerous other awards, including congressional recognition for her outstanding and invaluable contribution to her field.

When the initial stirrings for this book began to claim my attention, Miriam came mind as someone to include in the project. My impulse was prompted by more than the goodness I heard in her voice seven years before. Two days after I happened on that broadcast, I mailed her a copy of my graduate thesis, a lengthy tome on the development of the hero in the human psyche. I did not think she would actually read the whole paper. What I wanted most in sending it to her was just to connect with someone who shared my passion for the subject matter. Several weeks later she sent me a note thanking me for sharing my work with her. The note was so emotionally generous that I have it still.

I am too self-conscious to mention this when I speak to her on the phone to solicit her participation in the book. I give her the rundown, proffer an invite and, to my surprise, she agrees then and there to talk with me. We arrange to meet at her home in La Jolla four weeks later. When I hang up the phone, I lean back in my chair and laugh. "Who would've thunk it?" I say out loud. Then I remind myself that undreamed possibilities have always been fertile ground for the workings of grace.

❖ ❖ ❖ ❖ ❖

IT'S MAY IN Southern California, one of those magic, sun-drenched days when almost everyone drives with the windows of their car rolled down and cranks up the radio loud enough to feel as if whatever music they're listening to is coming from inside their own skin. The air is pungent with ocean brine. Even the asphalt on the road sparkles in the morning light. The rugged natural coastline of the Pacific on my right and the refined, tree-lined neighborhood of La Jolla Shores on my left attest to the varied expressions of California's beauty.

Miriam's sprawling ranch house is just off the main road. I walk the inlaid stone path to her front door and ring the bell. A slender, cultured woman in her mid-seventies, Miriam greets me warmly and invites me inside. She ushers me through the entry hall to a small study in the back of the house where we will spend the next two hours. There is an aesthetic about her, a sense of the artiste that is reflected in her eyes, her mannerisms, and in the decor of her home. Paintings and art ornament the walls and tabletops in a way that indicates they were placed by a thoughtful, creative hand. It's a home that's well loved, a home where love abides.

Miriam excuses herself for a few minutes to let her assistant know I have arrived. While she is gone, I settle in on the couch, lay my questions out before me, and set up my recording gear. I steal a furtive glance at the books that line one of the walls of the study—an assortment of novels, classics, professional texts, art and music references. Miriam returns and sits on a comfortable chair opposite me. I fiddle with the microphone and adjust the volume control one last time. "OK," I say, "Earth to Margaret and Miriam!" We laugh, and I begin our conversation by asking her how she would define spirituality.

"To me, spirituality is the search for and the connection with something that feels larger than oneself and the tangible world, something immense, something slightly beyond you, but also something friendly and mysterious that helps you make sense out of experience. It's also the surgeon's awareness of the relationship she has with another human being as she makes an incision at the start of an operation; it's the look on Audrey Hepburn's face as she talked with African children in a TV special I saw about her work with UNICEF. There's both a universal and a personal aspect to it."

Why mysterious?

"Because it's hard to define. If we brought a group of people together in one room and asked them each to define spirituality, we'd find certain commonalties, but there would also be descriptive elements that are unique to each individual. Each of us has to decide what spirituality is for ourselves.

"I think the search for the spiritual goes on for most of your life, so the definition of what is spiritual changes as you move through your life. Some elements stay with you, though. I remember an incident from my childhood—I couldn't have been more than six or seven years old—that was so magnificent I would call it a spiritual experience even today, though not in the traditional sense. I was playing outside and, for some reason, I stopped what I was doing and looked up at the sky. It was an intense blue, so blue that I immediately became absorbed by the color and my eyes filled with sky. I was so captured by the color, so filled with sky, that had anyone asked me at that moment what color my brown eyes were, I would have sworn that they were blue."

Her voices trails off and, for a moment, she becomes that young girl again. Then she breathes a discreet sigh. "It's unavoidable, I suppose, but I think spirituality has gotten a bad name. Sometimes I even find myself embarrassed to use the word because it's connected with—forgive me—so many sleazy or opportunistic operations. We often address the poetry of spirituality, but it's important to also define it almost clinically, to distinguish it from what's bandied about on Sunday morning television."

We talk briefly about these media pyrotechnics, the public and private machinations that seemingly occur in the name of all that is holy. Then I ask her to tell me what God looks like to her.

"I don't think in terms of an entity called 'God' but rather of an orderliness to the universe, a certain evolutionary, energetic motivation that moves things along in the world."

Do you have a relationship with or to that energy?

"I'm included in it, one manifestation of it, one of millions and millions of manifestations. I have a feeling of immersion in rather than connection to the energy. It's a very humbling experience."

How so?

"Because I realize that there are millions of people in this universe, each of us, like me, a little entity with wishes and hopes and dreams. I walk in my shoes, but everyone else walks in their shoes as well. Each of us is as valid as the other. I find that humbling."

Her words, and the sentiment behind them, move me. Despite her intelligence and accomplishments, she is a woman who is free from a sense of self-importance. I expect this is one of the things that makes her a good therapist and teacher.

How did you formulate your beliefs? How did your ideas develop?

"God was not talked about much in our family—not that it was ever taboo. I think I adopted this viewpoint very early in my life. As a young child, I read fairy tales and, though I adored them, I knew they weren't real. That people needed to be rescued or that they didn't know how wonderful they were until someone else intervened and sent them off to the ball was, for me, not how it worked. Somehow I knew I was both exceptional and unexceptional, special and just like everybody else. Juggling that paradox helped me to figure out the world. As I grew older and started to read scientific material, my reading confirmed my thoughts."

Is that paradox also about balancing a sense of the magic with the practical? The material and the spiritual?

"Yes. That time when my eyes filled with sky, I was open to the magical nature of experience and yet my life was eminently down to earth. Cinderella goes off to the ball in a pumpkin coach, but she also knows how to keep house. It's that sort of thing. It's a paradox we continue to juggle throughout our lives.

"Raising children is particularly like that. I remember once, when our children were small, we were preparing to head off for our summer vacation and intended to leave very early the next morning. My daughter asked me what we would eat for breakfast at that time of the day and I said to her, 'We will have dawn. We will have sun rising in the sky.' Her eyes grew wider and wider as I spoke. She was expecting a more practical answer, but this was just the right thing to say to her."

I did things like that with my children, too, I say. It was important to me to preserve their experience of wonder and awe, to give them a sense of the possible in what sometimes seems like an impossible world.

"Oh, definitely. There were some studies done several years ago which showed that people who have a high tolerance for outer chaos also have the increased patience to withstand greater levels of inner disorder. We all require a certain level of internal order or at least a sense that we're moving toward order. If you have a belief system that enables you rather than restricts you, you're more able to learn to deal with error within yourself or in others in a more forgiving way."

Finding my spiritual home certainly did that for me. Before that happened, I often felt emotionally and spiritually adrift.

"That's true for a lot of people. Or, sometimes people lose their connection to the spiritual—however they define it—and feel adrift. Maybe their belief system was borrowed, a hand-me-down from their parents that no longer fits. Many people simply don't validate their own inner wisdom and experience. This is particularly true for women because we've based 'correctness' or 'appropriateness' on a male model of what 'correct' and 'appropriate' are. The more public spirituality becomes, the more articulate we all become in talking about what we value. Therapy is also a way to scrutinize our personal experience and put it into a healthy context, to discover something we can believe in—even if it's not spiritual."

Our discussion turns to the work of Carol Gilligan, the Harvard scholar and researcher, who first documented the ways in which a woman's moral life and decision making differ from a man's. Gilligan validated what husbands and wives have deliberated over for eons: A woman's inner arbitrator focuses primarily on feelings and the preservation of relationships, while a man is more likely to base his decisions on principle or problem solving. I ask Miriam if and how these differences translate into our spiritual lives.

"I think that men and women can end up in the same place spiritually speaking, but our mechanisms of approach will always vary. We see this in the heroic acts of men, which have generally been more public—courage on the battlefield, that sort of thing—and the heroic acts of women, which are generally quiet and more private—volunteering at a battered woman's center, caring for a dying relative and so forth—not as easily observed or acknowledged given the tilt of newspapers and television toward the dramatic and sensational. They also occur mostly in the company of other women, children, the aged, and infirm. These are the ways women declare that another human soul is valuable and determine how life should be lived. Men are actually saying the same thing, but the ways they express these values are different.

"Even though current research says men now take a more active role within the family, a woman will always have a more intimate connection to the children because she carried them within her body. This gives her a profound respect for life and life maintenance. Whatever she chooses to do with her life, caring and relationship are what generally motivate a woman's originality and persistence.

"But, no matter what role she plays, if a woman has no sense of her own possibilities, of her own worth, she lives between despair and resignation. A woman doesn't need to become like a man in order to feel good about herself, but she *must* find a way to validate her own wisdom and experience. Whether she chooses to operate on the more private scale of one-to-one or the larger scale of one-to-five hundred, it's critical she sees herself as an agent of change, as someone who has an original perspective, as someone who has the guts and willingness to do what she believes is important."

We talk for a few minutes about how women will often suppress or minimize their wisdom or abilities in order to keep the peace. "I once wrote a poem about this," Miriam says with a gleam in her eye. "Would you like to hear it?"

I smile and nod. She clears her throat and straightens up in her chair, preparing for her recitation.

"It's called 'Sleeping Beauty,'" she says. "It goes like this:

Quick!
He's coming!
I have to lie down
And pretend I've been sleeping
All
These
Years.

I laugh at her performance. The significance of her words does not, however, escape me. She calms the unspoken storm behind her sentiments with the pragmatism of the bigger picture.

"It isn't just our self-perception or our role vis-à-vis society that have kept women in the background for so long; the environment we lived in also played a part in determining our function. Two thousand years ago, if you set out to establish trade routes in the Mediterranean, you were probably better off sailing with Jason than with Medea. At certain stages in our civilization, it was simply more efficient to have men do the things women now aspire to because they were physically bigger or stronger.

"Of course, all of that has changed in the last fifty years. Technology has been a great equalizing force. It doesn't take great strength or size to push a button. But, because pressing that button has the potential to unleash incredible devastation, we now have to temper the aggressive response to challenge or danger that is more characteristic of men with compassion and discretion. We must be more sensitive to how our actions affect others if we are to survive as a species."

Do you think there's an aspect to what occurs in the world and in a life that's fated or preordained?

"Yes, but in a very limited way. Rather than use the words 'fated' or 'preordained,' I prefer to say 'determined by circumstance and accident.' If you're born in Kosovo, you deal with a whole different set of experiences than if you're born in Southern California."

What about free will? How "free" do you think it is?

"I think it's limited by external factors: whether we're born male or female, by the expectations of the family and culture we're born into, by the opportunities we're given, and so forth."

Psychotherapist Victor Frankl talks about that crucial moment of choice before we act, the space between our thoughts and actions that is the ground of our decision making. How do you think that comes into play here?

"The development of that kind of competence is a gradual thing that increases as we grow older. As children, we can hardly muster the coordination and persistence to turn a door knob. As adults, we open a door all the time without paying any attention to the skill involved. The same is true about our ability to make conscious choices in our lives."

Years ago, writer Peggy Noonan said she thought the new frontier would be an inner one. Do you think this proved true?

"I would hope so. But Wordsworth also said—and he didn't even know the half of it when he said it—that 'The world is too much with us.' I think there will always be people who withdraw, who look inside, but I think, despairingly sometimes, that the world *is* too much with us for everyone to do that."

Yet there are certain questions most of us do eventually ask ourselves: "Who am I?" "Where did I come from?" "Who created me?" "What is my place in the world?" How would you answer these questions?

"I approach looking for those answers in terms of function and relationship. I'm a very important person in our family: a very important wife and a very important mother. I'm learning how to be a very important grandmother. I then expand this definition by substituting verbs for the nouns I used to describe myself. Saying 'I mother,' rather than 'I am a mother,' takes me beyond the caretaking of my own children and denotes an active connection to the world. It also puts me in touch with the whole range of who I am."

Where did you come from?

"From my parents' gene pool. When someone tells me, 'You're a lot like your grandmother,' they're saying something about the history and continuity of life. There's a connection to what came before me and a heritage that continues through me into the future."

Who created you?

"My parents. Not just biologically, but also in the way my father told me stories, how my mother fluffed up my hair, the way they held me when I cried. These things all contributed to who I am."

And what is your place in the world?

"To deal kindly with my neighbors. To tell jokes and sing songs. To cook a good meal for someone. To be ethical and decent. To act with patience, compassion, ingenuity, and candor—but not hurtfully so. This probably sounds very plebeian, but I think it's in these small ways that we let others know we love them."

I don't think it's at all plebeian. It's the essence of all great spiritual traditions. How did you learn the importance of these values?

"My parents lived their life this way. They were ethical people. It wasn't what they said but how they acted that was so instructive. My father was also a wonderful storyteller. In most of the stories he told me, I had an unseen friend who intervened on my behalf at just the right moment to ensure things turned out well for me, a little girl who sometimes ventured out farther than was wise, but who also learned about life and herself in the process. I think this was my father's way of telling me that it was OK to be adventuresome because there was kindness in the world, both specific and global; that people were good and, by and large, I could rely on that."

Who do you think your unseen friend was?

"It was a human presence—not something ghostly or supernatural—that was both my father's benevolent spirit and the spirit of goodness in the world. It taught me to proceed with caution but also helped me develop the optimism I needed to function successfully in the world I would some day live in as an adult. For example, I was able to make the commitment to get through graduate school with two young children—including getting up at 4:00 A.M. to study—and know I would be up to the challenge."

When you spoke about your place in the world, you didn't mention your work. Do you feel you have a mission, an assignment to carry out?

"Teaching and doing therapy. I want people to learn how to do things better, to respect and love themselves a little more."

Why is that important to you?

"It just seems like a better way to live. It's wider, not so confined or narrow. It's beneficial rather than hurtful. And I think it's a basic truism of our species that we grow to the extent we can participate in other people's growth."

Why not sell vitamins? How did you know this was the right work for you?

"Clearly my husband Erv's involvement in training and therapy was an important influence. I had also read a great deal of history and biography, and the glimpses my reading offered me into other peoples' lives fascinated me. Doing therapy seemed like a natural progression of my interests.

"After I got my degree, I was asked to teach a class in general psychology at the Cleveland Institute of Arts. I realized then that I liked to teach. I've also come to see that psychotherapy is a mutual process of education where both client and therapist teach each other what they need to know. Selling vitamins is fine, but for me, therapy and teaching are companionable with my interests."

Did you have any mentors or role models who guided your thinking or helped you along the way?

"This may sound like a case of arrested development," she says with a chuckle, "but the person I remember most is my kindergarten teacher. I adored her. I don't want to sound saccharine, but she was actively good, vocally good. She had a wonderful presence and made the atmosphere in the classroom feel so kindly and encouraging.

"I accidentally ran into her many years later, and it was clear she was still the same person I remembered her to be. After we said our good-byes, the phrase formed in my mind: 'I was right to have loved her so.' It wasn't a case of mistaken idolatry!"

We laugh. I ask her if there were others. She does a quick internal scan of her life, then replies thoughtfully, "There were moments when someone acted in a way or said something that touched me. Watching Fritz Perls and Paul Weisz do therapy was like that. And there were singers I knew only from their performance or from reading about their lives who affected me. But no one else impacted me like this teacher did."

In your book, *Eve's Daughters: The Forbidden Heroism of Women,* you write about how important it is for women to have heroes. Can you talk a little bit about that now?

"I think it's important for all of us to have heroes, and to have a variety of heroes, so we can see the different ways there are of being heroic and recognize the less obvious or less publicly acknowledged forms of heroism. Having heroes gives us a sense of inspirational power and awakens us to more opportunities for heroism in our own interactions."

How has our conception of the hero changed in recent times?

"Women are not as withdrawn from public life as we used to be—or if we do withdraw, it's part of a rhythm of withdrawal and public presence. And as we've become more vocal, many of our views have become accepted by the mass culture. Men are also becoming more comfortable with tender feelings and interacting with children. The male hero is no longer just the frontiersman who ventures out alone into the wilderness. He can also be the breadwinner rooted in family and community. And today, if you ask a young girl what she wants to be when she grows up, she might talk about being an astronaut or an attorney, whereas years ago, she was more likely to think that her only options were to be a nurse or a teacher. That women read hard news on television or step up to the microphone on the floor of the Senate is now commonplace. Of course, we could argue that we need to have the same representation of women in Congress that we do in the population, but the point is that male and female territories have expanded, and as a result, so have our emotional and spiritual horizons."

I glance up at the books that line the shelves of her study, and she follows my gaze. Were there books that inspired you?

"T. H. White did a series about King Arthur that I discovered about the time I was a freshman in college. In one of those books, Merlin tells Arthur the story of creation: On the seventh day, God gathered all the creatures together—still in their embryonic forms—and told them He would give them each whatever quality or physical attribute they wanted. Each creature comes before God and names its desire. He concedes to all their wishes and, as they leave, they metamorphosize into their fully developed animal form. The last creature comes before God and says, 'I don't want any special gifts. I trust Your wisdom and I will take my life as You made me.' God is very pleased by this and praises the creature, saying that it alone passed His test. The creature walks away and becomes Adam.

"I was young when I read this book—barely 'made' myself," she sighs. "But there was something metaphorical and mystical about that story that I really loved and could relate to.

"Another book in the series was called *The Ill-Made Knight*. As the story goes, the reason Lancelot tried so hard to be a wonderful knight was because, deep down inside, he was convinced he was not a very good person. It moved me because it was so human; we all know people like that. That book made it easier for me to see myself as a work in progress. It taught me to not be so hard on myself when I tried something I was not yet good at. Years later, I heard psychotherapist Laura Perls elaborate on this idea when she said, 'Anything worth doing is worth doing badly.' After all, we all have to start somewhere." Miriam smiles and her face lights up.

How do you deal with the reality of being human? Have you ever had a "dark night of the soul"?

"Of course. There were tragedies and trials that I was deeply involved in and could not walk away from. The challenge is to learn how to function creatively and lovingly with the limits and frustrations. I learned a lot about myself from these experiences. They taught me not to give up easily. I also had the help of others during these times who were very generous and supportive."

Do you have a spiritual practice?

"Every once in a while, when I have time, I meditate to quiet down. But for me, spiritual practice is making the bed, defrosting dinner, and so on. It's not magical or removed; it's about how I discover and reveal myself as I do things that are ordinary."

The simplicity and depth of her answer takes my breath away. No mountain top or ivory tower. Just the holiness of the moment.

Do you have any advice you'd like to pass on to others?

"Just to take time to pay attention to your feelings, your reactions, your wishes. Pay attention to yourself, to your inner voice. Do this in whatever way works for you, but listen and attend."

After a moment's reflection, she adds, "I also think it's important to explore other points of view. Doing this provides you with options; it broadens you. You discover that just because you made lemonade one way all your life doesn't mean you have to go on making it that way forever."

Yes. We get stuck, locked into the way we've always done things. Then it becomes hard to take chances. We hold back from life.

"Fear of injury—to ourselves or to another—can make us overly cautious. Don't let fear of short-changing your children or your relationship keep you from doing something you really want to do. Otherwise you end up with the sense of the road not taken."

It's a burdensome thing, I say, to live with "If only . . ."

"Yes. Regret. You can't go back in time and change what was, but you can change what you will do *now*. It's a good antidote, a good way to counterbalance past regrets. It's never too late to do what you want to do. Carried to extremes, this is obviously false. When I'm eighty and have arthritis, I may not be able to lift weights, but I can find ways to exercise at a reduced level. You have to be willing to look ridiculous! Don't be too invested in your dignity."

Is there anything you would do differently?

"I would have liked to have done more with my music and art. I was a singer. The voice has disappeared, but I'm thinking a lot now about how to bring more music into my life."

What do you think is your greatest accomplishment?

"The answer—and I really mean this—is that I don't know yet. But I think raising two decent, ethical human beings is one of my greatest accomplishments."

What do think is the secret to your success?

"That I always want to do my best—whether I'm preparing dinner or teaching a graduate course."

When the time comes and you leave this Earth, for what or how would you like to be remembered?

She smiles. "For my kindness, for my intelligence, for having an original perspective, and for my humor. That's not too bad, is it?"

Nope. Not bad at all!

Miriam Polster passed away on December 19, 2001. She will be remembered for all this and more by those who knew her and loved her best.

To Learn More About the Life and Work of Miriam Polster

Contact:
E-mail: epolster@ucsd.edu

Read:
- *Eve's Daughters: The Forbidden Heroism of Women*, Jossey-Bass
- *Gestalt Therapy Integrated*, Erving and Miriam Polster, Brunner/Mazel
- *From the Radical Center: The Heart of Gestalt Therapy*, Erving and Miriam Polster, Gestalt Institute of Cleveland Press
- *Women in Therapy: A Gestalt Approach*, edited by Franks and Burtle, Brunner/Mazel
- *Critical Incidents in Therapy*, Diane Hulse-Killacky and Jeremiah Donigian, Brooks/Coles

Four

Alma Flor Ada

Act, act in the living present!
Heart within, and God O'erhead!
—Henry Wadsworth Longfellow

THOUGH SHE IS the author of over one hundred children's books and scholarly texts, a Fulbright Scholar, and an internationally renowned educator, Alma Flor Ada is, to this day, a wide-eyed child held captive by the charm of a well-crafted story. Born to a family of educators, she grew up in the countryside outside of Camaguey, Cuba, in the turbulent years before the revolution and had an almost idyllic childhood immersed in the

tropical beauties of her homeland and the loving embrace of a large family. Her love for literature was constantly nurtured by her grandmother,
father, and uncle who were all master storytellers, and she knew at a very
young age that she would one day pass on the rich legacy of their stories
to other children. "How could I," she told me, "who had been so blessed,
not want to give something back?"

With that in mind, Alma Flor left Cuba at eighteen to attend college
in the United States. She continued her education in Madrid, earned a
Ph.D. in Spanish literature from the Pontifical Catholic University of
Lima, Peru, then did postdoctoral research as a Mary Bunting Institute
scholar at Radcliffe College at Harvard. Today, she is a professor emerita
at the School of Education at the University of San Francisco and is an
international expert on multicultural education. She travels throughout
the world working with teachers, parents, and children; serves on the
board of the Children's Television Workshop and Loose Leaf NPR radio;
and is an active member in a legion of national and international children's
literature and language organizations. Many of her books are published in
English and Spanish—to accommodate children who are bilingual, and to
acquaint young readers from both cultures with traditional Spanish stories—and have become cultural liaisons to the Spanish- and English-
speaking worlds. She has also won many prestigious literary awards for her
writing, including The Christopher Award, the Once Upon a World
Award from the Simon Weisenthal Center at the Museum of Tolerance,
the Latina Writer's Award for Children's Literature, and Argentina's Marta
Salotti Award, to name only a few. While Alma Flor continues to draw
heavily on her own childhood experiences for her work, she also gives
credit to her four children and eight grandchildren for inspiring many of
her stories.

Though her career has been prestigious and her literary output
prolific, Alma Flor has a more consuming passion in her life: She is a
devout spiritual seeker. Like her grandparents and parents before her, she
is a freethinker, and has explored her spirit through traditional and non-
traditional means. At every turn, she connects more deeply with the Great
Silence that is at the heart and soul of her seeking.

I first heard about Alma Flor from a friend who said of her, "Alma Flor
Ada is not only an advocate for children and multiculturalism, she is an

advocate for living the spiritual life." Though I knew little more about her than this, I heeded an intuitive prompting and invited her to participate in this book. She responded to my letter almost immediately, and we arranged to meet at an educational conference she would soon be addressing in San Diego. I found her to be open and unassuming, discerning and wise yet full of awe, intellectually and emotionally magnanimous—not all that far removed from the fair daughter of Cuba she once was who reveled in the wonder and mystery of life. Later, I learn that her name, Alma Flor, means "soul flower." Somehow, I am not surprised.

❖ ❖ ❖ ❖ ❖

IT'S MID-SEPTEMBER YET there are no signs of fall in San Diego, a city where summer often stretches out her golden arms well into November. I arrive at the bay front hotel where the conference is being held several hours before we are scheduled to meet so that I can sit in on Alma Flor's morning presentation. She is standing at the front of a large ballroom, talking in Spanish to a rapt audience of about two hundred teachers. She is a tall woman, in her early sixties, with stately bearing and an inner fire that is evident even from the back of the room. Words click off her tongue like castanets in the hands of a veteran flamenco dancer. Though I do not understand all of what she's saying, her dark eyes speak volumes and her audience sits enthralled. When her lecture ends, they gather around her and ply her with questions. I move into the crowd and stand off to the side, waiting to catch her eye and introduce myself. She looks my way and smiles, and I move toward her with hand extended. She is gracious and warm. We quickly make plans to rendezvous after her luncheon meeting, then I backtrack through the multitudes to the relative quiet of the hotel dining room.

Ninety minutes later, I knock at the door of the room where we are to meet. Someone chimes, "Come in!" and I enter the suite. Alma Flor sits among a group of women gathered around a large conference table talking and laughing. She nods in my direction then motions to a door opposite her. I move through a burst of laughter into the adjoining room and set up my recording equipment. A sliding glass door opens onto the boat harbor and a view of the Coronado Bay Bridge spans the not-too-distant sea. I pull up a chair and take in the view. She joins me fifteen minutes later with a tray of uneaten food in her hands and an apology for keeping me waiting. I offer her some time to eat and catch her breath. We sit in silence together and watch the boats bob in and out of the harbor. When she is ready, I punch in the tape recorder and ask my first question.

You've written so lovingly about your childhood in Cuba, particularly about the influence your grandparents had on your early life. They were proponents of what you call "free thought." How would you describe this belief system, and how did it shape your spiritual development—particularly growing up in a country that is predominantly Catholic?

"I have a very interesting heritage. Three of my grandparents were born in Spain. My maternal grandmother was a feminist and a strong opponent of imposed religion. My maternal grandfather studied in France where he became very interested in Eastern spirituality and Hinduism. My paternal grandfather was raised in Galicia, a region of Northwest Spain that is principally Celtic. And I suspect that my paternal grandmother came from a Jewish family that was once forced to convert to Catholicism.

"While it is true that within the Catholic Church there is great mysticism and compassion, given their backgrounds and the long-standing religious oppression that occurred in Spain by the Church, all four of my grandparents were very averse to organized religion. They were, however, highly spiritual people. Love governed their lives. They believed in generosity, kindness, and selflessness, and in the goodness of the human spirit. My maternal grandparents also believed in the capacity of the soul to perfect itself over many lifetimes. They didn't put a face to their Divinity, but they actively sought to be guided by Light and Peace. This philosophy was also later adopted by my parents, aunts, and uncles.

"After my mother and father married, they lived with my maternal grandparents and my mother's three sisters and brother in a large old house on what was then the outskirts of Camaguey. Considering the intellectual environment of our household, and because we lived close to nature, looking back, I think I must have been a pantheist as a child. To me, the Earth had life. I did not see any separation between myself and the natural world—or from other human beings, for that matter. The sky, the rocks, the trees, my family members were all one."

Are these values still at the heart of your spiritual practice?

"'Practice' is a word that stirs some emotion in me. As a matter of fact," she confesses, "I was a bit apprehensive about having this conversation because I don't engage in a specific spiritual discipline."

She looks at me somewhat tentatively—almost shyly. I assure her that form and structure are irrelevant to me, that what matters is that she has committed to live out her deepest values. She smiles and nods her head in silent accord.

"Fortunately, I shared these concerns with my daughter before I came here to San Diego. She helped me recognize that I am guided by spiritual practices I don't name as such: generosity, the impulse to give as much of myself as I can, respect for the beliefs of others, nonjudgment, support and devotion to even the simplest forms of life—certainly to children and to the particular individuals I consider my teachers. Listening is also part of my practice—not only that I listen to others, but that I teach others how to listen. My daughter saw me as someone who embodies my beliefs in action. Hearing all this, from her especially, was deeply healing because I was often taunted by neighborhood children when I was young, told I would surely go to hell because I had not been baptized and did not have any formalized religious practices."

How wonderful this naming could come through your daughter.

"I know!" she says happily. "This all happened yesterday. There we were, standing on the streets of San Francisco, people walking past us, having this profound and important conversation. And it all took less than ten minutes. For her to give myself back to me like that with such generous reflection was a gift. I must thank you for this, because if you and I hadn't planned to meet today, I probably would not have had that discussion with her."

Though she does not know it, her own generous reflection provides me with a gift: Considering how unstintingly the women in this book give of themselves to this project, I have privately entertained the hope that they too might yield some benefit from our conversations. Alma Flor is the first to satisfy my desire. But her disclosure takes me by surprise and I am unable to tell her how much her words mean to me. I quickly gather my Self unto myself, then steer our discussion back on course.

It sounds like your spiritual practice is similar to that of your grandparents'. Is this something they taught you or did you choose these values for yourself?

"I was very young when my grandparents died so I could not have learned anything from them on an intellectual level. It was who they were and how they interacted with me that was so instructive. My grandfather was a powerful presence. Though he was active politically and owned a busy newspaper, there was such an aura of peace about him—such profound grace and centeredness—that I could tell he was home the moment he'd set foot in our house. My grandmother often talked to me about spiritual principles, but more than that, she lived them. I learned generosity and kindness just by being with her. She has been the most influential person in my life, although she died before I was five years old."

She looks past me for a moment, out at the bay. "What had the most impact on me, however," she says, "was the trust these two people had in me. I was two when my grandfather died and barely five when I lost my grandmother, too young to have earned their trust by anything I actually did. What they were demonstrating to me was the trust they had in my soul. They were celebrating that which existed in me that was independent of my years."

How fortunate for you to have been exposed to this kind of valuing at such a young age.

"Yes. I was very fortunate. When I was about twelve, I began to search for more spiritual structure. I explored several different religions. Because the Church was all around me, I focused my search on Catholicism. I read the great mystics—Saint John and Saint Theresa—and longed to have their thirst for God. I yearned to be a Carmelite nun and spend my life in contemplation. But I was very torn because I didn't believe in hell and could not reconcile my feelings with what the Church taught about the existence of hell. My God was loving and compassionate, not one of retribution. Of that I was certain."

How did you resolve this conflict?

"There was a librarian in my home town who took an active interest in converting me. She introduced me to a Jesuit priest who helped me resolve the disparity between my belief in the total compassion of God and the Church's belief in hell. This priest was a very bright man. He told me that while Church doctrine maintained the existence of hell, nothing in any of the writings confirmed that anyone was actually *in* hell. Once I had this assurance, I was baptized in secret."

How did your family respond to your conversion?

"Though they had always told me I was free to choose my own religion, when I tested this in reality, I discovered that anything was acceptable to them except the Catholic Church. I believed in the Church of Saint Francis. They believed in the Church of the oppressors. Their view was shaped by their experiences, but so was mine. We argued a lot. It was a very painful time for all of us."

I understand. When I moved away from the religion of my childhood, my family was nearly bereft. I think that on some level, they may have interpreted my decision as a personal rejection. I didn't see that then. I couldn't understand why they were not as happy as I was that I had found a spiritual direction. It was very difficult for everyone.

"It was like that for me as well. To my family's great dismay, I persisted in my beliefs. I went to church every morning before school and even became president of Diocesan counsel for youth. Several years later, the librarian who befriended me helped me get a full scholarship to a Catholic college in Denver, Colorado. While I was there, I decided to become a Sister of Louretto and work for the poor in South America. I was actually accepted into the novitiate, but once they discovered my plans, my family put a stop to them. I continued my practice for a few years but ultimately gave it up. I have taught in a Catholic university and I celebrate those within the Church who are true to their beliefs. I also celebrate many aspects of Catholicism. But I am not now someone who chooses organized religion for herself."

Nowadays, it's not all that unusual for people to explore different religious teachings. Inquiry has value.

"Yes. I'm absolutely convinced that everything has a purpose. Nothing happens to us by accident. I don't believe there is someone, some place, pulling strings like a master puppeteer, but I do believe our lives unfold in a certain way."

How so in your case?

"I owe a great deal of who I am today to a woman named Elaine Marie whom I met by 'accident.' My former husband was very interested in Watsu, the type of bodywork she practices and, unbeknownst to me, he made an appointment for me to see her. Watsu is similar to Shiatsu but it's done in the water. The practitioner cradles you in their arms and gently moves your body into various positions that help the mind drop away and open to some very profound experiences. I wasn't searching for anything at that point in my life. In fact, I had become spiritually complacent. I had given up believing I could go deeper within myself—given up believing that there was more to life than just surviving, just working hard—so I was very reluctant to see her.

"But Elaine Marie helped me reach a new level of my spirituality. The work we did together took me into an experience that rekindled my spiritual seeking. It took me to a very deep place within myself of silence—and in this silence, Oneness. She also introduced me to Jeru Kabal's Quantum Light Breathing, a meditation technique that freed me of many old, useless thought patterns and helped me feel grateful for each breath I take— for the constant gift of life itself."

She says these last few words deliberately, softly, in praise and gratitude. She looks away for a moment, then back again at me, and there are tears in her eyes. She dabs her eyes with the corner of her napkin, then nods in my direction. I ask her what it was about Watsu that so affected her.

"In an effort to help me understand my own experience, Elaine Marie told me how this technique changed her life. Watsu was not just something she did and taught; it had also become her spiritual practice. This was very evident to me during my initial session with her. The loving tenderness with which she cradled and rocked me in the water allowed me to return to a place inside myself of total comfort, a place devoid of any concerns or anxiety. I accepted her love, unrequested yet so unconditional, because I myself was Love."

Alma Flor takes a deep, purposeful breath. Her body relaxes. Her words slow. The peace in the room is perceptible.

"Instead of fading, the memory of this first experience became brighter as time went on," she says. "Others began to remark on my new softness. My daughter said she had never seen me be so comfortable in my body. I was spiritually renewed. I began to receive Watsu on a regular basis.

Every experience was different. I gave each one a name. The first was the Watsu of Unconditional Love, the second was the Watsu of Forgiveness, the third of Belonging, the fourth of Gratitude, and so on. Each took me to a deeper place within myself.

"The seventh Watsu, the Watsu of Sharing, was consistent with my aspirations to give the best of what I myself receive. Elaine Marie said that giving Watsu was an even greater joy than getting it and so, once again, I put myself in her capable hands and became her student. As I learned to connect with the breath and heartbeat of another, to stand aside and forget myself, to be in constant awareness and totally present to someone else's needs, I began to see that Watsu was indeed a way of life. Shifting my full attention to the present moment in Watsu helped me be in the present moment in my life. I have since watsued relatives, friends, colleagues, and total strangers all over the world."

We exchange stories about other seemingly "accidental" encounters and she tells me about another such event that changed her life, her first meeting with Gangaji, a spiritual teacher who follows the teachings of Papaji and Ramana Maharshi.

"I was in a health food store in Maui," Alma Flor says with a laugh, "when a woman inadvertently stepped on my toes. She was flustered by what happened, and when I tried to put her at ease, she just looked at me and said, 'You need to see Gangaji.' I had no idea what she was talking about, whether this person was a man or a woman, but the radiance that filled her face as she spoke Gangaji's name piqued my interest. We talked for a short while and she invited me to come with her that evening to a gathering Gangaji was holding, but I wasn't sure whether or not I would go. We left it that if I was interested in attending, I would meet her later and we would go together. At the end of the day, I found myself close to the place she suggested we meet, at the time she said she would be there. So I went with her. It turned out to be an extraordinary evening.

"The meeting hall was filled with a large group of about three hundred people, all of whom were meditating. It was very peaceful. I sat down in the back of the room and closed my eyes. Within a few minutes, I began to have the most unusual feeling in my heart, almost as if someone was standing behind me, holding my heart in their hands. It was not an uncomfortable experience; I felt as if I was being welcomed in some kind of special greeting. In a few minutes, I began to feel as if my heart was connecting to something in front of me. I opened my eyes and saw this extraordinarily beautiful 'being' sitting in the front of the room. My heart was, indeed, linked to her. Such was my first meeting with Gangaji.

"I have had the privilege to sit in *satsang*, to listen to her speak, many times since then. Whenever I am with her, I experience the deepest silence. My mind—all its questions and uncertainties—just stops. I have also watched her on video. I have her picture on my desk. But even when I am not in her physical presence, my heart is in constant contemplation of the totality she embodies."

Reverence, gratitude, devotion, all pour from her heart like a great river. I will see the same response again when Olympia Dukakis describes her first meeting with Gayatri Devi, and when Sri Daya Mata talks about seeing Paramahansa Yogananda for the first time. My experience of this is always the same: In the face of what these women deem holy, I myself feel small and grand and still. Very, very still.

I move through the stillness and ask Alma Flor how, given all the varied influences in her life, she would now define spirituality.

"To me, spirituality is silence and the experience of Oneness that grows out of silence. It's not about going to some far off place. It's not about struggle. It's not about thinking what I do or do not deserve. Spirituality is Oneness. And we cannot all fail to be part of that Oneness."

And faith? How would you define faith?

"To me, faith is the deep knowledge that everything is as it should be."

That everything is perfect?

"Well, it's a perfection that may sometimes look imperfect to my limited vision. I accept what is because, deep inside, I believe things are just as they should be.

"I think I learned to do this as a child," she muses. "My Father and I would climb up onto the roof of our house to watch the stars, and he would talk to me about the magnitude of the universe. I remember him saying to me once that 'behind the stars, there is more and more and more.' I came away believing that the universe is filled with mystery, and that the mystery is perfect.

"To some people, this may seem contradictory to a life of social activism, to wanting to make the world a better place, but I don't see it that way. I have a responsibility to reflect on and plan actions which, from the perspective of my limited intelligence, are noble and loving. At the same time, I must have faith that whatever happens will be all right. In *action* I reflect on what is the best thing to do, but in *faith* I know that whatever I do will be OK."

She laughs. "Of course, there is a certain tension about this, like walking a tightrope, and sometimes I still get caught up trying to make things perfect."

Yes, the friction of opposites: action versus faith, doing versus being.

"I have had a life-long struggle with this," she confides, "somehow believing that I had to choose between social action and the spiritual life. When I was living in Peru—and in the midst of this struggle—I finally had a moment of revelation that took me beyond the conflict: I realized that when I brought goodness into the present moment, I was being politically active and deeply spiritual at the same time. I saw that these drives are not polar opposites, but are connected inside me as one and the same issue. It then became clear that what is of immediate importance to me is not whether there is an afterlife, or whether something remains of my spirit after I die, but that I live each moment of my life to the best of my ability. And the only way to do that is to be fully present, right here, right now."

She pauses for a moment to reflect, then she says, "Gangaji once told me something that really helped me deal with the various challenges of my life. She said, 'When pain appears, embrace it. It is the best teacher.' Pain and suffering are not the same thing, you know. One can experience tremendous pain, be it physical or emotional, and still not embrace suffering."

How so?

"Pain is a sensation that occurs in the moment, but suffering can become a part of one's essence. Though I may be in tremendous pain, if I embrace suffering, I become useless; I have nothing to offer anyone but my suffering. If I'm going to be of service to others, I simply can't do that. If, for example, my leg hurts, why should I only think about or feel that part of my body? Why not think about the other parts of my body that do not hurt? I don't need to be sad because I'm in pain. Happiness and pain are independent of each other."

Do you mean that you do not wallow in victim consciousness?

"It's more than that. I do not let pain change the essence of gratitude that is in my soul. I acknowledge that I have pain—I say, 'This is sad or difficult'—but I do not let pain alter the beauty of life, the magnificence and mystery of life, and my gratitude for the mystery."

I hold these words in the back of my mind for weeks, and bring them forward each time I nurse one of the aches that have the potential to become an obsessive preoccupation. Gradually, I begin to apply the words to the losses I still experience from my car accident—the decreased mental acuity, the memory loss, the narrow depth and breadth of visual field. At first, I am too attached to my pain, too much in need of it to justify my aberrant behavior and my grief to let it go. I did not hear her words in the way I hear them now. I did not feel them in my gut. Then one day, her words become an affirmation: Pain does not alter the beauty of life, the magnificence and mystery of life, and my gratitude for the mystery. Something frayed inside me begins to mend. I breathe easier. I no longer feel broken.

Unaware of how her words will eventually work within me, I simply ask Alma Flor my next question: Does she believe she has a mission or an assignment she was born to carry out?

"The word 'mission' sounds arrogant to me. I do believe I have a responsibility. I was born into a very literate family. As a child, books were a very important part of my life. My family supported and loved me; they gave me the self-assurance that allowed me to nurture myself throughout the rest of my life. How could I not help others to understand the importance of nurturing children? The importance of books? Life has been extremely generous to me. I would not be able to receive as much as I do without giving back as much as I can."

You once wrote that, "When we hear each other's stories, we begin to understand ourselves better and feel less alone." Did this factor into your decision to become a writer?

"My family are people who talk about the meaning of life and the responsibility we each have to life. I began to ask myself at a very young age how I could serve, what I could give back. The question is a constant in my mind still. The answer has been refining itself throughout my life. Being a writer and educator has been part of my journey. I feel privileged to be in a position where people want to hear what I have to say. But the most important thing I do in that role is to help others listen to themselves, to turn myself into a mirror so they can see their own beauty, see who they really are. When I tell my stories, it gives others permission to tell their own."

What would you say is the secret of your success?

"I don't think in terms of success. My work is just a humble effort on my part to try and give back some of what I have received. I still fall short of giving back enough."

There is an invisible wreath of thanksgiving that surrounds her as she says these words, a wellspring of gratitude that prevails over her own recognition of her very apparent abilities. She has been used by Life and the experience is an end in itself.

Given the chance, would you do anything differently?

"Anything I said would carry the implication that I had to deny the value of what was, and I simply cannot do that. Everything that has happened to me has contributed to the person I am today."

Do you have any advice for others?

"Find quietness in whatever way you can," she says softly. "Whether it's looking at the ocean or at a tiny blade of grass peeking through a crack in the sidewalk, find quietness. Then stay with it; let yourself be absorbed in it until you see your true Self. When that happens, smile! Rejoice! Because you've found your radiance."

Tejas. It's the Sanskrit word for Divine radiance.

"Yes. Divine radiance. We don't have to go far to find it. It's within us. We already are the radiance we seek."

She is quiet for a moment, waiting, watching for another thought to form itself in her mind. Finally she says, "And when you turn inward, do it with compassion. Forgive yourself for your mistakes. Give yourself the same love and understanding you give to others."

When you leave this Earth and all is said and done, how or for what would you like to be remembered?

A moment of reflection, and then she says—whispers: "My greatest joy would be that someone, having forgotten that I was ever instrumental in the process, was more in touch with themselves."

She looks out at the bay and then again at me. There is great tenderness in her eyes. We smile and express the satisfaction this time together has brought us both. As I pack up my taping gear, and each time I work on this piece in the months to come, I rejoice in how much more in touch with myself I have become as a result of being with her. I cannot ever imagine forgetting she was instrumental in this process.

To Learn More About the Life and Work of
Alma Flor Ada

Contact:
38 Miller Avenue, #81
Mill Valley, California 94941
Voice: (415) 383-8407
Fax: (415) 380-8126
On the Web: almaflorada.com
E-mail: almaflorada@yahoo.com

Read:
For a complete catalog of books by Alma Flor Ada please contact:
DEL SOL Books
29257 Basset Road
Westlake, Ohio 44145
Toll Free: 1-888-335-7651
Fax: (440) 892-5546

* *Abecedario de los animales*
* *Dear Peter Rabbit/Querido Pedrin*
* *Gathering the Sun: A Farm Worker's ABC in English and Spanish*
* *The Gold Coin/La moneda de oro*
* *Jordi's Star*
* *The Lizard and the Sun/La lagartija y el sol*
* *The Malachite Palace*
* *My Name Is Maria Isabel/Me llamo Maria Isabel*
* *Olmo and the Blue Butterfly/Olmo y la mariposa azul*
* *Under the Royal Palms*
* *Where the Flame Trees Bloom/Donde florecen los framboyanes*
* *Yours Truly, Goldilocks*
* *I Love Saturdays . . . y Domingos*
* *With Love, Little Red Hen*
* *A Chorus of Cultures: Developing Literacy Through Multicultural Poetry*, edited by Violet J. Harris and Lee B. Hopkins

- *The Power of Two Languages: Literacy and Bi-literacy for Spanish Speaking Students*
- *Authors in the Classroom: Transformative Education with Teachers, Student, and Parents,* co-authored with F. Isabel Campoy
- *A Magical Encounter: Latino Children's Literature in the Classroom*
- *Gateways to the Sun/Puentos al sol,* co-authored with F. Isabel Campoy, Santillana USA Publishers

Listen:
- "Como una flor," music and voice by Suzi Paz
- "Gathering the Sun," music and voice by Suzi Paz
- "Musica amiga," music and voice by Suzi Paz

View:
- *Writing from the Heart/Escribiendo desde el corazon,* Del Sol Publishing
- *Meeting an Author,* Del Sol Publishing

Five

Reverend Lauren Artress

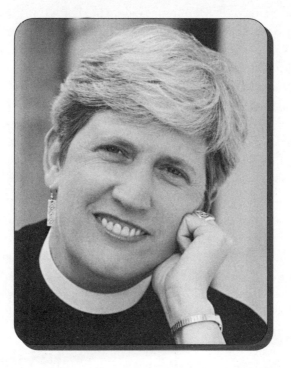

The nature of God is a circle in which the centre is everywhere and the circumference is nowhere.

—Empedocks

EARLY IN 1991, the Reverend Dr. Lauren Artress was, unbeknownst to her, about to undergo a life-transforming experience. Five years before, she had left a busy psychotherapy practice in New York City and moved to San Francisco to become Canon Pastor of Grace Cathedral, the third largest Episcopal Church in the United States. She arrived in San Francisco at the beginning of the AIDS crisis, at a time when the spiritual hunger in America was fast becoming an issue of grave concern for the traditional Church, and her pastoral and administrative duties grew exponentially. With the help of a grant from the Fund for the Enhancement of the Human Spirit, an endowment created by Laurence S. Rockefeller, she began to develop new programs at the Cathedral that specifically addressed the needs of the disenfranchised. Though her work was rewarding, the demands of serving a large congregation had begun to diminish her own reservoir of personal energy. In an effort to renew herself, Lauren decided to attend a seminar with psychologist Jean Houston, a former teacher and mentor. It was there, in what she later described as "one of the most astonishing events of my life," that she first walked the labyrinth, an ancient archetype of spiritual wholeness. The experience would take her into the sacred heart of a city halfway around the globe, and forever change her life and the lives of hundreds of thousands of people.

Simply explained, a traditional labyrinth is a narrow, continuous walking path that wraps back and forth around itself eleven times within the perimeter of a forty-foot wide circle. One-third of a mile in length, the serpentine trail starts at a single entry point, wends its way to the center of the circle and back out again. The labyrinth's intricate design is based on the principles of sacred geometry, a mystical science created by spiritual adepts in the Middle Ages who intuitively recognized the circle as a universal symbol of unity and wholeness, and the experience of pilgrimage as a metaphor for the soul's journey to the Divine.

The epicenter for this work and its best known example was and is to this day at Chartres Cathedral in France. It was there that thousands of medieval pilgrims came to make a symbolic journey to the Holy Land when actual travel to Jerusalem was not feasible. Walking the labyrinth was a way to internally connect with the holy ground of Spirit, to bring meaning and purpose to one's life, to create a sacred place within where the peace of God could be felt and the will of God could be intuitively discerned. Long held in relative obscurity, the labyrinth was, in modern times, known only to a select group of scholars and spiritual aspirants. Lauren Artress would change all that. She would bring the labyrinth into the twentieth-first century and carry it literally, in the form of a portable canvas, and figuratively, in her writing and workshops, around the world.

As a young girl growing up on the Chagrin River near Cleveland, Ohio, Nature was Lauren's first touchstone. The power of the natural world—it's prodigious genius, its ability to comfort and guide—connected her to Spirit. These early experiences stayed with her and animated her determined search for answers to the larger-than-life questions she was asking herself, especially after the death of her beloved grandmother. After completing her undergraduate work at Ohio State University, she entered a Masters of Religious Education program at Princeton Theological Seminary to pursue her growing interest in the relationship between psyche and Spirit. After a year as a social worker, she returned to school at The Blanton-Peale Graduate Institute for Religion and Health in New York City to become a psychotherapist, then opened a practice in Pastoral Psychotherapy in New York City. Several years later, she began teaching in the Spiritual Direction program at General Theological Seminary and met Alan Jones, an author and priest who was overseeing the program. In 1986, he was appointed Dean of Grace Cathedral and offered her the post of Cathedral Canon. Five years later, Lauren introduced the labyrinth at Grace Cathedral and soon thereafter, began training labyrinth facilitators. By 1995, her book, *Walking a Sacred Path: Rediscovering the Labyrinth as a Spiritual Tool,* helped make the labyrinth accessible to present-day spiritual pilgrims in churches, hospitals, schools, prisons, community centers, and private residences around the world. Today, her workshops and retreats help others integrate psyche and soul, develop intuition, nurture a relationship with the Divine Feminine, and make real the invisible world of Spirit.

I first heard of Lauren's work in 1998, several months before my husband and I took a dream-come-true trip to France. I had long hungered for France, particularly the little towns along the Loire Valley. As I researched that leg of our journey, I was led to Chartres Cathedral, and then to Lauren's work. Walking the labyrinth soon became part of our itinerary.

The first sighting of Chartres Cathedral from the highway takes your breath away. Its massive exterior commands the surrounding landscape for miles. The day we arrived, a mist rose from the earth to the heavens and enveloped the building in sacred mystery. It took us two days to find the labyrinth—partly because we needed time just to integrate the size and beauty of the Cathedral into our reality, but mostly because it was right under our noses, on the floor in the nave of the sanctuary covered by hundreds of wooden chairs. On her first trip to Chartres, Lauren moved the chairs so she and her colleagues could walk the labyrinth. We were not that bold. We simply stood in its center for a long while, then walked a small labyrinth in the garden in back of the Cathedral.

The following year, I was on my way to San Francisco when Lauren came to mind as someone to talk with for this book. She accepted my invitation to participate, but was unavailable to talk with me then. We set a date to meet three months later—a few weeks before she would return to Chartres with a group of women eager to connect with the presence of the Divine Feminine that the labyrinth, the cathedral, and France so embody.

❖ ❖ ❖ ❖ ❖

I BOARD THE commuter plane at San Diego Airport at the crack of a February dawn and arrive in San Francisco in little more than an hour. After a quick breakfast at an airport cafe, I make my way to a shuttle service that promises me a swift and comfortable ride to my destination. I wait forty-five minutes for a van that I am repeatedly told "will be here very, very soon," then jump into the nearest shuttle and hold on for dear life as the driver traverses the hills of San Francisco at warp speed. I arrive at Lauren's condo a few minutes after eleven, rather green—my breakfast nearly in hand.

Lauren buzzes me into the building and beckons me up the stairs to her living room. Her short, sandy-colored hair is turning gray and she wears little make-up. She is tall and hearty, in her mid-fifties. I can easily imagine her as a young girl skipping stones across the Chagrin River or perched in a tree inhaling the woodland tang of an Indian summer afternoon. The room has an easy informality about it. Nothing calls attention to itself, yet everything contributes to an ambiance that conveys thoughtful reflection. Its earthen colors and simplicity reflect her love of Nature.

We chat for a while about my transportation travails, Chartres, and our mutual love of France. She is easy to talk with, relaxed, a good listener, and a ready conversationalist. My first official question focuses on what she refers to in her book as the "Great Grandmother's Thread," an invisible, guiding presence that connects our inner and outer lives. I ask her if this is how she would describe God.

"It's one of the ways—a symbolic way—I use to describe that intuitive spirituality that tugs at us, that provides us with a clear feeling of being directed. Symbols transcend religious dogma; they're part of the collective unconscious. I think the thread is a good metaphor for the continuity of Spirit in our lives. The Great Grandmother's Thread puts us in touch with the Sacred and urges us to reach for deeper meaning. We feel connected to something greater. We feel we're here for a reason, to live in a way that lets the beauty that is inside of us come into the world and hopefully, be our gift, our contribution, to society.

"In traditional religion, we talk about God the Father. The Great Grandmother's Thread is also a symbol of feminine wisdom, of feminine spirituality, of the Divine Mother, as the Hindus call Her. She captures an understanding that's fallen into disregard, that's been feared in the West since the Middle Ages."

Your description of the Great Grandmother's Thread reminds me of what psychoanalyst Carl Jung called the *Hidden Immortal*, that part of us that initiates or fulfills our search for the holy.

"Yes, though I hadn't thought of it in that way before," she says thoughtfully. "To me, the Hidden Immortal is one way I define the Christ or Christ Consciousness, the imprint of the immortal upon the mortal soul."

How would you describe your God?

"I stand in the Christian tradition and understand that, in my being, I'm connected to Jesus as the Christed one—to Jesus Christ. I visit the various images of Jesus from time to time—brother, beloved, teacher, wise person, immortal being—depending on what's going on in my life. At other times, an embracing image for me is the feminine aspect of God, that of Mary or of Sophia, an ancient archetype of feminine wisdom. It's an image that is broad, that opens me to a world of gentleness and sorrow—and joy. And creativity."

We talk for a few minutes about France, specifically that it is primordial ground for Mary. She tells me that the veneration of Mary started there during the Middle Ages, and that Chartres was a focal point of Marian devotion. I felt it myself when I was there. To this day, when I think of France, I think of a midlife woman—full, knowing, a woman whose personal history has deepened her beauty and wisdom.

Lauren smiles when I tell her this. "My work with Chartres, though connected to the labyrinth, primarily focuses on rediscovering who Mary was and is. It may be controversial to say 'is,'" she says, "but the Divine Feminine, the Divine Mother, *is* a living force in the world. She is simply another way to understand God, or the Mother/Father God. For some people, this is a difficult concept to embrace. But the search for the feminine aspect of God doesn't undermine Christianity. Nor is it antithetical to Jesus. Jesus was supported by women and he befriended them. He acknowledged their spiritual nature and capacities."

And he manifested so much of his "feminine side," so much compassion and tenderness.

"Yes. One of the benefits of the labyrinth work we're doing through Grace Cathedral is that women and men are opening to this feminine, receptive side of their natures. Getting in touch with this can be a life-transforming experience because what we're really talking about when we talk about receptivity is how we can be open to growing and evolving into more enlightened human beings. In order to grow, we have to be open to new ideas and to the expansion of our own consciousness. We need to cooperate rather than compete.

"I still see a few clients for psychotherapy," she says, "and it's there that I see another aspect of God—God as an energy, a healing force that can be experienced within the human psyche, within others, and the world at large. Hildegard of Bingen, the twelfth-century mystic, called this *Viriditas*, 'the greening power of God.' People who are doing their interior work, who keep looking, opening, thinking, reflecting, not being mortified or shocked by the darkness in themselves and others, are receptive to this greening power. And it works wonders in their lives."

There's pain that's inherent to growth, I say, the conscious struggle and yearning to "become," and pain that's unconsciously imposed on us by self or other.

"Right. The Buddhists refer to this as pain that creates pain, and pain that ends pain."

Her comment stimulates a discussion between us about the recent shift away from thinking about God as an impersonal, punitive deity to thinking about God as an intimate confidant and comforter. Lauren tells me how she made that shift.

"One of the big benchmarks for me around this was the death of my grandmother when I was nineteen. It was a tremendous loss, one I didn't expect, and it created an open cavernous wound. I had a series of religious experiences then that quickly taught me that God was not just transcendent, not just the outer image I'd been taught to believe in as a child. That year at college, I attended the United Campus Christian Fellowship where we read some wonderful books together, like Dag Hammersjold's *Markings*, and had discussions about real life issues that helped me articulate what was going on inside me. Later, when I went into pastoral counseling, I began to see the ways psyche and soul were integrated within me, and experience what author and theologian Marcus Borg—and William James before him—called 'first-hand religion': the personal experience of God. Borg said first-hand religion is what people are looking for, but the Christian tradition teaches 'second-hand religion': religion imposed from the outside in—if you only just believe, then, lo and behold, you'll have the faith you need. It's a white-knuckle approach to God that doesn't work. We all need our own personal knowing, our own first-hand religion, to make sense of things and to handle the stress of modern life in a more fluid and graceful way. The hunger—especially for women—is for something much deeper than following the rules and being a good little girl."

This was certainly true for me. I was always watching, waiting, searching. Always searching. I was genuinely surprised though, that what I was looking for turned out to be God, that "first-hand" religious experience you spoke of. I never realized that kind of a relationship was possible. Did you always believe in God?

"Through Nature, I did. I was raised in the country and Nature was the overarching spiritual metaphor of my childhood. It stirred my imagination and grounded me. I still remember the fearful moments when the frozen river would rumble and crack and break up. The rushing of the water would literally shake our house! That event always signaled the resurrection of spring, and spoke to me about God's design woven into the cycles of the year."

Were you raised in a spiritual environment?

"My family went to church rather sporadically. I jokingly say we were 'emergency Presbyterians.'" She chuckles. "When we needed to marry or bury a family member, we relied on the Presbyterian Church. My mother believed church was important, so we went; but it was a stressful experience, partly because I wanted to sit with the adults in the sanctuary rather than go to Sunday School. My father didn't believe in organized religion. He was raised as a Christian Scientist and had a deep connection to Nature. He felt Nature was God's Bible and God's message to us—something I agree with."

How did you decide to become a priest?

"I went to seminary because of the religious experiences I had after my grandmother passed away, but I really had no intention of becoming a priest. I was and still am interested in how people change, in the integration of psyche and Spirit. To me, the Christian Scriptures are about transformation, about how we change our attitudes and values. I really felt my work in the world would be helping people do this.

"After seminary, I moved back and forth between the secular and the sacred, first as a social worker, then as a clinician and pastoral counselor. When Alan Jones asked me to be Canon Pastor at Grace Cathedral, I felt it was the next step in my journey so I took the position."

Has being a woman influenced how you function as a priest?

"Very much so. I function very differently than my male colleagues. For example, I put much more value on the experiential. I'm a lot more likely to preach a sermon that originates in an imaginative story rather than in an intellectual principle, as they often do."

In 1988, you and your colleagues created Quest: A Center for Spiritual Wholeness at Grace Cathedral. It's a very innovative program. How did it come about?

"We all knew things in the Church needed to change. We knew people were spiritually hungry, but we weren't sure what or how to change. So we took a long, hard look at mainline Christianity and isolated four areas we felt challenged the Church at end of the twentieth century: the denial of the feminine, the need to bridge Eastern and Western thought, the disregard for creativity, and the yearning for the mystical as a way to put people in touch with their own first-hand experience of God. With Laurence

Rockefeller's help, we began doing programs for the community around these issues. This eventually led me to work with the labyrinth."

What do you think the spiritual hunger in America is all about?

"I think people want to live with meaning and purpose, to be effective, creative, glowing, and flowing human beings. We want to connect with our right brain, our more creative nature, the symbolic world, the imaginative parts of ourselves that have been screened out through academia and the cultivation of the linear, logical left brain. In the last four hundred years, the pendulum swung toward scientific rationalism: if you can't see it, count it, or prove it, it doesn't exist. Christianity abandoned its mystical teachings during the Middle Ages and discouraged an inner, personal experience of God in an attempt to maintain power and control over the people—and especially over women. In Europe, women were banned from meeting together for over three hundred years, and at least forty thousand women were burned as witches because the Church didn't know how to interpret or guide the personal spiritual experiences of the masses. The veneration of Mary, our connection to Nature, these kinds of things were also eliminated from Church doctrine because they were frightening to those in authority. As a result, we learned to ignore the invisible world, the natural world, the domain of the right brain, and we denied the connection between body, mind, and Spirit. We can't live from only one hemisphere of the brain and be happy. If we can't create wholeness and balance in our lives, we can't be vibrant and alive. We end up experiencing a deep inner dissatisfaction. And, when we run from personal experience, from first-hand religion, we run from authentic Christianity.

"People today want clarity from their spiritual practice, something that speaks to the deepest parts of them. And we're tired of living with the guilt and the boredom of practicing a belief system that doesn't allow us to feel comfortable with being human—or that doesn't inspire us. We've got to stop hanging out there in the wind, living without meaning—or being unaware that it's meaning and aliveness we're searching for. As I said in my book, we need to change our seeking into discovery and our drifting into pilgrimage."

A picture emerges from my subconscious: I'm standing in front of an open refrigerator impatiently looking for something to eat, but not knowing what it is that will satisfy my hunger. I smile, then tell Lauren what I'm thinking.

She laughs. "Exactly," she says. "Fortunately, things have started to change. In the last fifteen years, many people have done a lot of inner work, studied different traditions, and gained a more universal under-standing of Spirit; we've followed our longing and let it take us to new ways of seeing the world. We listened and we learned. We stopped talking about the absence of meaning in our lives and started looking for ways to answer the challenges before us. It's so important to do what each of us feels inwardly directed to do. If we keep on, one day something significant happens—usually when we least expect it."

What makes the labyrinth such a useful tool for personal and spirit-ual growth?

"The external reasons are that walking the labyrinth is easy to do: it's accessible in a growing number of places around the country and there's no time limit to completing the process. It takes as little or as long as you want to walk. Internally, the labyrinth fills the need to capture our deep intuitive understanding of how the mystical world unfolds. Walking the labyrinth is a metaphor for the spiritual journey and a reflection on the spiritual life of the person who walks it. Something happens for most peo-ple as soon as they begin their walk. For some, it's 'Wow!'; for others, it's 'Whoa! I've got something I need to take a look at here.'"

The first time I walked the labyrinth in Grace Cathedral, I had one of those "Wow!" experiences. I had just started to make some necessary but daunting changes in my life that required me to lay claim to my personal needs. On my way to the Cathedral, I became embroiled in a conversation that tested my resolve and required me to make an assertive leap across this new threshold. Though I handled things reasonably well, the emotional residue from the experience left me feeling tenuous, as if I was made out of tissue paper. When I stood at the entrance to the labyrinth, I took a deep breath and somehow let go of my angst. My first step felt like a launch, almost as if I'd set sail for the New World.

After several rotations around the circuit, I began to notice a shaft of vibrant, sapphire-colored light that fanned out across the western perime-ter of the labyrinth. I traced the origin of the blue with my eyes to a stained glass window high above the cathedral floor. My gaze immediately fell to

the lower right-hand corner of the window, to the name—to my name!—
"Margaret" (which I later discovered was also the name of the window's
donor). I averted my eyes from the window to assimilate what I'd seen.
When I looked up again, two words from the Biblical verse etched on the
glass came clearly into focus: "will," at the beginning of the passage, and
"stand," in the middle of the passage. "*Margaret will stand.*" I gasped. In
that instant, I intuitively knew I would make it through this next phase of
my growth intact.

I hightailed it around the rest of the labyrinth with all the confident
expectation of a child on Christmas morn, stood briefly in the center in
praise, then retraced my steps back to my launch point. This too reflected
my inner biography, my desire to immediately integrate my newfound
affirmation of Self into my life. The walk had most certainly been just as
Lauren now described, a reflection on my life.

My own labyrinth experiences have been few and far between, but
their power makes me very curious about how walking it regularly has
affected Lauren's life.

"Early on, it took me out of the guilt I felt about not being able to do
a sitting meditation. I call myself a 'failed meditater,'" she says with a
smile, "because traditional meditative practices don't work for me like they
do for some people. The labyrinth does it for me because my body is moving. I'm not trying to contain or control my energy. It brings me into self-
alignment. It also gets me thinking about the blueprint of my life and
helps me start focusing on those things I want to manifest."

This reminds me of something you said in your book, that "when
we allow ourselves to be whole, we allow new visions to emerge in us and
in our culture." When I first read this, I was particularly struck by your
use of the word "allow." The labyrinth seems to provide a safe place
where people are more willing or open to letting these kinds of experiences occur.

"Yes, creating an experience of wholeness is about flow versus force,
about moving *with* the experiences of your life and not judging them or
condemning yourself. We each need to get out of the way of our own
growth. Saint Brendan said, 'You are the veil that hides the paradise you
seek.' Each of us has our own veil that keeps the immanent God, the greening power of God, the God who wants to birth Herself in us, hidden."

It seems to me that being able to go with the flow has a lot to do with faith—faith in oneself as well as in God. As a priest and as a psychotherapist, I imagine questions of faith are your daily bread and butter. How would you define faith?

"One definition I like is 'the ability to sustain ambiguity.' A lot of people think that if they have faith, they aren't supposed to have doubt or insecurity—and if they do, it means they're weak in faith. I don't feel this is the case. Faith is knowing Something Bigger than you is attempting to live Itself out through you. It evolves through each of us over time as an evolutionary process that moves the human race toward greater compassion, and it's a personal, individual experience in the present moment. Faith is also trusting the Great Grandmother's Thread, knowing that it's there, knowing that even if it leads you around a circuitous path, you will eventually find your center and be of service to the world."

Sometimes you're given a map, I say, and other times you walk in darkness.

"Someone once described this as faith that's constructed—where you see the vision, move to make it real, and then learn to love it—and faith that's created—where the vision unfolds from Spirit and it's loved from the minute it's conceived."

That's a beautiful way to describe it. Have you ever had a crisis of faith, a "dark night of the soul," where that vision is obscured or your faith is severely tested?

"I sure have."

How did you resolve it?

"I think it's something you grow through rather than resolve. It's like an eclipse of the sun or the moon; you just have to live through it. I remember once, right after I was ordained to the priesthood, I experienced a long dry period where nothing had meaning. I had such a busy, symbolic life on the outside that it seemed to rob me of a meaningful inner world. So, I decided to go to the desert—a good place to go given what was going on inside me—and I began to plan a trip to Israel. Just looking through the travel brochures caused an internal shift and, in a few months, my inner wellspring started flowing again."

She suddenly grows quiet, and asks for a moment to evaluate sharing something she rarely talks about. I close my eyes to give her some privacy.

"Sometimes," she says thoughtfully, "as an experience settles in, it feels right to talk about it. Since we're discussing how Spirit works in our lives, I want to share something with you now. Hopefully, it will be helpful to others."

I thank her for what I sense is not an easy tale to tell. I admire her willingness to share it, as well as how and why she chose to do so.

"The summer after my grandmother passed away," she says slowly, "I was a counselor at a camp for inner-city kids. We'd taken the kids out to the country. At the end of one particularly long day, I went for a walk. I was still in a lot of pain then and eventually, I sat down against a fence post to rest and reflect. It was a cloudy night. After a while, the full moon appeared from behind the clouds. Suddenly, the moonlight bounced off a nearby telephone pole and cast the sign of the cross at my feet. I felt like I was being claimed by this cross; all my fears of crucifixion, of taking on the burden of the cross, surfaced. I was so terrified that I ran down the road screaming."

The story ends. She takes a deep breath. "We often think of religious experiences as gentle and inspiring, but this was just the opposite! Swiss psychiatrist Carl Jung called this a 'negative numinous experience.' It can take a lot of work to assimilate it into your life in a way you can live with, but this kind of an experience is an important integration point, an opportunity to align the ego with the soul. It 'purifies the senses,' as it says in the Christian mystical literature. It also helps us get in touch with our 'shadow,' the unrecognized or unclaimed parts of ourselves we can't acknowledge because we're afraid of them. Admitting to our shadow—to our gifts as well as the parts of our personality we view as 'bad' or 'ugly'—dramatically changes our lives, and most people are afraid of change so they don't deal with these things head on. But we must face these difficult experiences because it's the key to becoming whole. I feel much more accepting about what happened to me now, some thirty years later. The experience also helped me understand the power of symbols in my life.

"Shadow work," Lauren goes on to explain, "also opens the door to improving the quality of our relationships—our relationship with God, with self, and with others. If we're not aware of our anger, our jealousy, our fear, our hurt feelings—or if we don't think we're capable of such feelings—we project them outside ourselves onto others. The unkind things we do—the back biting, the bigotry, the envy—occur simply because we don't know ourselves deeply enough to understand that whatever we criticize in another is also within ourselves. We don't have to love our shadow or dwell on the fact we each have one, but we do have to stop hiding from it. This doesn't happen all at once. It's a process. But unless we honor all the different parts of ourselves, we cannot function at our highest and deepest level. We might be technologically or intellectually sophisticated, but we'll never be wise."

Do you have a spiritual routine or specific practices that help you gain this kind of clarity?

Her eyes light up. "My answer reminds me of something mythologist Joseph Campbell once said when he was asked about his spiritual practice. His response was 'I underline.' Mine is 'I get on and off airplanes.' That's the biggest ritual I have in my life now besides labyrinth walking. I do dream work. I work with a spiritual director. I see a therapist when I can fit it into my travel schedule. About every three or four months I throw the *Runes* or the *I Ching*. I also participate in special events we have at Grace Cathedral, like the 'Women's Dream Quest.' And I pray—prayer that's a spontaneous springing forth, an act of love and compassion rather than a disciplined act of will. It's fine, of course, to have a specific prayer or prayer time, but each of us has to find that voice within us that carries our own natural sense of prayer, the impromptu outpouring of our soul."

Do you have a favorite prayer?

"That depends on what I'm focused on. Sometimes I say, 'Guide me, Mother of God.' Or I pray an affirmative prayer like 'I am the daughter of Light. Please guide me.' I like prayers that are gentle and inclusive of people of all faiths."

Did you have any mentors who helped develop or guide your thinking?

"Jean Houston was a mentor. Certainly Alan Jones. Laurence Rockefeller was not so much a mentor as a very thoughtful human being who understood about the evolution of consciousness. He gave the Cathedral a liberal grant and essentially said, 'Go ahead, Lauren, and manifest your ideas.' His generosity helped me begin to produce transformational events and work with large groups of people."

Hildegard of Bingen? Do you consider her a mentor as well?

"I think of her as my 'spiritual grandmother.' She was a strong, feisty woman, a great visionary and a mystic—one of the few people recognized by the Pope during her lifetime as an authentic voice of God. Every bit of her being was creative. She composed music, wrote ten books, she even had artisans paint her visions, all in an effort to magnify her faith so others could see its value. She thrived in the Benedictine Order at a time when women were viewed as second-class citizens. She was one amazing woman and I take a great deal of inspiration from simply knowing she walked this Earth."

I smile and say, "She was a woman with a mission," then ask Lauren if she believes that she too has a mission, an assignment she feels she was born to carry out.

"I do. I think we each have our own soul assignment, our own unique way of contributing to the world. It doesn't have to be something big. It just needs to be authentic, something that truly comes from within our own selves."

By "soul assignment," do you mean the development of a specific quality or the completion of a specific responsibility or task?

"The Danish philosopher Kierkegaard once said, 'Every human being comes to earth with sealed orders.' That's what I mean by soul assignment. It's something that tugs at you and pulls you along like the Great Grandmother's Thread. It's a driving force behind your seeking, your searching—and your creativity. It says, 'Hey, take a look at this! There's something wonderful here for you, some nugget to uncover.' Or it says, 'You're not quite on the mark here yet, but if you keep exploring, something will take shape.' I see this in a lot of people I work with, people who feel they're here for a special reason, who want to give back, to discover how they can be a contributing member of society."

Are you talking about what psychotherapist Erik Erikson called "generativity," the desire to pass on what you've learned or gained during your lifetime?

"That's part of it, but I'm thinking more about what Hildegard referred to as 'fully blossoming.' I think your soul assignment is more of a spiritual genetic code, something imprinted in your soul that you're born to live out. James Hillman talks about this in his book *The Soul's Code*. It's not predestination; rather it's something that unfolds over time."

And your soul assignment is . . .

"My work with the labyrinth is part of it, but I think a bigger assignment has to do with helping people integrate psyche and Spirit. A bigger assignment still is helping birth people's creativity. I'm not necessarily talking about the creation of beautiful objects of art but about creating wholeness within ourselves and within our society. Birthing our creativity is about how to heal the fragility of life and make the world a better place. We need creativity on all levels, a flowering of the masses, like what occurred during the Middle Ages, where people come forward to share what's inside them, to share their gifts."

How did you discover your gifts?

"I'm still finding that out. I feel like a rock tossed into a polishing tumbler banging against other rocks. As the hard, outer surface falls away, the hope is that more of my core is exposed and made beautiful. I've learned a lot about myself through trial and error and particularly through my failures. I don't have a lot of sensitivity around failure and rejection, so I don't get stuck when this occurs. I just let the bad ideas go or I follow them as they change into more effective ideas. It's part of the process.

"I think finding your gifts is a soul level issue rather than a job training issue. It's different from learning new skills. It's about looking at what you're good at, what you enjoy doing, what people respond to most in you. Ask yourself what creates that sense of flow and timelessness in you, what you enjoy doing. That's probably a good clue to what your gift is."

Given everything you've done, what do you think is your greatest accomplishment?

She briefly considers the question, then says, "Having the guts to follow my intuition, to trust and go with the flow." She laughs, then adds, "Of course, if I'd seen the whole picture at the beginning of my work with the labyrinth, I would have imploded with fear and disbelief!"

That's probably true about many things in our lives. Do you have any regrets?

"I have a whole list of them when I'm feeling uncertain about the future: I wish I had more administrative skills, more education, a broader network. The list can go on and on. But when I seriously sit down and reflect on my life, I'm very grateful for the role I am able to play. I love teaching and speaking. I love helping other people along on their path. It's both fun and a challenge."

Do you have any advice you'd like to pass on to others?

"Hang in. Trust. Don't get down on yourself. Become aware of those inner critical voices—and if you can't stop them yourself, *get help*."

When all is said and done, how would you like to be remembered?

"No one ever asked me this before." She rests her chin in her hand and ponders her response.

"As a creator," she says finally, "as someone who did what she felt deeply connected to; someone who followed a call and, as a result, was able to help address the spiritual hunger so characteristic of our times. That's how I would like to be remembered."

It is a description of a life that Hildegard of Bingen would no doubt say is "fully blossoming."

To Learn More About the Life and Work of
Reverend Lauren Artress

Contact:
Veriditas, The World Wide Labyrinth Project
The Presidio
1009 General Kennedy Avenue—First Floor
San Francisco, California 94129
Voice: (415) 561-2921
On the Web: www.veriditas.net
E-mail: LaurenArtress@veriditas.net

A full listing of workshops and events is available at Veriditas.net, including:
- "Walking a Sacred Path" at Chartres Cathedral in France
- "The Women's Dream Quest" at Grace Cathedral and other locations in the United States
- "Creative Leap: Negotiating a Life Transition"
- "Facilitators Training: Labyrinth Facilitation as a Spiritual Path"

Lauren Artress also leads workshops on:
- "The Labyrinth as a Path to Spiritual Transformation"
- "Hildegard of Bingen"
- "Meeting the Spiritual Hunger of Our Times"
- "Life Transitions"

Read:
- *Walking a Sacred Path: Rediscovering the Labyrinth as a Spiritual Tool*, Riverhead Books
- *The Sacred Path Companion: A Guide to Walking the Labyrinth to Heal and Transform*, Riverhead Books
- *The Sand Labyrinth*, Tuttle Publishers

View:
- *Rediscovering the Labyrinth*, by Grace Communications
- *The Power of Silence with Lauren Artress, Thomas Keating, and Thich Nhat Hanh*, produced by Wisdom Television

Six

Olympia Dukakis

*Wherefore let thy voice
Rise like a fountain for me night and day.*
—Alfred, Lord Tennyson

WE KNOW HER best as Rose Castorini, the intrepid wife from *Moonstruck,* the devoted friend Clarey from *Steel Magnolias,* and the clear-sighted Mrs. Madrigal, the landlord of indeterminate gender from *Tales of the City.* Olympia Dukakis has also played a senator, a countess, and a high school principal; she has been Jennifer Aniston's mother, Jack Lemmon's wife, a Jewish widow, and a Greek heroine—to name only a few.

An award-winning actress of stage, screen, and television, she has endeared herself to audiences around the world for her dynamic portrayals of the grand transformations and subtle accommodations that are the bread and butter of women's lives.

The daughter of Greek immigrants, Olympia grew up in Lowell, Massachusetts, in a neighborhood where ethnic discrimination, particularly against Greeks, was routine. She made her stage debut at thirteen in a benefit for Greek war relief and acting became her first love. Early in her career, she was advised to change her name to something less ethnic. She refused, despite the fact that it would have paved the way to a greater variety of roles, and remained undeterred in her desire to become an actor. After high school, she obtained a degree in physical therapy and worked as a therapist during the height of the polio epidemic. She saved her money, returned to school, and earned a master's in fine arts at Boston University's School of the Performing Arts. Degree in hand, she moved to New York City to pursue a stage career. Shortly thereafter, she appeared in a production of *Medea* where she met and fell in love with actor Louis Zorich. Their forty-three-year marriage produced three children and a lifelong repository of unconditional support.

In 1988, after thirty years of performing principally in New York City and in regional theater, and with fifteen years of teaching acting at NYU under her belt, Olympia won her profession's highest accolade, the Academy Award for Best Supporting Actress, for her portrayal of the Italian matriarch in *Moonstruck*. It was her first substantial role in a major motion picture. Later that year, she stood on the podium alongside first-cousin Michael Dukakis, then governor of Massachusetts, as he accepted the Democratic nomination for president of the United States, and shouted the names of her departed Greek relatives into the din of the crowd. It was, for her, a profound moment, a proud declaration of her ethnicity that she claimed for her entire family.

Olympia has gone on to appear in over seventy films, twenty-five Broadway and off-Broadway productions, twenty television movies, and over one hundred regional stage productions. Besides an Oscar, she has won, among others, a Golden Globe, a New York Film Critics Award, two Obies, and two Emmy nominations for her work.

One of her most personally memorable roles was in the play *The Trojan Women*. It opened her heart to what has become a profound relationship with the Great Mother, the feminine aspect of God long venerated in the ancient cultures of the Indus River Valley. In 1985, she met Srimata Gayatri Devi, an Indian spiritual teacher in the Vedanta tradition, and studied with her until her passing.

As an activist and popular speaker for women's groups, Olympia takes a strong stand for the health and safety of women and children, for the environment, and for equal rights among all people—not the least of which is the right to personal transformation. In 1992, she and several friends co-created "Voices of Earth," a nonprofit theater company designed to help women, including herself, explore their spiritual heritage and birth their own spiritual transformation. A grant from the Geraldine Dodge Foundation funded the creation of workshops and performance pieces inspired by the "Inanna Hymns," the ancient Sumarian stories that celebrate the Great Mother. Olympia describes the performances that emerged from these workshops as "emotional, physical, spiritual, and joyful" pieces that explored, through metaphor, issues unique to women's lives.

In all things, Olympia Dukakis is both vulnerable and a robust force for life. This was first obvious to me in her brilliant portrayal of Rose Castorini in *Moonstruck*. Beset by the growing disparities in her marriage, Rose goes alone to a neighborhood restaurant to have dinner and invites a lonely college professor who has just been rebuffed by his girlfriend to dine with her. After dinner, he walks her home and attempts to engage her in a liaison. In spite of her own needs for companionship, Rose luminously refutes his advances "because," as she says, "I know who I am." The way Olympia delivered that line, the self-awareness in her voice as she said those words, spoke to me about how to defuse the predatory desires that nibble away at our integrity and self-respect. It was also clear to me that no one could render such a delicately nuanced performance without being mindful of her own contradictions. Thirteen years later, when she accepts my invitation to participate in this book, I discover that contradiction is what feeds her, is grist for her spiritual and professional mill. What I also discover is that she is a woman who is unpretentious and down-to-earth—and a woman with a tangible and unreserved spiritual yearning.

❖ ❖ ❖ ❖ ❖

IT'S BONE COLD in New York City in March, but there I am, climbing out of a taxi in front of the cafe where I am to meet her, fairly oblivious of the chill in the air. I've been e-mailing Bonnie Kramen, Olympia's assistant, for several months now, arranging the details of this meeting. I reviewed the biographical materials Bonnie sent me, and staged an Olympia Dukakis Film Festival for myself, all to prepare for our conversation. I'm as ready as I'll ever be.

I pay the cabby, then walk inside the restaurant to get the lay of the land. The "joint is jumpin'," brimming with neighborhood regulars and intelligentsia from nearby NYU. I tell the hostess why I've come and ask her to reserve a corner booth for me for 2:00 P.M. She can make no promises, she says. "It *is*, after all, lunchtime." I spend the next hour walking the neighborhood. When I return to the cafe, my table is waiting. I slide into the booth, peel off the layers of winter clothing I've amassed around me, and set up my taping equipment.

Olympia enters the restaurant bundled in a nylon parka, a mustard-colored wool scarf tied fashionably around her neck and a black wool beret pulled down over her ears. The hostess points her in my direction, and as she walks toward me, she unwinds her scarf and stuffs the beret into her jacket pocket. She is much shorter and slimmer than she appears on screen. Her tussled hair is dark with an auburn hue. Her eyes, those rueful, intelligent, honeyed eyes of hers, draw me in. I smile and nod in greeting and extend my hand. She hits the table running, and begins our discussion even before she sits down. She is apprehensive, she tells me, "talking about women's spirituality in a world that has suppressed its existence for thousands of years." After ten minutes, I turn on my tape recorder and ask her to summarize the reasons for her disquietude.

"I always feel uncomfortable when I read one of these interviews because it never feels substantive enough or it feels very marginalized. It's not because there's a lack of sincerity, or even a lack of depth . . ."

Is it because it's hard to put something so subtle into words?

"No. I think it's because most of us talk one way and live another. There are a few people who truly, truly walk the talk—who are, as Merlin Stone wrote, 'women who have gone over the mountain.' The rest of us just talk the talk. The rest of us are still trying to find ways to live in the world with spiritual values. Myself included. We've learned certain skills, we've learned to prevail somewhat, but we've not made it over the mountain. I sometimes truly despair at ever being meaningfully altered and affected by the things I claim are so important to me."

She searches for the words that unravel the core of her discontent. It's easy to see she's struggling. Her eyes reflect her every thought.

"Oh! I know what it is!" she exclaims. "Most of us have contradictions about our lives, but when we talk with someone like yourself, we talk only about what we aspire to, what we smell in the air. We don't talk about the contradictions. I suppose those who have made it over the mountain still have contradictions, but not about their spirituality. They don't live in two worlds like I do."

She is clearly distressed by this paradox. This easy companionship she has with her vulnerability and her willingness to allow me to witness it occurs often during our conversation. Without giving it a second thought, I reach out and touch her hand, as if something I could do might be able to comfort her. She smiles at me.

"I recognize," she says with a sigh, "that the real pulse of life is transformation, yet I work in a world dominated by men and the things men value, where transformation is not the coinage. It's not even the language! Winning is everything in Hollywood. The 'deal' is everything. I understand the competitive thing because I had a real battle with it as a young woman. Because of my ethnicity, I felt I had to prove I was better—not as good as, but better—than others. Thankfully, it became clear to me that when I compete, I lose my connection to the passion I have for my work. Every once in a while, I come across a man who has the desire to collaborate and be conciliatory. But if I want to continue acting and have the potential for financial prosperity—something that came to me very late in life—I have to live with these competitive values."

She sighs, then tells me about the last time she saw Marija Gimbutas, the famed UCLA archeologist whose research into the goddess cultures of the Neolithic Era made a preeminent contribution both to the field of archeology and to feminist thought.

"Just before she died," Olympia says, "we talked about how difficult it is for me to make my work be about the things I feel are important. She pointed at me and said, 'Do it! Do it!' I carry out my private efforts, but I haven't yet said, 'You know what? I'm going to honestly make my life be about what I value most.'"

It's a hard thing to do.

"Yes it is. I feel it most in my work, because there aren't roles about women who are spiritually evolving. That anyone would even write something like that, something that's worth doing, would be a miracle! So I constantly play women who are damaged and out of touch, who are seeking without knowing, or knowing without the skills to transform their lives. But then, that's really the fate of many women today. Since I carry those same issues inside me, when I connect to that, it resonates in my work and I think women somehow feel the story is about them."

I tell her about my Olympia Dukakis Film Festival and how I observed that empathy in her performances. She turns and looks at me in mock horror, then hides her head in her arms.

"You had an Olympia Dukakis Film Festival!" she moans. "Oh my God!" We laugh.

The waiter has been hovering at a respectful distance, waiting for a break in our conversation. He now makes a beeline to our table. Olympia orders a burger. When he looks at me, she tells him with a smile, "She's working, I'm eating." I nod, ask for something to drink, and watch him scurry off to place our order. We pick up the thread of our conversation.

"I always look for ways to move the character to places within herself where it becomes necessary to confront something, to learn something new. Most of us are not real eager to grow, myself included. We try to be happy by staying in the status quo. But if we're not willing to be honest with ourselves about what we feel, we don't evolve."

She tells me about a book by the Catholic scholar Margaret Starbird, *The Woman with the Alabaster Jar: Mary Magdalene and the Holy Grail.* Starbird originally decided to write the book to discredit the reports that Mary Magdalene was married to Jesus and bore his child—stories she initially considered heretical. But her research thrust her into a personal descent that forced her to reevaluate her entire belief system, for she discovered that, at least as far as she was concerned, the accounts were true. "Being the woman she is—which is honest—she couldn't lie to herself about what she found," Olympia says. "Her self-honesty was extraordinary.

She's still a Catholic, but now she works within the Church to effect changes in how women are seen."

Olympia looks me straight in the eye, shakes a finger and declares, "You see, *her* life and *her* work are together. I'm not saying she doesn't have problems, but she doesn't get up every day and think 'A' and then go out and deliberately do 'B.' That's what I do."

This seems painful to you.

"It's very painful," she says. Her eyes reflect her pain.

I want to ease her heartache, one I'm not all that unfamiliar with myself, but all I can think of to say to her is that at least she can name her pain, that a lot of us walk around not knowing why we're unhappy, not knowing why we feel so conflicted. She nods her head in agreement. Then I tell her that I think this struggle to bring our inner and outer worlds together is an ongoing part of the spiritual life, that when we face these contradictions, we can then choose how we will walk our talk.

"I understand this now," she confides. "In 1985, I became very involved with Gayatri Devi, a spiritual teacher, who helped me see this."

How did you meet her?

"My husband, daughter, and I were in therapy because of issues that came up after he had a terrible automobile accident. The therapist said everyone was OK except me, that I was behaving as if we were still in crisis. He said I had to do something to focus on myself, by myself, or he wouldn't see me anymore. I rooted around for something to do and a friend suggested I go to a retreat center in the mountains. I had my doubts—it seemed to me like a camp for precocious adults!—but I went anyway.

"The only weekend I was free was during what they call their 'Spiritual Weekend,' so I signed up for that. Friday night, the presenters sat on a stage and talked about their upcoming workshops. There were rabbis and Cambodian monks and Indian swamis and Protestants and Catholics and Native Americans. It was a whole smorgasbord! And there was this little lady in saffron robes. I was very moved by what she said, but of course, I didn't permit that to influence me! I decided to go with a shaman because I'd been reading a lot about shamans at the time."

As she tells this story, a calm comes over her. She is a wonderful storyteller—funny, self-effacing, and poignant—and paints the scene with brushes steeped in the rich palette of her emotional wellspring.

"The workshop I went to was like a bad acting class! Everyone was try-ing to get in touch with their feelings—beating drums and howling—but I stayed with it. The next day, the leader asked us each to share why we'd come to the retreat. Everyone gave such esoteric and spiritual reasons—and there I was because my therapist told me that if I didn't do something about myself, he wouldn't see me anymore! But when my time came to talk, I got very choked up and said, 'I'm here to open my heart.' I don't know where that came from, but that's what I said.

"The workshop continued with much sage-burning and carrying on, but I just couldn't do it anymore. I walked outside toward a little house where I heard the chanting of women's voices. I looked in the window and saw the woman I'd been so moved by the night before sitting in lotus posi-tion on a slightly raised platform. I walked in and sat down. Gayatri Devi was a *bhakti*, as they say in India; hers was the path of devotion to God. She was talking in an animated way about the Great Mother, about Her role in the Vedanta tradition. The more she talked, the more I cried. I didn't know why I was crying. It wasn't that I was sad; I was just crying."

I tell her that I know that kind of crying, when someone touches you in a place so far beyond what your conscious mind can articulate that all you can do is cry.

"You know that kind of crying too? Good!" She slaps the palm of her hand on the table, pleased not only that I understand what she is talking about but that I too have had that kind of cry.

"I didn't make too much of it though at the time. After all," she says parenthetically, "I *am* an actress!" We laugh.

"After the break, I went over and asked Sudha—Ma's assistant at that time, and the one to whom the mantle was passed after Ma's death—if I could speak with Ma, with Gayatri Devi. She told me it would be impos-sible to see her, that Ma was totally booked. I wasn't too upset because I already knew something about what Ma had been talking about. The truth was, I had secretly gotten involved with the Great Mother on my own, thinking I was the only person on the planet to do so. I had no idea other people were interested in Her."

How did that come about?

"I did a play called *The Trojan Women* that brought up a lot of spiri-tual questions for me. Then I read a book called *Perseus and the Gorgon*.

After that, I went to every bookstore I could find to get books about the Great Mother. One day, I was in a store here in the Village, and Merlin Stone's book, *When God Was a Woman*, fell off the shelf and landed at my feet!"

She holds up her right hand as if she is taking an oath. "Honest to God," she vows.

And then . . .

"Then, months later, I'm having a massage and I hear a voice that seemed to come from the back of my head, an androgynous Presence, say the words 'Celebrate Her'—meaning I was to celebrate the Great Mother. I started to cry and cry and cry. Finally I said aloud, 'I know how to suffer, but I don't know how to celebrate.' And the Voice replied, 'You are of Her, and you know how to do it.' My awareness of this Presence remained for a while after that, but I told no one about the experience.

"Several months later, I'm going up the stairs at the subway at 42nd Street, on my way to NYU to teach. I'm in a hurry and feeling angry because people are in my way and I couldn't walk as fast as I wanted to, and I hear the Voice again. It said, 'Turn around.' I turned around and saw everyone scrambling up the stairs. Then the Voice said, 'She loves everyone. All these people; everyone.' It really took my breath away. I started to cry, so grateful was I for this love."

She begins to cry. She's there again, climbing the stairs in the subway, hearing the Voice, feeling the Great Mother's love.

The waiter arrives with our order. The time it takes to set our food before us gives Olympia the chance to regain her composure. She scarfs down a few bites of her burger, then takes me back to that weekend in the mountains and her first meeting with Gayatri Devi.

"So when I heard Ma couldn't see me, I was OK with that because, as I said, I already knew about the Great Mother. I started to walk outside when Sudha came over to me and said Ma wanted to see me. I froze and said, 'It's OK,' but Sudha said, 'No, Ma *wants* to see you.' So I started up the hill to where Ma was sitting—to a table and two chairs facing each other under some trees—and as I walked, my awareness of all external sound left me. It was as if I were walking in a vacuum. I sat down and told her my name and what brought me to the retreat. Finally, I told her about the two times I heard the Voice.

"She became very alert, then asked me some questions about the Voice. Then she said, 'What are you afraid of?'"

Tears begin to run down Olympia's cheeks. "I said, 'I'm afraid of this love, afraid I would be lost.' And Ma said, 'Lost in the sea of Her love?' I said, 'Yes. I'm afraid if I allow myself to feel it, I won't come back. I know what that is. I've psychologically let go before and struggled to come back.'

"Ma looked at me for a long time, almost as if she were x-raying me. Then she talked to me and her words made me feel I would be all right, that I could receive the Great Mother's love—which is still hard for me to do—and give Her love—which is easier. You know?"

Before I can answer her, Olympia digs into her jacket pocket and pulls out a small book of prayers written by Swami Paramananda, an Indian monk of the Ramakrishna Order. "I want to read something to you," she says. She reads me some prayers, not as an actress but as a *bhakti*, filled with the devotion that inspired words she has since made her own.

> Great Mother Heart, how tender art Thou
> Thy love, transcending all my iniquities,
>   pours upon my life its benign sweetness.
> How oft my imperfect nature lies mortified
>   and ashamed in Thy protecting bosom,
>   overwhelmed by Thy unfathomed tenderness.
> Who art Thou that givest this endless bounty to me,
>   meritless and ignorant?
> Divine Mother Heart. Proof of Thy unceasing care,
>   I find in every turn of life.
> With many arms dost Thou shield me.
> With many hearts dost Thou love me.
> With many minds dost Thou guide me to the road of safety.
> Forget I may at times when dark clouds gather;
>   but to have seen Thy face of love
>   and known what is not known,
>   save when Thou dost lift the veil,
> Is joy forever and crowning glory of Life.

"That's so hard for me to take in, to really let myself have that," she whispers softly. I reach for her hand again and she reads me another of Swami Paramananda's beautiful prayers:

> Glory to Thy all-conquering love;
> Yea, Thy love is my armor, my impenetrable shield,
> My unfailing safeguard,
> I bathe in Thy love and am refreshed;
> I feed on Thy love and my soul-hunger is appeased.
> What need have I of ought else,
> When Thou dost fill me and surround me
> With Thine inexhaustible and all-filling love.

"That was the love Ma was talking about," she says.

She is quiet now, lost in thought. She manages a half-hearted smile, then loses herself in her lunch. I shift the direction of our conversation, and ask her how she would define spirituality.

"Well, there's something open-hearted about it. I really understood how important this was when my mother was dying from Alzheimer's. Her defenses went away and she was no longer suspicious or critical. Her heart opened.

"So why does this seem part and parcel of spirituality? I guess because in order to be open-hearted, you have to trust, or be willing to trust—but trust with open eyes. You have to look at the reality of things. Sometimes there's darkness and pain. That's part of life, too."

Being open-hearted in the face of contradictions?

"Being open-hearted when the world pretty much looks like a place your heart should be defended and protected against."

It's the stuff grown-ups are made of. Some words of Simone de Bouvier come to mind: "One is not born a woman, one becomes a woman." I ask Olympia what she thinks about this.

"I think we're socialized out of being women, and then we have to find our way back to it. That's hard to do. Sometimes I feel as if four thousand years of silencing women, of the fear of women who were burned in oil or eviscerated in front of their daughters, is imprinted deep within me and has altered my DNA."

Yes, I say. I think we are connected to each other in ways that defy logic. How did you become a woman? What experiences . . .

"Let's not kid ourselves," she admonishes. "It's still going on. I'm still struggling, thinking and reading and talking and writing and noticing—constantly noticing. It's an ongoing process."

I nod my head in agreement.

"These days, maybe because of all this New Age stuff, I hear the word 'crone' a lot. People think of crone as a destination you arrive at, not as a time in your life when something is still going on. You never 'arrive.' It's not over because you're fifty or sixty or seventy! I think we're in endless transition—and that goes on till we die. In that sense, maybe Simone de Bouvier was right.

"Stories about the ongoing dramas in our lives as we age are not being told because women find it difficult to be honest about what's going on—about, for example, our heightened sexuality as we age or about living in a society that only values youth. We have to be honest with ourselves—and with each other. We have to talk about our real lives and our real needs."

Spiritual transformation is an ongoing process, but Western civilization is so goal-oriented that we focus on the end rather than on the process itself.

"Yeah. The reality is you don't arrive, you don't have a crone ceremony and suddenly get wisdom."

Years ago, I heard Ram Dass say that we're all born with certain core issues we deal with throughout our lives, but as we evolve, we become aware of those issues sooner and it takes less time to work them through. Do you think this is true?

"My sense of transformation is much more synergistic. Much more mysterious."

Not so formulaic?

"Yeah. I also think we have to open our eyes to what others tell us and see if it works for us before we buy into it. I fall prey to this myself. We have to be cautious. At least, I do. I bought into a lot of things when I was growing up that were right for someone else but that I later discovered weren't right for me."

Me too. I think a lot of us did.

"A lot of us still do. I talk to women's groups all over the country and see women struggling with this. The fear of not being accepted, of being different, of not having a man, all make it hard for a woman to do what she really believes is right for *her*. And, if we want to change things for women, we can't tear away at the fabric of each other's lives like some feminists do. Women have got to work together. We've got to recognize and acknowledge the bravery it's taken to live the lives we've lived, to get up every day and take care of our children and our homes, to keep our churches and schools going, to plant trees in our parks—all these things. It makes me want to cry when I think about what women do! And we get *buhpkis* for it. We aren't even recognized by ourselves for what we do!"

Sometimes it's easier to recognize our potential in another. That's why I often show your movie *Moonstruck* in the women's retreats I lead. That heart-stopping moment when your character refuses to sacrifice her integrity on the altar of her conflicting needs can be a powerful mirror for others to see the need to maintain their own integrity.

"'Because I know who I am,'" she utters, repeating the words Rose used to jettison her libidinous dinner companion.

"Wasn't that incredible! It's amazing how many women talk to me about that one line. Why? Because they finally saw something in a film that reflected a woman's view of herself, that wasn't a man's view of how women are. There it was. I got a similar response when I did *Steel Magnolias* because it was a film about the profound friendships and loyalties women are capable of."

How important do you think the kind of knowing Rose had about herself is to living a spiritual life?

"I think we have to be careful about what we label as a prerequisite for spirituality. I don't think you have to know a lot to have a spiritual life, but knowing gives life richness."

I take a moment to think about her response. She looks at me with a glint in her eye. "So," she says, "what else you got?"

I smile and ask her to tell me how she conceptualizes God.

"God is not something I think about but something I experience as an energy, a Presence. I do find it easier to pray to a female Presence or an androgynous Presence. I once asked Ma about this and she said, 'One God, many paths.' Whether you pray to Jesus or to the Great Mother or to Buddha, that's just the path you choose as you evolve towards something within yourself that is of God."

Have you always believed in God?

"I don't think I thought about things like that when I was young. I stopped going to the Greek Church because I'd get nauseous on the trolley. I hated being there and thought the priest was mean. My best friend was a member of the Salvation Army so I went there for a couple of years, until they wanted me to say I was saved by the blood of Jesus. I couldn't do that, so I quit.

"In my late teens and early twenties, I went to a lot of different churches. I was looking for something but didn't know what it was. When my children were born, I didn't have them baptized because I felt baptism was about erasing Original Sin—something the Church said children got from their mother—and I absolutely refused to believe women carry Original Sin. My daughter became a Pentecostal Christian and was eventually baptized, and both my sons married Catholics. I'm very happy for them. They found their own way. My husband is a fall-away Catholic, but with a vengeance. He's actually more of a feminist than I am."

When did you realize what you were looking for?

"In my forties and fifties, when I first heard the Voice."

Do you follow any particular tradition?

"I don't have a formal tradition; I go on my own experience. When I was a kid, I'd kneel down at the side of my bed every night before I went to sleep, and my mother and I would say a Greek prayer to the Virgin Mary."

She repeats the prayer in Greek, then translates it for me:

> *Holy Mary, give me your help and never let me stray*
> *   far from you.*
> *And make me a good child, so that I love knowledge.*
> *And to my good parents, give everlasting health.*

"Years later, Ma asked me if I remembered any prayers from my childhood. I remembered this one and thought, 'Well, look at that! Thanks to my mother, even when I was young, I was connecting to a female Presence!'"

How do you now explore your spirituality?

"Through prayer and meditation. And I do Iyengar Yoga. The physical world is also an important part of my spirituality. Trees, for example, are a tremendous source of connectedness to my heart. A tree only aspires to be a tree. It doesn't compete with other trees It adjusts to whatever obstacles it has below or above the ground. It doesn't complain. It's such a beautiful living presence, such a teacher."

I tell her how, years ago, I tearfully clung to a tree during a rock concert hoping to connect with a deeper source of happiness than what the world had thus far provided. Though I didn't know what it was that I was looking for at the time, that tree started me on my spiritual journey.

She smiles at my story. "Once, when a group of us were having lunch with Ma, someone began to pontificate about what he thought life was all about. Ma turned to him and asked, 'What does a mother want for her child?' It was quiet for a minute, then someone else said, 'Happiness.' Ma said, 'That's it. All you need to concern yourself with is what brings you *real* happiness.' She boiled the whole thing down and made it easy."

Yup. We make it so complicated!

"Women especially do this. We fragment ourselves; we take care of everyone else to the point where we don't really know what makes us happy. We need to reclaim a sense of play and reclaim our creative initiative. We need to find out what works for *us*. Once we do this, we find a way to move forward with our lives. We stop being so fragmented and regain a sense of ourselves."

The same sense that Rose had in her moment of decision?

"Yes. It's that feeling of 'I know who I am.' It's also the willingness to *not* know who you are, and to permit that transformation from not knowing to knowing to occur.

"Marija Gimbutas used to say that the heart of the goddess is transformative energy, the same energy that turns the seed into the plant, the tadpole into a frog, the cocoon into a butterfly. In ancient times, these animals were sacred because their transformation illustrates what life is really about. It seems to me that how we understand transformation and how it exists in our lives is also a big part of spirituality. At least it is for me. It's something women understand intuitively and intimately through our bodies—if we have the courage to claim that kind of knowing."

I know your relationship with Marija Gimbutas was very close. Would you consider her a mentor? Have you had other mentors?

"Oh my God, have I!" Her eyes light up as she talks about the women who have been important to her.

"I'm so fortunate to have had Ma, Marija Gimbutas, and my mother, though they all passed away within three years of each other. Esa Bollen, a Pilates instructor I got to know in California, was a wonderful woman to talk to and be with. Betty Meador, Merlin Stone, Barbara Walker, and Vickie Noble—blessed women who have been out there when there was no net—were also mentors to me through their books and friendship."

Connections this strong can be a source of great comfort, particularly during hard times. Have you ever had a "dark night of the soul"?

"Yes, I've had a number of these experiences. I dealt with them by instructing myself—by willing myself—to go forward into the darkness, by facing whatever I thought would be the worst part of the darkness."

Later it occurs to me that this warrior spirit of hers is also the seat of her vulnerability. It takes great courage to be vulnerable, to look fear in the face, to sit with the unknown, because you never know where you will end up. But doing this has its rewards: gradually, the fear diffuses, it loses its power. In some seemingly miraculous way, this letting go bestows access to an inner font that allows you to live with greater meaning.

Olympia tells me a story that illustrates this process: "Many years ago," she says, "at a point when I was finally beginning to feel good about myself, I got a good review that threw me into quite a spin. I'd felt bad about myself for a long time, like I was just a black pit inside, like there was no real person inside. So when I got this review, I was literally lost. Who was I if I was not that darkness?

"I happened to be in therapy at the time, and I told the doctor I couldn't get through this experience without drugs. We argued. He said I could have two aspirin and that was it! 'You'll get through this the way you've done everything,' he said, 'with willpower.'

"I had to do a play that night, but I was so upset, I just sat in his office the rest of the day. I finally went to the theater, but I almost passed out on the subway. I got some smelling salts, put them in my pocket in case I needed them, and told the stage manager to watch me in case I started to fall. I got through the play and didn't need the smelling salts." She smiles.

"Now, if I feel the darkness coming on, I pray, 'You are my impenetrable shield . . .'—that prayer I read you earlier. It helps me tremendously to say that, to *know* that.

"Talking to certain people, like my daughter, also helps. She recently visited me in London, and just before I went to the theater, she asked me if I wanted to pray with her. She said this incredible prayer. It just poured out of her. It took me years to learn to pray like that, but my daughter knows how to do it and she's in her thirties! Isn't that great?"

She is beaming, *kveling*, a Yiddish word that, loosely translated, means to be filled with pride at another's accomplishments. I smile and nod my head. After a few moments, she glances over at the large clock that dominates one wall of the cafe and tells me her time is growing short.

I make an appeal for a few more questions and she acquiesces.

What role do you think your marriage plays in your spiritual development?

"My husband—because of who he is—helped me see myself, helped me know myself. At one point after I awakened to the Great Mother, I was worried about something and he said, 'Why don't you ask the Great Mother what to do?' I had a little altar upstairs, and he said, 'Go on up and ask Her.' It was so helpful.

"Before we got married, we promised to support each other in whatever we each wanted to do—even if we disagreed with what that was. He has always done that for me—more and better than I. He has never, ever, ridiculed or diminished anything I've done. You don't stay married for forty-three years because of sex or even because of love, but because your partner is a real friend to you, because they respect and regard you."

I nod, then I fire off my remaining questions. She answers each in a few precise words:

Do you believe you have an assignment, a task you were born to carry out?

"I used to think so, but I don't know if I do anymore."

What do you think is your greatest accomplishment?

"That I had children, raised them, and somehow we held it together in the midst of some horrendous things that happened."

What do you think is the secret of your success?

"That I have a real passion for my work and an appetite for life."

Do you have any advice you would like to share with others?

"Only what they ask of me. I'm not a wise crone. All I know is that we keep transforming; we never end."

Last question: When all is said and done, how would you like to be remembered?

"I think this being remembered business is much ado about nothing. I don't think I have to be remembered. My children will remember me intensely, my grandchildren will remember me less intensely, my great-grandchildren will laugh and say, 'You know, there was somebody in my family whose name was Olympia.' And that's it. Then we're gone from memory. What? Somebody's going to read a theater book and see that I did this, that, and the other thing?" She laughs.

That's it then, I tell her.

She smiles, gathers her jacket and scarf around her, and takes my hands in hers. "Good luck with this book," she says. She pulls her beret over her head and slides out of the booth. Three hours have flown by. I watch her go. I watch those in the cafe watch her go. She stops and shares a few words with the hostess, then disappears into the crisp March afternoon.

To Learn More About the Life and Work of Olympia Dukakis

Read:

- *Ask Me Again Tomorrow: A Life in Progress*, HarperCollins

View:

- *An Intimate Portrait: Olympia Dukakis,* Lifetime Biography Series
- Many of Olympia's films are available on DVD including: *Moonstruck, Steel Magnolias, Mr. Holland's Opus, Look Who's Talking, Dad, The Cemetery Club, Mighty Aphrodite, Picture Perfect,* and the Showtime miniseries *Tales of the City*

Seven
Riane Eisler

Women never have young minds. They are born 3,000 years old.
—Shelagh Delaney

IN 1987, RIANE EISLER published a book called *The Chalice and the Blade* that was a bold and scrupulously documented piece of scholarship. The book traced the evolution of social consciousness from the Neolithic Age to modern times and chronicled a view of societal restoration that was a radical departure from conventional wisdom. Readers learned about the existence of agrarian "partnership societies" that were egalitarian in nature, rooted in life-enhancing female images, and organized around traditional feminine values of nurturance and connection. They discovered how these peaceful people were overrun by aggressors from the more arid regions of the globe, "dominator societies" that used violence, manipulation, and fear to subdue their conquests. They also saw, perhaps for the first time, how this evolving hierarchy had, for thousands of years, distorted and suppressed partnership values in order to control the masses. Riane Eisler not only took this remarkable story to the people, she championed the nonviolent ethos of the ancient partnership societies for modern times. She promoted social development through gender balance and multiculturalism, and demonstrated viable governing alternatives based on cooperation and mutual regard. Her book celebrated women but it also celebrated the potential of every human being for caring. For many people—particularly women, children, and minorities—it was a call to freedom from a deep source of pain and social oppression.

The Chalice and the Blade was translated into seventeen languages and rapidly became an international best-seller. But it took more than ten years of intensive research and a lifetime of personal experience to write. When Riane was seven years old, Nazi soldiers stormed her parents' home in Vienna and forcibly dragged her father off to Gestapo headquarters. Her mother's courage saved them that night; her indignation and protest miraculously procured her husband's release. The family fled to Cuba where they lived for seven years until they were allowed to immigrate to the United States. When the war ended, Riane learned that most of her relatives had been exterminated in the Holocaust. It was a defining moment, one that would eventually compel the woman she would become to probe the origins of cruelty and violence in the world and lead her to her life's work.

Riane and her parents eventually settled in Los Angeles. She went to high school, studied sociology and anthropology at UCLA, and began a career as a social scientist with the Rand Corporation. Several years later, she returned to UCLA to earn a law degree. Then one day, she came across an ad in the newspaper that changed her life. A fledgling woman's center— one of the first in the United States—was looking for an attorney to help them incorporate and Riane volunteered for the job. She began to connect with other women who, like herself, had started to question the traditional roles of women in society. Though she knew little about feminism, she pored through the existing literature. Soon thereafter, she began teaching classes at UCLA on the legal and social status of women and children, and quickly became a pioneer in what came to be known as women's studies programs. Her subsequent achievements as a cultural historian and evolutionary theorist are now central to feminist theory and the human rights of women and children.

Riane has gone on to write other books about the efficacy of partnership values in modern society, and now serves as president of the Center for Partnership Studies, a nonprofit organization she founded in 1987 with her husband, social psychologist David Loye, and several other colleagues. The Center offers training, self-assessment tools, curriculum, coaching, and networking for educators, business professionals, and community and government leaders interested in implementing partnership values in society. She speaks at conferences worldwide, serves as a member of the World Commission on Spirituality and Consciousness, the World Academy of Arts and Sciences, and the World Business Academy—to cite just a few. *Macrohistory and Macrohistorians* named her as one of the twenty most important long-range social thinkers in the world. She is also the mother of two grown children and grandmother of four grandchildren.

Her research and scholarship, and her personal history, have led Riane to anchor her spiritual life in one enduring and universal tenet: love. After a break from the Jewish observances of her childhood and a growing exposure to other religious traditions, she began to incorporate a variety of beliefs into her thinking. Though she has gradually reconnected with her Jewish roots, she has come to believe primarily in the ever-present authority of kindness and in the joy she finds in connecting with others—particularly her family. I observed this in action when we met at a peace conference we both spoke at in San Francisco—she as the keynote speaker and I as a workshop presenter. Her consideration for others was unstinting.

My first decisive awareness of her work came when a professor in my graduate course in cultural anthropology described Riane's account of the comings and goings of the matriarchal societies that lived in the great Indus River Valley between 7500 B.C. and 3500 B.C. Like most people, I believed that the evolutionary narrative I had grown up with was a fairly accurate rendering of the world story—well, at least what we knew to date. The necessity to judiciously reconfigure history as new information came to light was a matter of course. What horrified me as my professor talked was the realization that I was so entrenched in the hierarchical spin—and so unaccustomed to questioning what I'd been told—that I had, with few reservations, bought the existing historical nine yards and all its inaccuracies lock, stock, and barrel. I felt outraged at the ruse that had been imposed on society and at my own naiveté, yet validated by the newfound logic with which I now perceived some of society's ills. This experience became a turning point in my life, one that cued me into the politics of deception and fueled a new resolve to develop a more inquiring mind. Years later, when the fates drew us together at the peace conference, I determined to make a way to Riane and invite her to participate in this book.

❖ ❖ ❖ ❖ ❖

SEVERAL WEEKS BEFORE the conference, I send Riane a letter about the book and suggest that perhaps we might find time to talk in San Francisco. But I do not hear back from her. Undaunted, I pack my tape gear in preparation for a windfall of instantaneous consent. Such bravado, I muse, is testimony to my growing experience of the way boons such as this have become integral to writing this book. When I arrive at the conference, I whoop out loud when I learn I've been invited to attend a private luncheon with Riane that will be held after she delivers her keynote. I clear my calendar for the rest of that afternoon on the off-chance that the wind will indeed blow my way.

We gather in the ballroom of the hotel the next morning for a series of announcements and accolades. Riane is finally introduced. She rises from her seat, walks up the stairs like a swan sailing across a lake, and takes her place behind the podium. In her late sixties, she is tall and lithe and elegantly dressed—refined in the European tradition. I expect her commentary to be incisive, and it is. But I do not anticipate the lilting quality of her voice, the gentleness that flows through her to the audience. She reminds me of a symphony conductor who, having mastered the technical execution of a concerto, yields to the innate longing of the music to be heard. People consistently smile as she talks and nod in silent agreement with her words.

When she finishes her talk and the applause dies down, I make my way to the luncheon, holding the thought that, should the opportunity arise, I will tell her about this book. Our hostess seats me almost directly across from Riane and halfway through the salad, she tells her about my work. On an impulse, I ask Riane then and there if she might be interested in participating. She turns away for a moment to think. "Why yes," she says, "I think that would be lovely. Let's see what we can do today."

Voila!

It's several hours before Riane and I are able to make our way through the crowd to my hotel room to talk. I've set up my recording gear in advance of her coming, but by the time we get to my room, it's clear she is worn somewhat thin from the demands of the day. I relinquish my desire to begin our conversation and we spend the next two hours talking about our lives in all the good ways women do. We part with an embrace and the promise to meet again. After a series of futile attempts to reconnect, we determine to continue our discussion via telephone. Had I not brought my recording equipment to San Francisco, we would not have had that time in my hotel room to get to know each other and thus, make such a warm connection when we talk again on the phone. We spend the first twenty minutes of the call catching up. I start our "official" conversation by asking her what God looks like to her. Because she has written about a variety of feminist issues, and particularly because her work teems with references to feminine images and myths, I make an assumption about her response. Her answer reminds me that I serve my companions best when I purge myself of even the most understandable expectations and remain open to the adventure of another's life.

"This is a very interesting question," she says, "because I don't have a personalized God, an image of a woman or a man. In fact, there is a vast divide between my experience of the Divine and my scholarship. I use the word 'God' in my writing because it's common terminology, but I don't think of the Divine as 'God.' I think there is a mystery in the universe that we, as bright as our species is, simply don't have the capacity to understand. We don't know what's beyond what we perceive with our senses.

"Obviously there's something—what I like to think of as some very wonderful energies. When I begin to tap into them through meditation, I realize that I am—that we all are—both the center of the universe and the most infinitesimally unimportant part of the universe. I get in touch with something that is far beyond me yet within me, as well as a part of the world I live in."

What do these energies feel like inside you?

"When I'm in touch with them, I really don't know whether they are inside or outside of me. 'Outside.' 'Inside.' These are just artificial boundaries we've learned to make. What I experience is a sense of being at home in the universe, a sense of joy, of calm—and at the same time, a certain excitement at being in touch with That which makes everything seem all right."

Do you have a personal relationship with these energies?

"Not really. But I do make an effort to connect with them and bring them into my life. Sometimes I use Thich Nhat Hanh's 'calm smile' technique where I breathe in calm and breathe out smiles. I like that a lot. Sometimes I watch my breath. Sometimes I do a moving meditation where I raise my arms very, very slowly above my head. I created this meditation—what I now think of as my chalice meditation—after I noticed that many of the goddess images from prehistory hold their arms above their shoulders in a position that forms a chalice. Doing it gives me a surge of energy and then a feeling of being very centered. I love doing it! It's very calming. I prefer this to a sitting meditation as it allows me to access that calm much faster."

After we get off the phone, I practice Riane's chalice meditation. Doing it reminds me somewhat of Tai Chi and of walking the labyrinth. There's much to be said about the ability of deliberate, conscious movement to fill the present moment with peace.

"Walking fast or running by the ocean is also part of my spiritual practice," she continues. "It clears me. If I just walk slowly, I stay in my head. I spend a lot of time there and need a break from all that intellectual activity, so I run in spurts. I do this almost every day at the end of the day. It gives me a wonderful sense of calm, just as I have when I meditate."

Riane's deep love for her family is, as she now tells me, also connected to her spirituality. "When I feel love for my daughters, or when I look at my little grandchildren, this is also, to me, a spiritual experience. It's not a specific practice; it's my life."

So you see no separation between your spirituality and your daily experiences?

"No, I'm very blessed in that. I feel so much joy sometimes when I immerse myself in my life, when I become fully conscious of my life. It's hard to express."

When life has been harsh, I say, it can be difficult to put your appreciation for whatever becomes your bounty into words.

"Yes. Gratitude is a big part of my spiritual practice. I'm very thankful for everything that's been given to me. For my husband David. For my children. For the incredible miracle of my grandchildren. I'm grateful to walk on the beach by the beautiful cypress trees near my home. I'm grateful to do the work I do and that, in my small way, I can make a contribution to the world."

How did you form your conception of the Divine? Did your work or the myths and images you write about influence your beliefs?

"Actually, my own beliefs have little to do with the things I've written about. I think of myths more as social constructs than as something having to do with this mysterious energy I feel inside and outside of myself.

"For some people, myths and images open them to a different perception of themselves and of the Divine. They think, for example, of the Divine in more pleasurable, feminine terms. My beliefs evolved more from the rational, cognitive part of my nature. Of course, there are myths and images that verify my beliefs, that particularly support my belief that we don't have to conceptualize the power that governs the universe in the punitive way we were told to do in the Judeo-Christian traditions. At the core of many world religions are symbols and stories of love and connection that were masked or changed in order to perpetuate the subordination of women. From my perspective, it's important to unmask those stories so we can change the injurious ways we relate to one another."

In your book *Sacred Pleasure*, you wrote: "My own spiritual journey, a sometimes tortuous and sometimes joyous quest, took me not to an isolated mountain, but to a new way of looking at my day-to-day life that was very different from what I had been led to expect." How so?

"The mystical literature is mostly about the person who goes off some place and has a solitary experience. That's hardly been the case with me.

My experience is one of connection. Even when I meditate and go inside myself, I find I'm connected to something."

You've also written about the profound absence of connection you felt after your family settled in Cuba and the challenges you faced as a young Jewish immigrant growing up in a predominantly Catholic country. For instance, you told your classmates at the Methodist school you attended that you believed in Jesus just to keep from being further ostracized. How did you reconcile these experiences within yourself? Your feelings of not-belonging?

There is a poignant silence. "With difficulty," she murmurs. "But one of the wonderful things that happened to me as a result of all this disparity was that it suddenly dawned on me that there are a lot of very different ways to think about God, and that I didn't have to think only one way in order to be a good person. I even began to incorporate some of these beliefs into my own thinking.

"For example, I was very attracted by the concept of the Madonna, the loving mother. She wasn't mean, she wasn't on the cross suffering—and thereby focusing my own attention on suffering—and she wasn't punitive. I now know that this loving countenance is part of human experience, even during periods in our history when violence and abuse are dominant. When we are hurting, we all want someone we can go to and say, 'Take care of me. Love me. Help me.'"

Were there specific experiences that shaped your spiritual beliefs?

"Certainly my childhood was a big influence. I was raised in a faithful Jewish home. Care for and responsibility to others was a value that was lived by my family and those around me. I learned by example rather than from anything I read in a prayer book."

She is quiet again, and I wait in respectful silence of thoughts that are hers alone.

"I was alone when I saw the newsreel that told the world what had occurred in the concentration camps—the horror of it all. I ran out of the movie theater, went down to the ocean, and swam out as far away from shore as I could. Though I wasn't conscious of it at the time, I think now this was an attempt to regain some sense of power and control in my life. Back then, it was an automatic response to what I had seen. I just wanted to get away. Much of the passion that now animates my life, my research and writing, is a result of that experience. I want to make this a better world."

How shocking it must have been, particularly to a young girl, to see that film!

"It was very shocking. I had prayed every night for my relatives, my grandparents, aunts, uncles, and cousins who had to stay behind in Europe. When I found out they had died, and then when I saw that film, I just couldn't believe it! Nothing made sense to me. This was the place in my life where I broke with the God of my childhood. I no longer believed there was one all-powerful, all-knowing entity who gave orders and who expected those orders be obeyed. To me, that's the ultimate dominator fantasy. I do not think the universe works this way."

The passage in her autobiography that describes this event is very moving. When the letters arrived from Europe telling her parents what happened, Riane desperately tried to make sense of it for she did not want to face the possibility of "a world bereft of God," the God she had so trusted to take care of her family. Seeing the newsreel had been the last straw, the ocean her only means of escape. She swam out to a raft that had previously seemed beyond her reach, convinced that if she went the distance, she would be endowed with the ability to survive anything. It was an act of will that lit the darkness in her heart and taught her how to handle the challenges in her life.

"I've gradually reconnected with the Jewish traditions I valued as a child," she says, "but I do not now have a faith that revolves around some other-worldly intervention that will make things better on this Earth. I'm not waiting for somebody to come and save me or save humanity, for a messiah who will waft us off to some better place. I think it's up to us to create that place here on Earth. Either we're going to do that ourselves or we're not."

You put your faith in yourself?

"Well, no, I can't even say that because when I'm scared, I pray. I don't know to whom or what I'm praying to, but if someone I love is ill or in danger, I pray. It's a habit I acquired in childhood.

"I also know I can only do so much. I believe in what we can all do together. I believe people bring about social and personal change. I believe we can relearn partnership rather than dominator ways of relating to each other and to our Mother Earth and thus, make this world a better place."

Given the pain and suffering people have endured for millennia—the cruelty, the separatism, and the humiliation—what do you think has allowed our species to not only survive but to flourish?

"I think it's our enormous human need and capacity for loving, for caring, for empathy. It's *that* part of us I put my faith in. I believe that our capacity for love is a wonderful, mysterious thing. I also believe there is an evolutionary movement towards love in the universe, a self-organizing process around love that's moving us toward what we call higher levels of consciousness."

I understand what you mean about love being "evolutionary," that as we mature as individuals and as a species, we deepen our capacity to love. But I never thought about love as being a self-organizing process before. That's very interesting.

"The more evolved a species is, the more loving it is. Some species of lizard babies are preprogrammed to get out of their shells very quickly so they don't become lunch for their parents. Mammals are much more caring. And if human children don't have some modicum of love, they don't make it. Now, is there something or someone else behind all that? Something we call the Divine? I don't know."

Are you still asking yourself these kinds of questions?

"Sometimes. But they're no longer urgent matters for me. For example, after I finished college, I thought a lot about the whole notion of infinity. Where does infinity come from? What comes after infinity? But I just couldn't get it. Finally, I decided that our brain just isn't wired to understand the concept, so I gave up thinking about it."

Did you make peace with the idea or did you think the answers were just beyond what your brain was "wired" to comprehend?

"I felt I was wasting my energy to think about such things; that I could do something else with my time that was much more productive. I think it's wonderful that we ask these questions, that humans are curious about such things. But at a certain point, I felt like a rabbit on a treadmill, as if I was going around and around but not really getting anywhere because there are no empirically established ways to directly get answers to these kinds of questions."

I tell Riane about a game I play with my grandsons that starts with my telling them that I love them more than whatever arbitrary number pops into my head. The play continues as we go back and forth, each of us raising the numerical ante of our love until one of us says, "I love you infinity." When this first occurred, my eldest grandson's enthusiasm was brought to a grinding halt. Had we reached the outer limits of our love? Then a light blazed in his eyes and he said, "I love you infinity plus one." In that moment, we shattered the divide of authoritative science and the fixed boundaries of the intellect and soared into the limitless regions of a child's love.

Riane laughs at my story. I ask her if her conclusions about the nature of infinity and other ultimate verities satisfy her.

"No," she says, "but I've stopped letting the questions distract me. I do think about these things from time to time, especially as they relate to my own life. For example, I love my husband David very much. I hate to be apart from him. It took us such a long time to find one another. We're home to each other. When I think that someday he may die before me, that I may be without him again, it's upsetting. But then I think, 'Well, there's nothing I can do about it.' So I don't dwell on it—on things I know are beyond my control."

In a universe where there is little we can control, how did you ensure your voice will be heard?

"I really didn't start to find my own voice until I discovered the women's movement in the '60s. I had worked in the civil rights movement and my involvement was authentic; it was a voice I wanted to support but it wasn't *my* voice. I didn't know much about feminism or how integral it was to my life; but in the course of my work, I met other women who, like myself, felt invisible or devalued in their lives, who felt forced into the straitjacket of arbitrary roles. Until we started talking about these things, we each thought our feelings were exclusive to us—or a sign that something was wrong with us because we were uncomfortable with the way things were. Something in me clicked. I realized that what we were all experiencing was a social rather than a personal problem and that we'd better get together and work on it.

"I started to read the feminist literature—though there wasn't much of it in those days—and it was fascinating. I was excited, emotionally and intellectually, and felt very empowered. There were so many wonderful ideas and courageous lives to consider, like Charlotte Perkins

Gilman, who struggled with madness because of the imprisonment she felt in her 'traditional' marriage. I realized that my own impulse to not adjust to domination and being controlled was healthy. I finally got it that the subjugation of women is basic to a dominator way of living. Not only did this kind of treatment harm me personally, but it harmed women—and men and children—throughout history. So I moved from the personal to the political and assumed a leadership role in the women's movement."

In your book *Sacred Pleasure*, you make the statement that the way we view our intimate relationships is a major determinant to how we construct our political, economic, and social relations. Could it follow that our efforts to move beyond dominator values of competition, subjugation, and control to more cooperative partnership values are a reflection of the age-old struggle within our own consciousness to champion good over evil?

"That's a thoughtful question," she declares. She takes a moment to contemplate her answer, then says, "I don't think we can understand our world in terms of simple linear cause and effect. There are a lot of factors at play; it's a multidimensional process. But if by 'good' you mean empathy, caring, and mindfulness, and by 'evil' you mean abusiveness and domination, then my answer to that question is 'yes.' Humans develop beyond the cellular level to the point where we end up self-organizing around the concepts of good and evil. When people self-organize around their authentic human needs, when they move beyond denial and break out of what I call the 'social trance,' when they stop accepting domination and trauma as part of the status quo, partnership values flourish."

It's so interesting, I say, that even in the most traumatic circumstances, there are people who don't get caught in the social trance.

"I have given much thought to what it is that allows people to survive. One thing that helps is faith, but what we have faith in is crucial to our own survival and to whether or not the circumstances that brought about the horrors we endured are perpetuated. One of the main obstacles to changing things for the better is this belief that 'somehow, it—brutality— was meant to be.' The whole point is to change our thinking so that we no longer use any excuse to accept brutality."

What do you have faith in?

"I do not have faith in an otherworldly entity that orchestrates violence for his or her own amusement. I do have faith in the push of evolution towards love. This sustains me somewhat because, as I said earlier, at least I know I can do something to improve my own relations and help the world. If all we do is work on ourselves, if we don't also change the larger structures of how people learn to relate to one another, we won't get very far."

Do you think change proceeds from the inside out or the outside in?

"I think it's like the chicken and the egg; I'm not sure which comes first because it's such an interconnected process. I do know that if you change your personal relationships toward the direction of partnership, the beliefs that guided your behavior will support the development of other partnership relationships—partnership-oriented families, social structures, workplaces, and communities. This begins to change the rules that govern even a wider web of relationships, including our economic and political relationships, that eventually support partnership relations across the board. It's an upwards spiral, but growth doesn't just proceed from one level to another. There are a lot of feedback loops. It's more like an inter-connected web. The self cannot really be helped in isolation from the relationships around it. I write a lot about this in my new book, *The Power of Partnership*. It's a new genre of self-help books that I hope will be useful for personal and social transformation."

Did you have a mentor who guided you or inspired your thinking?

"There were people who inspired me: my mother, her courage that night when she stood up to the Nazi officers who came to loot our home and take my father away, and a family friend who took a special interest in me as a child. But I've never had that one special teacher."

Do you have a Golden Rule, a principle that guides your decision-making?

"I don't know that it's a 'Golden Rule,' but I try always to be aware of goodness. I try to be kind. As an example, if someone who makes their living as a telemarketer calls me at dinnertime to sell me something I have no interest in, I easily find it within myself to be courteous."

She laughs and confides, "I do have a temper though and I lose it sometimes, but I also have a lot of love in me and I don't believe in rationing it. I think the more you give love, the more you have love."

You've come a long way from the young girl teetering on the edge of belonging. It's not uncommon for people who have escaped the prospect of physical or psychological annihilation to feel as if there is a reason why they were saved. Did you ever wonder about this?

"During the last few years we lived in Cuba, I had a real impulse to do something to change the world. But when I came to the United States, this got lost for a while in the shuffle of growing up. I was fourteen and had been an outsider for such a long time—I desperately wanted to belong. That impulse didn't surface again until many years later. After I'd gotten back on track, I went to visit an old family friend who, in the course of our conversation said to me, 'Life has a way of taking care of those it chooses. Since you were chosen to be saved, there is good in store for you.' It was good to hear and very affirming."

What do you think that purpose is?

"To live a good life as best as I know how. I must become more conscious of how to do that personally, but I must also do something to change the conditions that distort consciousness and behavior and make people brutal and uncaring."

What do you think is your greatest accomplishment?

She takes a moment to reflect. "Actually, I think my greatest accomplishment has been some of the changes I've brought about within myself, my own attempts to alter behaviors rooted in anxiety and control that I learned from others. I'm hardly terrific, but I'm working at it. I've gotten better."

What do you think is the secret of your success?

"Success is a strange thing; it's hard to define. Whatever success I've had I attribute to the fact that I work very hard at what I do. I also have an enormous curiosity, a passion for understanding and exploring. I'm very adventurous intellectually. I think that's my greatest strength.

"In a way," she says thoughtfully, "always being an outsider was very helpful to me too, because it put me in a position where I had to be myself. I had to say, 'This is who I am and that's OK.' I gained self-acceptance. But mostly, I feel I was just very, very fortunate that somehow, in spite of everything that happened in my life, an inner core of me remained intact. That's not so much a secret as it is a miracle." Her voice softens as she says the words.

Given your knowledge and experience, what advice would you give to others?

"Seek your own way. We all need teachers, but I think we must pay the most attention to our inner teacher, to the authentic voice of love and sanity I believe we're all born with. I've had to unlearn a great deal in order to move forward; I've had to question much of what I'd been taught and pursue my own answers. That questioning has been the central motif of my own personal emergence as well as my scholarship.

"So, my dear," Riane says, "now you know my whole life story."

Not quite. There is one last question I want to ask you: How would you like to be remembered?

She takes a minute to think about this. "I guess as someone who contributed to building what I call a partnership way of living. I'm immensely grateful that others have found my work useful to their inner growth and, beyond that, to their own efforts to become conscious agents for positive change."

Her voice resounds with thanksgiving. On that note, our conversation ends.

To Learn More About the Life and Work of
Riane Eisler

Contact:
The Center for Partnership Studies
P.O. Box 51936
Pacific Grove, California 93950
Voice: (831) 626-1004
Fax: (831) 626-3734
On the Web: www.partnershipway.org
E-mail: center@partnershipway.org

Read:
- *The Chalice and the Blade: Our History, Our Future*, HarperCollins
- *The Power of Partnership*, New World Library
- *Sacred Pleasure: Sex, Myth, and the Politics of the Body—New Paths to Power and Love*, HarperCollins
- *Tomorrow's Children: A Blueprint for Partnership Education in the Twenty-First Century*, Westview Press
- *The Partnership Way: New Tools for Living and Learning*, Holistic Education Press/partnershipway.org
- *The Gate: A Memoir of Love and Reflection*, iUniverse.com
- *Sex, Death, and the Angry Young Man: Conversations with Riane Eisler and David Loye*, Matthew Callahan, Time Change Press
- *Women, Men, and the Global Quality of Life*, Riane Eisler, David Loye, and Kari Norgaard, UN Conference on Women in Beijing, partnershipway.org
- *The Equal Rights Handbook: What ERA Means to Your Life, Your Rights, and the Future*, Avon/iUniverse.com
- *Dissolutions: No-Fault Divorce, Marriage and the Future of Women*, McGraw Hill/iUniverse.com

View:
- *Tomorrow's Children: Partnership Education in Action*, Media Education Foundation, www.partnershipway.org

Listen:
- *The Chalice and the Blade*, audio version read by Riane Eisler, New World Library

Eight

Le Ly Hayslip

Thou didst turn my mourning into dancing.

—Psalm 30:11

FROM PEASANT GIRL to best-selling author and international ambassador, at first glance, her story is pure Cinderella. But for Le Ly (pronounced Lay-Lee) Hayslip, there was no glass slipper and no Prince Charming—apart from Buddha. Born in 1950 in a small village near Danang in Central Vietnam, Le Ly was reared to love God, revere her ancestors, and honor her country. She spent her childhood working alongside her parents in the rice fields and playing with other children in her village. Then war broke out. By the time she was twelve, Le Ly had become an impassioned freedom-fighter, maneuvering the swamps and back alleys of Vietnam undetected by soldiers on either side of the conflict.

During the next four years, she was imprisoned, raped, and tortured. She gave birth to a son. Separated from her family and no longer able to avail herself of their counsel, Le Ly learned to listen to a quiet inner voice that celebrated the religious ideals of her childhood. After years of struggling to create a life for herself and her child, she immigrated to the United States as the wife of an American civilian. He died two years later and she remarried. Widowed yet again, Le Ly worked at a variety of jobs to make ends meet and raised three sons alone.

In 1986, she returned to Vietnam for a visit and was stunned by the devastation that ravaged her homeland. Its pastoral beauty in ruin, its people adrift and demoralized, Le Ly vowed to do something to help restore her country. The following year, she formed the nonprofit EAST Meets WEST Foundation to provide medical and educational facilities for the children of Vietnam and help heal the wounds of war for both the American and Vietnamese people. Eager to raise money to support the work of her foundation, Le Ly wrote a frank and stirring account of her life that she titled *When Heaven and Earth Changed Places*. In 1994, Oliver Stone adapted it and her second book, *Child of War, Woman of Peace*, into the riveting film *Heaven and Earth*. Five years later, Le Ly created a second nonprofit organization, The Global Village Foundation, modeled on the Peace Corps. Today she devotes much of her time to her writing and to creating an international peace center that will be located in Southern California.

I first learned about Le Ly's remarkable life after reading an excerpt from her book in *The Norton Book of Women's Lives*. Several years later, I saw her at a writer's conference in San Diego. I noticed her immediately. Petite, with black hair and eyes, there was a dignity about her that made her stand out in a crowd. She was at the conference to speak about the benefits of having a literary agent, yet what I remember most about her presentation was the fierce loyalty she had to *her* agent. It was that single-mindedness that connected the woman before me to the uneducated peasant girl turned freedom-fighter turned social activist I had read about years before. Later, when I met Le Ly, I understood that in all things, she is a warrior in the venerable tradition of her ancestors.

❖ ❖ ❖ ❖ ❖

IT'S BEEN SEVERAL years since I saw Le Ly at the conference and I am well into planning this book. I have been trying to locate her to invite her to participate in the project but have been unable to track her down. Finally, it occurs to me that I can probably contact her through her agent. In a few weeks, Le Ly telephones to say she has received my invitation and is happy to talk with me. We arrange to meet at her home which, I am amazed to discover, is only ten minutes from my own. She is the first of the fourteen women I will talk with.

I prepare for our conversation by reading her books. Her story is both personal and historic. Sometimes I read into the night—because I am engrossed in the intrigue and valor of her life and cannot put the book down. Sometimes I read only in spurts—because I feel her anguish and must remove myself from her pain. I come away from my reading realizing that she is a woman who has lived fully in two very different worlds.

This is no more evident than in her home—a five-bedroom tract house around the corner from the famed La Costa Golf Course. On the outside, the house is typical of those that pack the winding streets of most middle-class Southern California suburbs. A cadre of arched windows dominate the building's stucco exterior. A brass wind chime bestows a greeting as I brush by it on my way to the front door. Le Ly greets me in casual dress, slacks and a sweater, and no make-up. She ushers me into her living room and my eyes immediately gravitate to a large movie poster mounted over her couch, a billowy blue and green pastoral scene that was used to promote Oliver Stone's film of her life. Red-tasseled kites and family photographs hang on the walls; Asian artifacts decorate tabletops and bookshelves. A loft she built when she bought the house juts out halfway across the living room. She added the room so she could have a Buddhist temple in her home—a place for meditation and a shrine to honor her ancestors. During our conversation, her eyes frequently drift upward toward the loft, almost as if she is mentally placing herself at her altar as she talks.

Directly across from the living room is a large office that is the material hub of her house. Bookshelves line the walls from floor to ceiling. Photographs taken during the filming of the movie and of Le Ly with various United States legislators and world leaders lean against her books alongside the many humanitarian awards she's received for her work. Her desk is piled high with papers. The phone and fax machine ring every few minutes.

She is about to leave for another trip to Vietnam and excuses herself to attend to some pressing last minute details. I sit on the couch in her living room while she talks once, twice, three times to New York. Watching her, seeing the obvious dedication with which she works, reminds me of something her father told her: that though a woman may be called upon to do many things, her first duty is to "defend life with a warrior's strength." When she joins me on the couch, I open our conversation by asking her what these words mean to her given what she is now doing with her life.

"As a child, my father often told me about our ancestor Phung Thi Chinh, a great warrior woman. In 39 A.D., she commanded an all-male battalion of Vietnamese soldiers who were fighting to defend our homeland against Chinese invaders. Phung Thi was seven-and-a-half months pregnant when she accepted her commission. In the midst of the conflict, she went into labor. She delivered her child on the battlefield, strapped the baby to her back and, sword in hand, cleared a route through the Chinese ranks that helped the Vietnamese win the war. When I first heard the story, I thought my father wanted me to be a fighter like she was. Later I realized he was actually teaching me that a woman's role is not just to bring life into the world but to uphold it, to fight for what she believes in. So, this is what I do now."

This fidelity to life permeates everything about her—it shines in her eyes and is reflected in her candor. This makes it very easy for me to ask her something I've been curious to know about since I first started to read her books.

I noticed that whenever you wrote about God, you used a lower case "g." Can you share with me your reason for doing this?

She smiles. "I'm often asked this question. I did this intentionally," she says, "not out of disrespect or because I am not a religious person, but because I wanted to distinguish my view of god from the view held by some people in the West."

What do you see as the difference?

"My god does not punish you or send you to hell if you do not believe in him," she declares. "My god does not pit people against each other in wars and say, 'Use this bomb or that airplane to kill your brother who is fighting against you.' I don't understand this kind of big 'G' God. My little 'g' god is loving and compassionate. My little 'g' god loves everyone equally and wants us to live in peace. He also knows everything about me—who I really am—and I know who he is. This is all that matters to him—and to me."

You also frequently use the phrase "as fate or luck or god would have it" in your writing. What's the connection there for you between these three concepts?

"Fate is what you are born to do; it is your destiny—the road map you follow as you go through your life. Luck is what comes to you because of your efforts to be virtuous. Good luck is like a bonus you earn as a result of the good you do. god is the energy, the spirit, that pervades everything in the universe. god is in the sky, in the trees, in the rocks. god is also inside each one of us. When you live your destiny and work hard at being honest and compassionate, then god is pleased with you. When fate, luck, and god are in harmony in your life, you are home free."

Home free?

"Yes. When you play your part to the best of your ability, you no longer have to worry about what's going on in your life because, ultimately, everything turns out OK. It's the law of cause and effect."

What goes around, comes around. Karma.

"Yes. You cannot harvest what you do not plant."

She is comfortable talking about spiritual things, as comfortable as she was just a few minutes ago conferring with her colleagues in New York. She moves from one to the other—from the material to the spiritual, from East and West—with relative ease. I ask her how she bridges the gap, how she manages to be so at home in both worlds.

"god walks with me when I walk, sleeps with me when I sleep, eats with me when I eat. There is never a moment in my day that I am separate from god or that god ever leaves me. I cannot live without my god."

Her explanation is simple, yet so profound: I do it all with God, in the unchanging presence of God. Omnipresence has no borders or limitations.

"My only real fear in all of this," she says, almost as an afterthought, "is that I might do something to make god or Buddha unhappy with me. If I break a political law, they can punish me or lock me up in jail for years. That doesn't matter to me. I've been there before. Big deal! But if I break a spiritual law, then god is unhappy with me and I feel very, very bad."

There is no hint of anger or remorse in her voice about the indignities of her past. Nor is there any fear at what her god might "do" to her if she displeases him. There is only genuine concern at the prospect of disappointing her dearest Friend and Well-Wisher. In that brief moment, the depth of her relationship with her god is unmistakable—and so very touching. I ask her how she came to develop this kind of a connection.

"I was born into this approach. In my country, god is a part of our everyday life. We don't go to church; we have an altar in our home. We have no technology. We live simply and close to nature. We are mostly villagers, farmers. We grow the rice we eat. What is left over, we give to the duck in our yard. This duck lays the eggs we eat and also rids our garden of bugs so we grow better food. Everything depends on everything else. When you live this kind of existence, day in and day out, you see that each creature has something it was born to do, and you understand how life is interconnected. You also learn how important it is to lend a hand to others, to help them evolve. In this country, if you have ants in your house, you buy some bug spray and kill the ants. In Vietnam, if you have ants in your house, you put a small piece of meat in the yard and redirect the ants outside. Buddha's teaching of compassion is not just a philosophy; we put it into practice every day of our lives.

"This is how my ancestors worshipped god from the beginning of time. They taught us by the simplicity and dedication of their lives to live honorably, and we revere them for that. We pray to them for guidance. We follow their way. We breathe the same air they once breathed. We breathe in and out with them in every moment, with those who have come before us and with those who will come after we are gone. Our ancestors—past and future—embrace us every second of our lives. Each generation has an obligation to those who come after them to live honorably. I am the ancestor of my great-great-grandchildren, so it is also important that I live in a way they will take comfort in."

Does following the ways of your ancestors free you from the press of decision making, the strain of having to determine "right" from "wrong"?

"It's not that simple. My father once told me that freedom—physical, political, and spiritual freedom—is something that must be won and won again. Freedom is constantly choosing the right path at the right moment—at *every* moment. No one can do that for you. You must choose freedom again and again. When you do this, you win the battle, whatever it is. You are victorious. You also cannot take freedom for granted. If you do, it will not be there when you need it most."

Her response cuts right to the heart of impeccable decision making: make the right choice at the right moment—in every moment. I'm curious to know what she does to still the waves of personal opinion and desire that inhibit the ability to know the right path and moment.

Her eyes gravitate toward the loft and her face softens notably as she talks. "I spend a lot of time at my altar. I talk with my ancestors every day. Sometimes I pray or talk with god, sometimes I meditate. Sometimes I read spiritual books or listen to various spiritual tapes. Sometimes I just look at my altar. It's very beautiful."

And the goal of your spiritual practice?

"To learn how to become a human being," she says, as if it's as plain as the nose on my face.

A human being?

"Someone who is real, who has fully lived their life in accordance with the truth of their own soul. Like Mother Teresa, for instance. She was just a woman, but when she died, people called her a saint."

She asks me, "Wouldn't you like to be a saint? Wouldn't you like to be liberated?" Before I can answer she says, "I would! We have women's liberation. We have liberation of human rights. Why not liberation of our own souls?"

How strange, I say, that in a nation founded on the pursuit of a multitude of freedoms and inalienable rights, soul liberation is not on the list. In Eastern spiritual traditions isn't enlightenment the primary goal of life?

"I live a spiritual life so I can pay off my karmic debts from the past and put 'deposits' in my spiritual bank account that will go toward 'buying' my future liberation. It's like a mortgage. I can pay off the principle or the interest, or I can pay off everything all at once. If I miss a payment, I pay a fine. If I continue to miss my payments, I get bad credit. It's no different in the spiritual life. When you pay off all your karmic debts, you are spiritually free and clear."

You've found a way to make sense of things, to make the world and its apparent inequities work for you. Have you always been able to do this? Amidst all the insanities of war—the terror, the torture and rape, the homelessness, and the loss of your dearly loved brother and father—how did you make sense of it? Did you ever feel as if God had abandoned you?

She is genuinely surprised by my question. "How could god ever abandon me? god does not tell us to fight or kill each other. War is man-made. You have to separate yourself from what happens to you if you are to survive. When bad things happened to me, I just watched what was going on as if I was observing something on the beach. Buddha helped me through this. Like a loving parent, his teachings guided me back to the root of love, to god."

She pauses for a moment to reflect. "Compared to you or other people, maybe I've been through a lot, but compared to millions of Vietnamese, I've been through nothing! I created certain karma in another incarnation and in this life I repaid that debt. I was born at this time in history in Vietnam to be a part of that war. How could I blame god for that? god is only love."

Did you ever doubt your ability to make it through?

"Sometimes," she says. "I *am* human. But those doubts were just thoughts. They never stayed with me long enough to make a difference. Why should I beat myself up? I just changed my thoughts by doing or thinking something different.

"A thought is like a magnet," she explains. "It taps into a specific frequency that creates or draws negative or positive results, depending on the quality of the thought. Whenever I felt scared or hopeless, I would think about something happy, something uplifting, something bigger than myself, something not just for myself. Then I would feel better.

"This is Buddha's teaching: You make your own heaven or hell. You're only a victim, truly a victim, when you feel like one—when you're knocked down and don't even try to get up. Someone can rescue you, but only you save yourself."

Did you find value in your suffering?

"Suffering always changes me. It makes me stronger, wiser. It creates compassion for others. It helps me grow spiritually so I can better help others. It motivates me to change my thoughts and then change my actions so I can move out of a karmic cycle that is self-destructive.

"As a result of those difficult experiences, I understand people better. I also understand myself better. I know who I am and how to live my life. I have a deeper understanding of karmic law, of universal law, of spiritual law. Suffering has been a good teacher. Today I lecture before an audience of a thousand people and receive an ovation, not because of anything I learned at a university, but because of what my life has taught me."

She looks directly at me and a slight smile forms across her lips. "I said in my book, 'god is not cruel, just practical.' Cruelty exists in this world, but god is not cruel."

Her comment puts a subtle spin on my thinking about my own suffering. Though I want to avail myself of every opportunity for self-betterment, I admit to a preference for those methods that subject me to as little pain as possible. I do recognize, however, how easily distracted I become from the rigors of due diligence and cannot, in all honesty, say that I would be as clear or tenacious about what I want for my life had I not fully experienced all that I *don't* want for my life. Le Ly's words help me to pull back from the emotion that surrounds those difficult experiences and see them more as the requisite practicalities of self-mastery.

Experience has obviously been a good teacher for her. I ask if she also had any mentors who helped her formulate her beliefs.

"My father, of course. And the other elders of my village. When I look at my mother now, I see how important she was in my life. But when I was growing up, her words would go in one ear and out the other." We laugh together at her comment. Some experiences transcend cultures.

So many people are unable to leave their unhappiness behind them. You seem to have done this. In your book you wrote that, as a young girl, happiness was "the ability to live according to your ancient ways." How would you now define happiness?

"Happiness is dancing in the light. It's watching what goes on around you and staying balanced no matter what's occurring. There is always yin and yang, good and evil, black and white. You cannot have one without the other. But you can keep your balance and be inwardly happy in spite of what goes on outside of you."

How?

"By consciously choosing goodness. By not taking anything for granted. By helping those who are less fortunate than you are."

By way of example, she tells me about something she does when she is in Vietnam to ensure that she does not take the pleasures of a good meal or the company of her American friends for granted: She invites the homeless and hungry people who live near a restaurant she frequents to share a simple meal with her. When they sit at her table, she treats them with dignity. "Eating at a table, in a restaurant, helps them feel like human beings again," she tells me. "Though I am in the company of beggars, I am happy because I am sharing my good fortune with them."

As she talks, she moves back in time—recalling not only the experience she just described, but the young girl she once was, the young girl who daily combed the streets for her next meal. Thirty years of living in the West has molded her into a successful businesswoman and a force to be reckoned with. I ask her how her views about the spiritual life have changed over the years.

"The material world does not mean as much to me as it did when I was younger," she says. "The real world to me now is the soul. You can't destroy soul. You can't lose soul. When I die and come back in another body, my soul will stay with me. Soul, to me, is reality."

With whom do you share your spiritual life?

"I have a few friends I talk to about these things, but I think it's rare to find someone who has the same understanding you have, who will not argue with you or condemn you for your beliefs. When people share your understanding, they do more than just talk to you; they give of themselves to you. They may disagree with you but they support you. If people are not with you, you have to let them go and move on.

"So, who do I talk to? I talk to god. I share my life with god. My spiritual life is powerful and strong. It's joyous. It helps me, just like a lover, to make every day a little easier. A human lover may sometimes cheat on you but not god. god will never betray you. god will never hurt you."

The phone rings. Le Ly excuses herself and goes into the other room to answer it. When she comes back, she tells me she has just made some important contacts that will facilitate her work overseas. She is very pleased with the possibilities that await her. It seems superfluous, given what just transpired, to ask if she believes she has an assignment, a mission she was born to carry out, but I ask the question anyway.

"After I returned from my first trip to Vietnam, I made a contract with god: I said, 'I want to write a book about my experiences—not my story but the story of your children in Vietnam who need a name and face. But you must help because I don't know anything about writing a book.' My part of the agreement was to work twenty-four hours a day, seven days a week, to give the project my love and passion and then give the money I made to the poor. god's part was to make it happen.

"So, god sent me a writer and an agent to help me. Then god sent me Doubleday to publish the book. It got reviewed on the front page of *Los Angeles Magazine* and Oliver Stone made it into a movie. I formed EAST Meets WEST Foundation and went to Washington, D.C., and knocked on doors. Gradually, things began to open up. The United States eventually lifted the trade embargo and relations between the two countries were completely normalized. We built many medical and educational facilities for the children of Vietnam. That work is still going strong today." Though she does not mention it, her efforts were largely responsible for the reparation between the two countries.

"For the next ten years, I went back and forth to Vietnam—sometimes with U.S. veterans—to build schools, medical clinics, medical outreach facilities, and homes for orphans. Vietnam is a nation of sixteen thousand villages, all of them below poverty level. People still live without electricity, without adequate sanitation or water. There are no vocational training programs, no parks and recreation facilities, no cultural centers to preserve our national heritage. In 1998, the Vietnamese government finally passed laws that allowed the rebuilding process to begin. A year later, I formed the Global Village Foundation. I have spent the last few years recruiting educators, students, and philanthropic organizations from around the world to come to Vietnam and help establish schools, clinics, vocational workshops, and a cultural center where the old train the young in the arts and crafts of village life. Now, I am looking for land in Southern California to develop a Pan Asian Cultural Center that will be a resource for students and scholars and a haven for pilgrims—including Vietnam vets and Americans of Asian descent—and tourists. The center will bring the best of the entire Pacific Rim to America—arts and crafts, music, theater, food, home and garden furnishings, and agricultural methods that use sustainable resources and minimal energy. There will be open air theaters, shops and markets, footpaths and gardens, flower and herb fields that all connect to a central village. It's quite a big project."

How did you know it was your mission to do all this?

"When I went back to Vietnam for the first time and saw what was going on there, I knew I had to do something. In the beginning, I was in darkness. I didn't know what to do! Then a little light came in. I followed it and it got bigger. If all I had was ten dollars in my pocket, I'd buy gas and drive to L.A. and talk to someone who might be able to help me. If nothing happened, at least I knew I had made an effort. I just kept at it and did what I thought was right for me."

Given all you've achieved, what do you think is your greatest accomplishment?

"Being true to myself no matter what other people think of me. This is not always easy, but it is vitally important to do this." I nod my head in agreement.

Do you have any advice for others?

"Be who you are; be a good human being, a quality human being," she says. "Work hard. Spend little. Give more than you take. Treat everyone the same, rich or poor. Spend time alone so you can discover how you respond to things when you are not under the influence of others. Do the best you can at whatever you choose, and try to have fun while you're doing it! There were times when I had to sell my house and pawn my jewelry to make my dream happen. There were times when I was so tired and frustrated I cried. But through it all, I did and do this work because it brings great happiness to me and to others."

She pauses and, once again, looks up at her altar. "But most importantly, I would tell people to connect with god. god will never leave you. god will never let you down. Don't let a day go by without knowing that god is looking after you."

When you leave this Earth, when all is said and done, for what or how would you like to be remembered?

"Of course, people will remember me differently depending on who you talk to. I want to be remembered not for all the good things I've done—or for all horrible things that happened to me. Let them simply say of me, 'Ly Le was a lady, just an ordinary woman.' I think that would be very nice."

We end our conversation on that unassuming note. I thank her for her time and extend my hand in farewell. We smile at each other for a few moments. The phone rings. She takes the call and I take my leave. I glance up at her altar, then at her on the phone and wave good-bye. No, I think to myself, Ly Le Hayslip is anything but "an ordinary woman."

To Learn More About the Life and Work of
Le Ly Hayslip

Contact:
The Global Village Foundation
P.O. Box 13656
Carlsbad, California 92013-0656
Voice: (760) 929-9174
Fax: (760) 929-9735
On the Web: www.globalvillagefoundation.org
E-mail: LHayslip@aol.com

Read:
- *When Heaven and Earth Changed Places*, with Jay Wurts, Plume
- *Child of War, Woman of Peace*, with James Hayslip, Doubleday

View:
- *Heaven and Earth,* directed by Oliver Stone, Warner Brothers Studio, 1993

Nine

Zainab Salbi

I'll shade him from the heat, 'till he can bear
To lean in joy upon our father's knee.

—William Blake

ZAINAB SALBI WAS a young undergraduate student at George Mason University in Fairfax, Virginia, when the idea first came to her to form the relief organization now known as Women For Women International. She was reading *Time* magazine, reading about the reports of the genocide in the Balkans, of the ethnic cleansing, of the repeated and systematic rape of an estimated twenty thousand Bosnian women by Serbian soldiers. As the stories unfolded before her eyes, her thoughts turned to her own child-hood in Baghdad, to growing up during the Iran-Iraq conflict and to liv-ing under Saddam Hussein's watchful eye. She was on intimate terms with the vulnerability war engenders, with the fear of annihilation and the per-vading sense of disconnection and loss that are the consequence of war. She also knew what lay in store for these Bosnian women—particularly the strain of trying to shape a life in the aftermath of war. As soon as she came to the United States, fighting broke out in the Persian Gulf and Zainab was unable to return home or even communicate with her family. She took a series of part-time jobs to make ends meet. The loneliness she felt, the uncertainty, was almost more than she could bear. As these famil-iar images played themselves out on the pages before her, she vowed to use her life experience to help these Bosnian women. It was, she believed, her moral and spiritual responsibility to do so.

In the days that followed, Zainab telephoned various relief organiza-tions in Washington, D.C., to volunteer her services. Agency representa-tives were sympathetic to the situation, and to her desire to help, but no one was, at this early stage of the conflict, prepared to provide aid to Bosnia. With no experience in disaster relief organization, no professional contacts, and no funds of her own to draw on, twenty-three-year-old Zainab Salbi did the only thing she could think of to do: She backtracked through the list of organizations she had telephoned and asked total strangers to help her form a nonprofit organization to support the women of Bosnia. One group—the All Souls Universalist Church in Washington, D.C.—liked her idea and agreed to act as the administrative arm for her fledgling project for one year. It was just enough time for her to get Women For Women in Bosnia up and running.

Today, Women For Women International serves indigent women in Sudan, Bosnia and Herzegovina, Kosovo, Colombia, Rwanda, Nigeria, the Democratic Republic of the Congo, Afghanistan, and Iraq. The organization provides emotional support and financial aid to women through a one-to-one sponsorship program. It offers job training—including leadership development and human rights awareness—that teaches women how to grow a postwar economy. And it funds a micro-credit lending program that provides capital to create women-owned entrepreneurial ventures. In 1995, just two years after it was founded, Women For Women International was honored at the White House for its grassroots achievements. To date, it has raised over $24 million in direct aid and loans, and helped fifty-five thousand women become self-sufficient.

Zainab travels frequently to the countries her organization serves, as an ambassador and an activist. These trips have grown easier since she and her husband, Amjad Atallah, first visited Croatia on a fact-finding mission late in 1993. The stories they heard and their experiences with the women they met affected them deeply, and dramatically altered their lives.

I initially heard about Zainab's work in October of 2000 when she appeared on *The Oprah Winfrey Show* to discuss the sometimes visible/sometimes veiled humiliation and violence experienced by women today. I'd been thinking about this very issue for weeks, often contrasting it to the autonomy and privilege I felt in writing this book. That afternoon, in the midst of what I had believed were simply my private thoughts about human rights, I turned on the television to give my mind a respite, and there was Zainab, a young woman of incredible poise and compassion, saying almost the same words aloud that I had, minutes before, said to myself. There was a presence about her, a defining radiance—the same fusion of passion and humility that animates all the women in this book. Now that I had found my way to Zainab, I would not let her go.

The next day, I visited her Web site and invited her to participate in this book. She was living in London, working on her master's degree in developmental studies at The London School of Economics. Since she would not be back in the States for several months, we arranged to meet during a trip I would soon make to England—a trip I had planned six months before I knew Zainab Salbi existed. Note: This interview took place when Iraq was still under Saddam Hussein's rule, and the Salbi family connection to him was not public knowledge.

❖ ❖ ❖ ❖ ❖

WE MEET ON a cold, blustery English morning right out of the pages of a Dickens novel, at the flat of friends who have offered to provide sanctuary during my visit. Zainab arrives promptly at eleven. Though I know she is thirty-one-years old, I am still struck by her youthful appearance. She is tall and model slim, with short, black hair cropped stylishly close to her face. Her dark eyes light up as we embrace in greeting.

We have exchanged at least two dozen e-mails in preparation for our conversation and there is, by now, an easy familiarity between us. "I feel as if I know you," she says as we walk down the hall to the sitting room where we will spend the next few hours. I feel as if I know her, too. In addition to what I have read about her, she reminds me of my own daughters— warm, confident, and decidedly more aware than I was at thirty-one.

There is an ardor, a spark about her that lies just beneath her words and punctuates her speech. I notice it immediately. As our conversation progresses, it catches fire and burns white hot. She asks me why I decided to write this book and about the other women I have talked with, and absorbs my response like a sponge—not because my words are particularly wise or instructive, but because, like me, she is intensely interested in the inner workings of women's lives. She wonders aloud why I would want to talk with her, especially since she does not have a Western religious practice. I believe, I say, that our conversation will unfold in a way that will more than support my desire to talk with her. And it does. The stories she shares and the way she reveals herself through her stories prove to be windows into her soul. She adjusts herself in her chair and we begin to talk about the things that have brought us together. I turn on my tape recorder and ask her to tell me how she would define spirituality.

"To me, spirituality is ultimately about seeing our Source—no matter what we each call It—as the same. It also involves acting on our responsibility to help others, especially those who are less fortunate. We must each do something to improve the world, even if it's only that we pick up a piece of paper on the street. I feel very strongly about this."

What does this Source look like to you?

"No matter what your religion, if you live anywhere in the Middle East where I was raised, the teachings of Islam permeate the culture. There is no specific image or person that embodies the Islamic conception of God. God is everywhere, anywhere. God is part of you. I was raised to follow the teachings of Islam, so I believe this as well. I talk with God in my heart. Depending on the situation, I ask, 'Why is this happening to me?' Or I say, 'Thank you. Thank you, God.' I feel comfortable and happy with this connection. We all have something we create for ourselves to make sense of things. This is what does it for me."

In one of the articles I read about you, you describe yourself as a "Universalist." Would you elaborate on this?

"What I mean by 'Universalist' is that I don't believe in nationalism or in grouping people only according to a geographical location or outer characteristic. Culture, religion, ethnicity are man-made social constructs that influence our lives, but we are more than these limited constructs. We are one humanity, the human race, and we have a responsibility to help each other regardless of what group we belong to. It's only natural for people to drift towards others of like mind or color or geographical location, but I don't think these things should restrict us from relating to everyone simply as human beings. If we act based on what we have in common with each other rather than on what's different about us, we can really help one another."

She lingers for a moment in her own thoughts. "I'm not trying to essentialize human experience," she explains, "to disregard what makes us each different or unique—or to say that one way will help everyone. I realize that our experiences of race, ethnicity, and class do affect who we are and the challenges we face. But we have to act humanely toward each other. I can disagree with someone politically—and God knows I do!—but when it comes time to ensure that they have access to food, medical care, education, shelter, and so on, their political views become irrelevant to me."

Do you have a Golden Rule that governs your thinking?

"I believe Spirit, or God—the name is not important to me—is influencing my life and, as I said, that this Spirit is everywhere all the time. Believing in God is what is important to me. This belief, more than any particular religious teaching, is what guides my life.

"Gratitude is also a big part of my spirituality. I feel very fortunate to have the people, the love, I have around me. I'm grateful for the big things, like being able to come to London for school, and for the really small things. I don't take anything for granted."

Do you engage in any regular spiritual practices?

"My spirituality is really more a view I have about life that helps me make sense of the different experiences I go through than something I do. It helps me deal with my challenges and enjoy my happy times. I do pray every day and try to silently reflect on and contemplate my life. This strengthens my connection to God and my ability to deal with my challenges."

Were you raised in a spiritual environment?

"My parents were not practicing Muslims. They were not religious but they were very spiritual. They lived by the principles that are the foundation of all religions, of all moral teachings. They taught me to be a good person, to help the poor, to not lie or steal, and to thank God every day for what we had. These concepts were not just words to them. My mom would give my brothers and me money—she would actually put it in our hands—and tell us to give it to the beggars on the street. She wanted us to experience the act of giving for ourselves. I still believe these things are the essential elements to being a good person."

How did living in the midst of the Iran-Iraq War affect you?

"I was eleven years old when the war began," she says. "I grew up in that war. It was by no means similar to what happened in Bosnia or Rwanda—or even the Gulf War—but it was war nonetheless. I saw Iranian planes and missiles land near our home, kill people I knew.

"In spite of what went on throughout my childhood, I had a good life. You learn to make a good life for yourself in a war. It's a very interesting paradigm that people who haven't lived through war don't realize: Life can continue and you can still have fun even when you're being bombed. You make life work. You make life happen."

How do you do that? Making life "work" even in the most privileged circumstances is difficult.

"My mom was a fun-loving person who was determined that we would not be miserable just because war was raging. For example, during the bombing of Baghdad, many families we knew all slept in one room. The reason? They thought that if they were going to die, if a missile were to hit their house, at least they could die together. But my mom insisted we each sleep in our own room because she wanted us to live as routinely as possible. She wanted us to feel normal and happy. She reminded me somewhat of the father in the movie *Life Is Beautiful*."

Zainab tells me the first of many remarkable stories she will share with me this day. Her stories are raw and initially startling, but the courage and tenacity they contain are stunning.

"Once, when I was in Bosnia," she begins, "I was walking in an alley and I heard this incredible music coming from inside a building that had been nearly destroyed by shelling. I asked the woman I was walking with about it, and she told me that we were passing the music school, and that what we were hearing was the conservatory students practicing their lessons. There we were, in the middle of the siege of Sarajevo, listening to children play this beautiful music! Life *has* to keep on going. You can't hide in a basement all your life. You can't stop, you know? You make the choice to go on. This is part of the reason I started Women For Women. I wanted women who were victims of war to know that life goes on."

A brief pause, then she says with a shy smile, "But, to be honest, I had no idea what I was getting into at the time."

With regard to the situation in Bosnia or to setting up an organization?

She laughs. "Both, actually. Iraq was closed to any news about the international community. It was only after I came to the United States that I even realized there were other wars going on in the world besides *my* war. It was quite a shock!

"So when I heard about what was happening in Bosnia, I felt I was in a unique position to help these women and I wanted to do so. It seemed natural and humane given the circumstances. I tried to volunteer, but every place I called said they were not set up in Bosnia and that they couldn't do anything until they were. I was very frustrated. I kept thinking, 'There are rape camps in Bosnia! How can they tell me to call back in six months?'

"I tried to sponsor a child in Bosnia or Croatia, but I couldn't do that either. That's when I decided to form an organization myself. I liked the sponsorship format and wanted to give the money from the sponsors directly to each woman so she could decide how to spend it. This seemed very respectful to me; it would demonstrate trust in her and help her feel more in control of her life again. The Unitarian Church in Washington, D.C., invited me to attend a board meeting to present my idea. There I was—twenty-three-years-old and scared!—talking to a room full of dignified, elderly people in English, my second language. But they agreed to sponsor me for a year. Even then, I didn't realize what I had committed myself to."

When did you understand what you'd set in motion?

"The turning point came when my husband and I went to Croatia late in 1993. Bosnia was under siege at the time, so most of the refugees went to Croatia because it was an exit point. That's why we went there. We decided it would be good to meet the women and see for ourselves what they needed and exactly how we could help them. We were recently married and had been saving money for a honeymoon in Spain. After a brief honeymoon in Florida, we did some fund-raising, and pooled what we raised with the money we'd saved for Spain and went to Croatia."

Zainab turns to face me directly and rests her arms on the arms of her chair, as if she's steeling herself for what she is about to tell me. It's not a story that is easy to tell—or easy to hear.

"The first day we were in Croatia, we met Ajsa. Someone just put her in front of us. She'd been impregnated in a rape camp, then released when she was nine months pregnant. Her child died two months after it was born from multiple medical complications. She was totally devastated.

"Before she was imprisoned, Ajsa had been married with two children and had a life of some distinction. She didn't know where her family was—and after all that had happened to her, she didn't want to see them again. She no longer felt worthy of her old life. She cried the whole time we were with her."

Zainab shakes her head in sad remembrance and I place my hand over my heart, hoping to assuage the ache I feel.

"My husband and I didn't know how to respond to her," Zainab says. "I was afraid that if I cried in front of her I'd only add to her burden. I couldn't tell her that I understood her pain, because I didn't. I had never experienced anything like that. I just listened to her and absorbed as much as I could. Afterward, we went back to our hotel and spent the whole night crying. Ajsa put a real face on what was happening for us; her story wasn't just something we read in the newspapers. It was then that I began to understand what I had taken on."

For me, Ajsa puts a face on the work Zainab is doing. She takes me beyond the pictures I've seen on the Women For Women Web site and brochure, beyond any intellectual construct, even beyond my own desire to help. Zainab's story takes me to Ajsa, into her presence, into her suffering and shame—and into my own. Like Zainab, I have never had an experience like Ajsa's. But that part of me that has felt lost, that part of me that has felt violated and ashamed, grieves. I offer up a silent prayer for Ajsa's well-being.

"Another turning point came," Zainab says, "when I realized I needed to move beyond my original idea to only help rape victims. While we were in Croatia, someone asked me how I planned to identify the women I wanted to help. Was I going to put up a sign that said, 'Rape victims line up here for aid'? Singling them out like that would only be another slap in the face; it would stigmatize them even more. I didn't want to do that.

"About that time, I met a woman who told me about escaping from the Serbian soldiers when they came to destroy her village. She was shaking as she described how she and her two sons ran into the mountains, how she turned back several times to see her house in flames. For her, this was the most traumatic event of her life. She wasn't raped, she wasn't held in a concentration camp; none of that had happened to her. But the image of her house burning totally scarred her. Who was I to say that because she was not raped she did not deserve aid?

"I decided then I would not ask a woman what happened to her. I would not ask if she were married or widowed or single or what she believed politically or spiritually or what her ethnicity was. This was irrelevant. What was and is relevant for me is that she is a human being who is poor and needs help. There isn't one definition of a victim; there isn't one definition of the most horrible thing that can happen to a person. You can't compare atrocities. You can't compare human misery."

Zainab's statement startles me, partly because it's so obvious, partly because her delivery is so unpolluted by the emotion I normally associate with human misery. It goes beyond the narrow peripheries of predicament and sectarianism, beyond our very human tendency toward insular self-indulgence and our proclivity to raise our own sufferings to the level of victimization or martyrdom. I think about her statement again and again in the days and weeks to come. And I think about Zainab, what her stories reveal about her and her commitment to live out her spiritual values in her daily life.

There were more trips to Croatia—and to the other countries her organization now serves, including Iraq. More women to help. So much suffering. I ask Zainab how she keeps from getting pulled into the pain the women share with her.

"At first, I didn't know how to deal with what I was hearing, and their stories took quite a toll on me. I actually had second-hand post-traumatic stress. I cried a lot and had nightmares about being raped. I empathized too much and internalized their pain. When we returned to the States, I'd feel guilty about taking a shower or I'd deprive myself of something new because they didn't have these things. I finally reached a point of total exhaustion.

"A therapist helped me see that I couldn't get drawn into their pain if I was going to pull them out. Depriving myself would not help them live a better life. I needed to enjoy my life and take care of myself so I could have the inner resources to support them."

This is a challenge many women—particularly spiritually oriented women—deal with at one time or another. We deprive ourselves or we take care of everybody else and stretch ourselves too thin or we don't create healthy emotional boundaries because we think that by taking care of ourselves, we are abandoning the other—that we are being selfish or "bad."

"Yes. Now I don't get so involved in their pain that I can't give them hope. I say, 'OK, where can we go from here?' When I hear their stories, I still cry with them—you can't not cry with them—but I handle myself differently. And because I've seen many of them a few years down the road, after they've regained some confidence, I am able to tell those who are beginning this process that they too will be OK some day. For many of these women, it takes years to get back to where they were before the war. But they have showed me that one of our great strengths as human beings is our ability to move on."

What inspires you most about them?

Without hesitation, she responds, "The strength of their spirits."

And what do you think is the source of this strength?

"The Rwandese are very religious people, Catholics who integrate their religion into every aspect of their lives. They're calm. They seem at peace with themselves. They start every meeting we have with them with a prayer. Clearly, their faith affects how they internalize and deal with the tragedies of their lives. Bosnia, on the other hand, was a socialist country before the war and religion was discouraged. Strength is more a part of the Bosnian women's cultural identity. They are angry and bitter, yet they use these feelings to motivate themselves to go on.

"My own analysis—one not based on any formal research—is that religion is one of the primary ways many of the women I work with bring understanding to what they've experienced. It can give them a framework to process or disengage from their misery and deal with their challenges."

By way of illustration, Zainab tells me about a deeply religious Rwandan woman she met who lost her six children in a brutal massacre. "She was in church praying with her family when the soldiers came," Zainab says. "The bullets began to fly and all her children were killed. They all fell on top of her as they died. When the soldiers came through the church to execute the survivors, they assumed this woman was dead because she lay still underneath the bodies of her children."

I gasp. Thankfully, there's more to this story. "She was pregnant at the time this happened," Zainab says. "She left her home, moved to another town, and had her baby. By the time I met her, she had adopted five children who had lost their parents in a similar incident that occurred in their town. Taking those children helped her give meaning to her own loss."

Tears run down Zainab's cheeks as she talks. "After she tells me her story, this woman looks at me and says with a big smile, 'Thank you for being here, for coming all the way from America and listening to me. And thank you to the people who made your trip possible.'

"This woman is thanking me? It was I who should be thanking her! I feel so privileged to work with such women. I see this kind of strength over and over again."

I retell this story many times in the weeks and months to come to diffuse the initial horror of it and, as Zainab has done, to draw from its strength.

"I've come to respect the women we help as unique individuals who know what they want and know what's good for them," Zainab says. "My responsibility is to support each woman in her process, to give her exposure to different options, but ultimately to let her choose what's best for her, what she feels will restore her dignity.

"A lot of humanitarian organizations use photographs of crying women—the conventional image of the refugee—in their appeals for support. In our photos, the women are dressed nicely; some even have make-up on. They take the initiative to do this. They want to be photographed this way because they want to feel good about themselves. They may be running in the streets to avoid the snipers surrounding their city, but somehow they manage to be well-groomed. I admit this took some getting used to at first, but eventually I realized that their appearance is the only thing they have power over. It's also a way to remind them of life before the war. 'What do you want us to do?' they once said to me. 'Just because we're in this situation doesn't mean we must stop loving ourselves.'"

Then and there, I make a conscious choice to focus on the nobility of these women as Zainab does, to see them in terms of their strengths and gifts. This doesn't eliminate my concern for them or my sorrow, or my desire to want to make this world a better place. To my surprise, it provides me with some necessary detachment.

"Step by step," she continues, "they find ways—small ways, at first—to regain their power. For one woman, it was a simple gold bracelet she had received from her sponsor. It was all she had and it became her connection to life itself. It was not the material value of the bracelet that was important to her but the friendship it symbolized. Someone out there cared about her; someone was there for her if she needed help. Every time I saw her she'd say to me, 'Have you seen my golden bracelet?' She'd show it to me again and again. It had such a powerful impact on her."

Given what you've seen and experienced, how do you explain these kind of events? Do you believe in fate?

"I think I do," she says thoughtfully. "To what extent fate dictates my life or I dictate my own fate, I'm not yet sure. But I don't believe I should be passive and let fate lead me where it will. I *must* take an active role in getting where I want to be. Some things happen you don't count on, that take you in directions you don't count on, but even then you have a choice about how you're going to respond.

"I've been through a lot of things in my life," she says, "war, divorce, the death of my mom—and I'm only thirty-one! I believe there's a reason for everything that's happened to me: Everything has led me to improve who I am. I always try to look at my life from the perspective of what I'm supposed to learn from an experience. Once I figure that out, it helps me get through the difficulty."

Has what you've seen or experienced ever shaken your faith?

"When the Gulf War broke out so soon after I arrived in the States, I was very upset and confused. I was angry at God because I was separated from my family, and also because I realized there were so many wars in the world. I would say to myself, 'Zainab, how could you be angry at *God*?' But I was.

"I used to be embarrassed to say that out loud to anyone," she says reluctantly. "I was afraid people would think I was being blasphemous. Now I understand that my relationship with God is like any relationship I have with someone I love. It's very personal and it goes through different phases. Being angry was a phase I was in which, like everything else in my life, led me to become a better and stronger person."

She looks down at her hands resting in her lap, and goes about the intricate business of harvesting a memory from a tangled web of fragile thoughts and feelings. "My mother's death was a very difficult thing," she confides. "I loved her very much. I took it for granted that she would be around for a long time, so it was quite a shock to lose her. One of the lessons I learned from her death was not to take anything or anyone for granted. It's also something I've learned from the women I work with, because everything they cared about has been taken from them. Who's to say this won't happen to me some day?

"Ultimately, my mom's death helped me realize how important having a spiritual life is. She was very ill before she died and knew her time was coming. I watched her contemplate her life as a way to deal with her death. I saw her ask for God's help. She handled her death with such dignity and peace. It was so moving. Though we all seek this in different ways, she showed me how strengthening my inner life could better help me deal with the external world."

The room fills with a tangible peace and Zainab plumbs the veiled province of memory once more. I wait quietly until she is ready to share her thoughts.

"I don't know how people deal with losing someone they love if they don't believe there's Something out there—if they don't believe their loved one will be OK, that things will eventually be OK for them as well." She sighs, then looks at me. I nod my head in silent agreement.

Was there someone besides your mother—a mentor—who guided your thinking?

"My mother was a big influence in my life but she wasn't my mentor. She was very supportive and I loved her very much, but her life was not an example for me—and she knew that. She wanted me to have more than she had.

"I think my mentor and my best friend is my husband. I connect with him on so many levels. He is the person I consult when I have a problem; he is the one who gives me spiritual and moral support. I met him two years after I came to America during a very difficult period in my life. He helped me regain my sense of self and become who I am today. I love him very, very much," she whispers.

During the first three years Women For Women was in operation, all the money she and her husband raised, and almost everything he earned in his job, went to help the women. Zainab took no salary even though she was working full time for the organization. It was an emotional and financial strain for them both, she says, but it was also a statement of his belief in her and the work she does.

I have noticed throughout our time together that whenever she talks about her work, her eyes light up. The more she talks about it, the more ebullient she becomes. I ask her if she thinks her work is an assignment, something she was born to carry out.

"When I was fifteen, I told my mom that when I grew up I wanted to do something to help women—*all* women—but I didn't remember I'd said that until after I started the organization. Because of this, I guess I think of my work more as my calling, my path, rather than an assignment. It fulfills my soul. When the women I work with express their gratitude to me, I say, 'Don't thank me. I love what I do. If I ever go through what you've experienced, I expect that you would help me, too.' If tomorrow something should happen and I have to do other work, I'll feel lucky to have had this opportunity.

"I used to be embarrassed that I was so excited about my work," she confides, "but I have to be honest about who I am. My passion attracts people to join me. Others see my commitment and invest in it. I think that's one reason why Women For Women has grown so quickly."

Where do you get that passion? How do you create it?

"I don't think passion is created; I think it's there because I love what I do and because my work fulfills me. I get so happy when I see a woman take even a small step forward in her life!"

Months later, as I am working on the final edits of this conversation, I reach for my dictionary and, on a hunch, look up the word "enthusiasm." It comes from the Latin *enthusiasmus* and means, among other things, "akin to possession by a god." This makes sense to me—not that Zainab is "possessed," but that there is a goodness about her when she talks about her work—and a kind of rapture. She seems Spirit-filled. I've observed this in all the other women I've talked with for this book as well.

I know you're only thirty-one, I say, but given what you've done with your life thus far, what do you see as your greatest accomplishment?

"That I've been able to draw a smile on at least one woman's face. This makes me very happy. This is what makes me most proud."

Any advice to others?

"A lot of young people talk to me about their career choices. They've told me that even though they like art, as an example, they're going to go into computers because that's where the market is. I don't necessarily agree with this approach. You may do something well, but if you don't love what you do, you won't really be happy. Life is too short to waste. Do what you believe in. Follow your passion."

We come to the final question: I'm especially interested to know how someone with so much life ahead of her would like to be remembered.

She takes some time to think about her answer. "Helping others makes me happy," she says distractedly, as if she's processing her thoughts out loud. "I do it as much for myself as for the people I help. It's selfish as well as selfless."

She's quiet for another moment and then she says, "While this is very important to me, I think I'd really like to be remembered as someone who did not cause harm or hurt to anyone."

Her response triggers something in me too subtle to name at the time. We exchange thank yous and chat informally as she gathers her scarf and coat about her. I walk her to the door and we embrace as she leaves. Each time I hone the text of this conversation, I actively petition for the "A-ha!" that will decode my unknowing. Finally, finally, it comes to me: A decision to "not cause harm or hurt to anyone" is a conscious and disciplined act of will, a sometimes difficult task given the crosscurrents of emotion one must tame and the faith one must maintain to withhold retaliation.

Helping others brings satisfaction, but noninjury to others brings self-mastery.

We all read each other's lives from the pages of our own. Several years later when her memoir is published, I learn that Zainab herself fled from an abusive marriage, a marriage arranged by her parents to get her out of Iraq, and that her family suffered great emotional pain at the hands of Saddam Hussein. Though the intention behind Zainab's words was very different from my own resolution, I have become, through her life, more in touch with my own.

To Learn More About the Life and Work of Zainab Salbi

Contact:
Women For Women International
1850 M Street, NW, Suite 130
Washington, D.C. 20036
Voice: (202) 737-7705
Fax: (202) 737-7709
On the Web: www.womenforwomen.org
E-mail: info@womenforwomen.org

Read:
• *Between Two Worlds: Escape from Tyranny: Growing Up in the Shadow of Saddam,* by Zainab Salbi and Laurie Becklund, Gotham Books
• *A Woman's World: A Training Manual About Women's Social, Economic and Political Role in a Civil Society,* published by Women For Women International
• "Mass Rape: Natural, Cultural, or Social?" *Journal of Sacred Feminine Wisdom,* 1996
• "The Role of Microcredit in Poverty Alleviation in a Post Conflict/Transitional Society: Bosnian Villages as a Case Study," Making the Transition Work for Women, World Bank Conference, June 1999
• *Women, Philanthropy, and Social Change: Visions for a Just Society,* edited by Elayne Clift, University Press of New England

Listen:
• *Octaves Beyond Silence: A Benefit CD for Women Survivors of Sexual Torture and Violence,* featuring Ani DiFranco, Indigo Girls, Eve Ensler, and others, www.octavesbeyondsilence.com. All proceeds benefit Women For Women International.

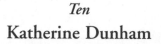

Ten
Katherine Dunham

People of Orphalese, beauty is life when life unveils her holy face.
—Kahlil Gibran

FOR MOST OF her ninety-five years, Katherine Dunham could rightly be described as a vital and luminous presence. Dancer, choreographer, anthropologist, and humanitarian, her talent breathed life into the world at a time when women, particularly African American women, had little national influence let alone global renown. Though she loved to dance as a child, she began her professional career as an anthropologist at the University of Chicago in the 1930s. It was there, at a lecture on cultural anthropology, that she first understood the ways in which dance was a reflection of the fundamental belief systems of a society. At that moment, she forever merged her childhood passion with her scholarly pursuits.

In 1935, Katherine received a prestigious Rosenwald Fellowship to study the indigenous dances of Jamaica and Haiti and began to explore her interest in movement as a medium of individual and collective expression—particularly religious expression. She surrendered herself body, mind, and soul to her research, both as a social scientist and as a spiritual aspirant. The consequences of her field work reached well beyond the scientific community: She brought the rhythms and movement of the Caribbean to the world stage and was the first to make black dance an accepted art form. She broke the color barrier of classical dance and paved the way for future dance icons such as Alvin Ailey and Arthur Mitchell. And she pioneered a technique that immersed her dance company in the language and culture of the work they performed, a practice that took them individually to a greater vision of humanity and collectively to over fifty countries.

During most of her forty-year dance career—a career that spanned stage, film, and television—Katherine collaborated with her husband John Pratt, a Canadian-born costume and set designer who passed away in 1986. Among the highlights of their work together was a 1963 production of *Aida*. In accepting this assignment, she became the first African American to choreograph for the Metropolitan Opera.

Katherine's personal and professional associations include George Balanchine, Marlon Brando, Eartha Kitt, Harry Belafonte, Whoopie Goldberg, Jonathan Demme, and a host of United States presidents and international royalty. She counts among her many accolades a Kennedy Center Honors Award, the Albert Schweitzer Music Award, the Urban League's Lifetime Achievement Award, and the Presidential Cross of Brazil. Though she has not performed publicly since 1965, she continues to use her talent and celebrity to make a difference. In 1962, she accepted a position with Southern Illinois University as a Visiting Artist in Fine Arts. Five years later, she took up residence in East St. Louis, Illinois, near an inner city branch of the university, and formed the Performing Arts Training Center. For the past forty years, she has provided classes in dance and the humanities to the city's young people in an effort to help break the ongoing cycle of poverty and violence in that community. On several occasions since she began the program, her students have performed at the White House. In 2000, she moved to Manhattan to work on *Minefields*, the final volume of her autobiography, to teach, and to oversee the renovation of her school and museum in East St. Louis.

Not surprisingly, Katherine's inner work has been equally rich. The courageous and diligent probing that characterized her scientific life impelled her to take part in the Caribbean ceremonies and customs she documented—rites that had been hidden from Western eyes for centuries—and led her to some of the great minds of the day: Erich Fromm, Margaret Mead, Krishnamurti, and many others. Katherine also became one of the first international celebrities to use her fame to draw public attention to various humanitarian causes at home and abroad. She created dances that protested the inhumane treatment of victims of the Spanish Civil War, the racial murder of a young black teenager in the 1950s, and the segregation she and her company encountered as they traveled around the world. In 1992, at the age of eighty-three, she fasted for forty-seven days on cranberry juice and water to demonstrate her objection to the repatriation of refugees who attempted to leave Haiti when a coup overthrew their democratically elected government.

My first experience of Katherine Dunham came not in a theater but in a doctor's office. I was casually fanning through a *National Geographic* and came upon a photograph of her, a glorious image spread across two pages of the magazine. She was sitting barefoot on a carved wooden bench, turbaned and draped in an exotic batik fabric, left leg extended, looking like an African queen. There was grandeur and pageantry about her but it was her dignified bearing and innate grace that made the photograph a visual feast. I did not know all of who she was then, for only a few short biographical statements accompanied the picture, but I asked the receptionist if I might have the magazine nonetheless. Why I wanted it was not entirely clear to me; all I knew was that I had to have it. Ten years later, I found the magazine buried beneath a pile of things in my office. Once again, I fanned its pages. Once again, my heart stopped when I saw the photograph of her, for by then I was actively researching women to talk with for this book. Over the next few weeks I called all over the country to try and find her, to no avail. Several months later I saw her name on a

Web site and sought her out. Eventually, I was led to Madeline Preston, her assistant in New York, who told "Miss Dunham," as she refers to her, about my desire to talk with her. Two months later I flew to New York to meet her.

❖ ❖ ❖ ❖ ❖

IT'S BEEN THREE years since my automobile accident, and a year-and-a-half since I roamed the streets of Jacksonville, Florida, in fits and starts making my way to Grandmother Twylah. I have grown much more confident about maneuvering around a strange city since then. My increased comfort is due, in part, to the remedial therapy I am doing, but more to the realization that despite my diminished abilities, I am being led by a Guidance System that far exceeds anything I can muster on my own.

Case in point: As my time to meet with Katherine grows close, I begin to feel apprehensive about being on unfamiliar turf, particularly in New York City. The hustle, the noise, the immediacy of a city are all potential triggers that could cross my internal wiring and induce a *fugue*, a neurological overload that temporarily reduces my brain to bouillabaisse. To nip that possibility in the proverbial bud, I become vigilant about my travel arrangements. Among other things, I call a friend of a friend in New Jersey to get her advice about the easiest way to travel from Newark Airport, where I will land, to Manhattan, where I will stay. I do not tell this woman about my neurological soup or what airline or flight I will be on, and we make no plans to connect when I'm in town. Yet there she is, standing at the gate as I disembark from the plane, holding a makeshift sign with my name on it. She is as surprised as I am by her presence at the airport. "I just felt compelled," she tells me by way of explanation, "to take you into Manhattan." As we motor down the turnpike, it's clear that I could not have made this drive on my own without immense difficulty. She delivers me to my hotel and three days later, she drives in from New Jersey and takes me back to Newark Airport. My stay in New York is neurologically uneventful.

The hotel where I'm staying is very near Katherine's apartment, close enough to walk there on the day of our meeting. I arrive with time to spare. Elderly men and women, all of whom have the sophisticated air of the City about them, stroll through the lobby. The receptionist notifies her of my arrival and directs me to an elevator that takes me high above the New York skyline to her seventeenth floor residence. Madeline greets me at the door and escorts me into the living room where Katherine sits on the couch.

She is still beautiful at ninety-five. Her white hair is cropped close to her head and her amber-colored skin is lustrous. She wears a simple sweater and slacks. A small woven throw is draped across her legs. As she reaches for my hand in welcome, the rows of bracelets that girdle her wrists jangle like a tambourine. But it is her eyes, black and glistening like the ocean at midnight, that claim my attention. And her smile. The two seem indelibly linked, hot-wired in simultaneous agreement with her heart to glow at her behest.

As I set up my taping gear, Katherine tells me that she is in New York to conduct a Dunham Institute at City Center for students and friends. Her description of the event is modest. I later learn that City Center has actually staged a series of week-long public conversations and a retrospective to celebrate her life and work. The phone rings and she excuses herself to take the call. As she talks, I glance at the things she surrounds herself with—and take an armchair excursion around the world. Artifacts from Africa and the Caribbean and an elegant array of European collectibles fill the room. Photographs of her dancing—including a four foot reproduction of her leaping mid-air across the cover of *Look* magazine—hang on the walls. Madeline, a former Dunham dancer herself, forewarns me that there is always something happening at the apartment—phone calls, visitors, and such—as Miss Dunham remains connected to a vast global family. This international aspect of her life and the perspective it affords her provides a good starting point for our conversation. She hangs up the phone and indicates she is ready to begin. I ask my first question.

Given the variety of people and belief systems you've been exposed to as an anthropologist and as a dancer, how would you define spirituality?

"I think spirituality is that part of us which is beyond this material body we inherit and identify by our own name or use to move from one place to another. It's the recognition of a thing or things infinite. There's a touch of transcendence associated with spirituality that, when we connect to it, allows human beings to rebound from the dreadful occurrences that happen to us and helps us move beyond the guilt and inferiority we feel about our mistakes.

"My travels have convinced me that there are many ways to tap into one's spirituality. Dance was one of the things that certainly helped me touch this part of my Self. As I learned to give myself over to the rhythmic motion of the dance, I discovered how to use my body to express my deeper feelings and ultimately, to reach for something beyond the body that would not only captivate my beholder, but also allow me to feel satisfied no matter what else was going on in my life."

Many people use the vocabulary of war—words such as "battle" or "victory"—to describe the spiritual life, to describe life in general. Is dance your metaphor?

"I don't know that I would go so far as to say that life is a dance—though, for me, dance has been a major part of being alive—but I would certainly say that dance has a lot to do with life in general. The Eskimo dance, so do the Pygmies. Birds dance. Even elephants dance at their funeral grounds. If you study the cave drawings done millions of years ago, you always find a depiction of people gathered together in dance. Every society in the world uses dance as a way to express its deepest feelings and to bring about cohesion within the group.

"Dance is universal, something needed and desired by our species. I've worked with people who were unable to walk, veterans injured in the war or people incapacitated by illness. Yet when those of us who were able danced before them, their eyes filled with light. They could not dance, but something inside them did."

The image of a life-sized statue I once saw in a museum of the Hindu deity Nataraja, the Cosmic Dancer, comes to mind. I wonder—does her God dance?

"As a child, my conception of God was influenced by Bible pictures that depicted God as an old man with long, curly hair and words streaming from his mouth in a cloud. When I grew older, I understood this image could not possibly be accurate for everyone; people who lived in Timbuktu or other parts of the world would not envision a God who looked like this. I have been in fifty-seven countries in my lifetime, and one of the gifts of my travels is the realization that each of us has an internal image of God that is based on our culture, our religion, and our own unique relationship with our Deity. It was then that I stopped thinking about what God must look like and began to form a personal relationship with God."

She pauses for a moment and smiles. "Eventually, I distilled God into a quality rather than a being having a specific form or shape. To me, God is the convergence of goodness in man and a melding and dispersion of that goodness. God is a collective of good thinking, of right thinking and actions, that makes life easier and more beautiful. And, in my mind, beauty is always associated with God. While I recognize that there is ugliness in the world—in man and in Nature—I am careful not to get immersed in it. By staying with the positive and the beautiful, life becomes, for me, easier and more comprehensible."

Have your beliefs changed or evolved over the years?

"As I've grown older—I will be ninety-six on my next birthday—my thinking about God has remained pretty much the same. What has changed is that now I don't feel as possessive about God as I did in other periods of my life."

Possessive?

"Possessiveness not in the sense of holding on to God—though whenever I was up against a difficult situation, I did hold on tightly! This enabled me to live through such occurrences without any particular abrasions or scars. But when I was younger, I used to take great pleasure in feeling that I knew the workings of God better than other people, in thinking that I had a corner on knowing about the things of Nature and of God. I now see that thinking, that exclusivity, as a phase; it was a way to help my soul survive. The more I became aware of God, the more I wanted my soul to survive, but sometimes, out of sheer ignorance, I didn't go about that in the right way.

"That period of asserting my own thoughts did, however, help me to separate myself from everyone else's thinking. Once this separation occurred, I began to develop a relationship with God, one that was not better or worse than anyone else's but was unique to me. I also came to understand that each of us is in a definite and distinct relationship with God, a relationship that is unique just as each flower in the universe is unique."

So initially, you tried to impose your beliefs on others as a way to affirm or anchor those beliefs within yourself.

"I did, though I wasn't aware that this is what I was doing at the time. I thought I was trying to help them. Fortunately, I began to realize that the more you become aware of God, the more you ask of yourself, not of others. What also follows is that you want to share the best of yourself with people, and you want to participate more fully in life. You reach a place where you realize you have a choice: to admire the beautiful waterfall from a distance or to stand in its midst and let it pour over you. I've found that participation is the best part of being human."

She leans toward me, as if she is marshaling my attention for what she will tell me, but there is no need. I am riveted, a devoted audience of one.

"Have you ever listened to a musician or a conductor who is making music solely to open a path to others, to spread music to her listeners? What an experience! It's almost as if she has bared her divinity to you. It's quite different from someone who uses her skill, her technique, to create something for herself."

Yes. You feel vulnerable and powerful at the same time.

"Very true. I think this is how it is with all art. Whatever the medium, when art is permeated with a desire to share the higher expression of oneself, it goes beyond the art—the music, the painting, the dance—and fills the atmosphere. It draws others in and gives them something of the inspiration that flowed through the artist when she created the piece, something she felt about the whole universe."

She stops and looks at me from the corner of her eye. "Am I too far out there with this?" she asks with a twinkle.

No, I say, I think I know what you mean. There's a reciprocity that occurs, an exchange between the artist, the art, and the audience that's bigger than any one of these elements or even the combination of all the elements.

"Yes. I'm not sure where this conviction comes from, but I believe it to be the case whenever anyone gives the best of themselves to another— certainly artistically and spiritually." Bracelets click and clatter in rhythmic sway as her hands choreograph her thoughts in the air. Even when she sits, she dances. How I wish I would have had the opportunity to see her perform.

Katherine suddenly apologizes for not being a better hostess and offers me something to drink. Madeline retreats into the kitchen and bring us each a tall glass of Coke. We sip our drinks for a few minutes and chat informally, then I ask her about the religious traditions she draws from.

"I was raised in the African Methodist Episcopal Church, but I didn't attend church regularly until I was a teenager. I can't tell you why or how it began, but I also had an interest in Eastern religions long before I was even old enough to know where India was on the map. My brother might have been the first one to mention such things to me. He was a philosopher and very interested in metaphysics. Later, when I was at the University of Chicago, I was greatly influenced by the beautiful dancing of Shankar, a prominent Indian dancer of the day. My admiration for his work drew me into a milieu of people who followed Indian thought, who lived in the beaming sunlight of their gods and took their life sustenance and joy from Eastern philosophy.

"Later, when my husband and I lived in Hollywood, we connected with Krishnamurti, an Indian teacher who had a colony of followers in Ojai, California. He would often come to our house on Sunday mornings for brunch, and we would engage in wonderful philosophical discussions. He was a very interesting man."

How did your time in Haiti impact your spiritual life?

"I was almost a full-fledged anthropologist by then. I came to Haiti at the urging of Melville Herskowitz, the professor who outlined the direction of my field work, and the great Franz Boaz, one of the legends of anthropology. Boaz told me, 'You will do something not one of us has done.' He was referring to the fact that because I was black and a woman, I would be able to gather data no white man had been privy to before. So I went to Haiti with that purpose in mind.

"I saw a completely different kind of religious devotion there than I had ever seen. Believers focused on a whole pantheon of gods, emissaries of a supreme God who was somewhere in the picture but not really given much attention. There was a god for water, for planting, for birth and death, for this, that, and the other; each governed an aspect of your life. Though it was not something I sought out, I managed to become a respectable *hounci* or follower. This engendered respect on the island and thus, gave me access to ceremonies I would not have otherwise had simply as a scientist."

She is quiet now. Still. Inside. "My perspective on my time in Haiti has changed throughout my life," she says slowly, intentionally. "It's difficult to say how much of their religious practices I was actually drawn to—how much of my participation in their ceremonies was motivated by my own intellectual curiosity—and how much was motivated by the hot breath of the anthropological masters for whom I was running front and guard. Sometimes I was drawn into relationship with what I was experiencing, and other times I remained outside of the experience and observed what was going on strictly as a scientist. However, I can say this much: My participation in these rites did not bring me closer to the God I now know and love."

You say in *Island Possessed*, the book you wrote about your work in Haiti, that you also had some undefined personal needs that unconsciously drove your curiosity. Were you seeking a spiritual direction then or a way to bring greater meaning to your life?

"Because I am a creative person, I am always searching for answers, for new ways to do things, for deeper understanding. This was true even as a child. For example, until I was fourteen, I slept in a tiny room that must have, at some point, been a closet. It was barely big enough for a single bed and a small dresser. It did have a window, however—and I was delighted with that. Almost every night, a bright star was visible through that window. I don't know what star it was, but in some mysterious way, seeing it every night became an answer, a confirmation of my existence and of what I was thinking and becoming. It justified my being; it validated my creative and sensitive nature in a family that was not accustomed to providing me with that reassurance. That star was home; it was life itself. Its presence had a great influence on me."

I think I understand something of her relationship to that star, how it ordered her thinking and affirmed parts of herself she learned to keep secret from others, how it gave her a kinship to something besides her secret longings. For a creative person who has not yet discovered their avenue of expression, finding that sense of belonging is something akin to a mythological quest. I know. Though I had no star to reassure me, I had long, intimate conversations at night with an unseen but palpable Presence I called The Magic. The Magic filled me with uncharacteristic bravado about my ability to master my life—and sometimes, joy. I did not know then that I was talking to God, for my childhood understanding of Spirit was circumscribed by the superstitious wives' tales of my playmates and the patriarchal doctrines of orthodox religion. I knew only, as Katherine knew about her star, that there was something sacred about The Magic, but I never talked about It. I think I was afraid I would be ridiculed or, worse yet, that I would have to give It up because It didn't conform to what I'd been taught to believe. Katherine tells me that she too, kept her relationship with the star secret. She also tells me how fortunate she felt to have had an older brother she adored, who supported her and guided her thinking. We talk about him now, and about others who mentored her at the beginning of her career.

"Yes, my brother Albert, for as long as he was alive, was very helpful to me. Professor Herskowitz was a great mentor, and certainly Franz Boaz, though I only saw him once. And Erich Fromm, of course. I was finishing my last year at the university when he came to Chicago. In his own way— and because he was a great mind, a great analyst—he managed to get inside me and slowly ease away certain unproductive beliefs I held at that time. I would come to him with a question about something, and he'd start our discussion with a laugh, then go straight to the heart of the matter. Or he would keep asking me questions until I myself saw the folly of my thinking. He was in my life at a time when I was up against a great deal of racism—a difficult thing to deal with, particularly for a young person. Fromm also helped me pay more attention to the feelings of others rather than always being centered in my own feelings. He did a lot to arouse a conscience in me. He was a great influence in my life, more than I ever realized back then."

You were a pioneer as an anthropologist, a dancer, a civil rights activist, and a woman. You must have been confronted with some extraordinary personal and professional challenges. How did you make it through?

"What I say to you now I say without feeling sorry for myself: I have had many very difficult times. I got through them because, as I said earlier, I held on tightly to God, and because I knew that eventually, things would change. Change is a law of the universe. Nothing ever remains the same. I'm a great believer in change. I very seldom find a person or a situation that I think is beyond change.

"I'm also a great proponent of optimism. By optimism, I do not mean simply thinking that 'tomorrow will be better.' Optimism is much more than that. Everything can be miserable and then, suddenly, I'll look up and see a tree in the sunlight and I'm aware things are wonderful."

Is your optimism related to what you said earlier about having an awareness of the beauty in life?

"It's not just about beauty. I have a willingness to see that even in the midst of bad times, there is something good somewhere that I can appreciate. This facility has allowed me to have quite a wonderful, productive life."

Is this willingness part of your spiritual practice?

"My spirituality is not something I practice but something I am, something I live. I have protested against social injustice in Haiti, in Spain and Brazil, in the United States, and all over the world because I believe we must each live and act in accordance with the knowledge that we are a part of Something Greater than ourselves. We must also take an intelligent stand against injustice. We must not give in to things that are destructive or contradictory to our deeper beliefs. If we fight irrationally or emotionally against injustice, or if we concede to indignity, we simply cannot achieve our full potential as human beings.

"I've always believed that there is some sort of great empathy in the world that would direct and protect me if I only deeply connected with it. As a result, there have been many times when I used my life, my position, to make a statement about injustice, a statement in action or in words."

She tells me now about one such occasion, a protest she staged in 1944 when the Dunham Company was performing in Lexington, Kentucky. The city was segregated then. There were signs everywhere that said, "For Whites Only." "I was quite weary of these less-than-subtle racial slurs," she says, "and from a long struggle with the theater owner about his policy of refusing to allow black people to sit anywhere in his theater except the upstairs gallery. It was all very trying.

"My performance was sold out that night, so my first thought was to refuse to go on to protest the situation. But the theater owner got wind of my plans and called the police. He said they would take me to jail if I didn't perform. So I decided to do something else to get my point across.

"I took one of those 'For Whites Only' signs and pinned it to the back of my dress. When I danced, I turned my back to the audience frequently to make sure everyone saw the sign. At the end of the performance, when I came out to take my bow, a sympathetic stage hand held the curtain open longer than usual. I stood on stage and said to the audience, 'As long as people such as I cannot sit in this theater next to people such as you, I cannot perform here again.' Many people in the audience were weeping. It was very moving. This stand desegregated the theater and allowed other performers such as Paul Robeson and Marion Anderson—who were scheduled to appear there shortly after our troupe left—to play before an integrated audience. Gradually, local restaurants and hotels followed suit and Lexington became more desegregated. It didn't happen overnight, but the part we played in breaking down the racial barriers in that city gave me a great deal of satisfaction and hope."

What you accomplished, particularly given the challenges you faced as a child—the early death of your mother and the harshness of living with an abusive father—is quite miraculous. Would you frame your accomplishments in those terms? Do you believe in miracles?

"Of course I do. To me, as an example, my Rosenwald Fellowship was a miracle. It took me places and put me in the company of people who looked out for me and offered me a helping hand. I don't outwardly call these events miracles, but within me I know that I have lived by a series of such happenings, many of which have come at very dark points in my life.

"I also believe I was put here by a major Power to accomplish certain things—things I've done in the past and things I am still doing—in education, in thought, in providing affirmations of life to people who have none of their own. This, to me, is also a miracle."

Is it also your mission?

"Yes. Many, many years ago, I was walking out of a large, empty room in a museum, and I heard, but I didn't hear—I heard with a sense that was not hearing—an interior voice say, 'You must never forget that you are here to teach.' It was tantalizing! I had always known this about myself on some deep level, but never had it been as clear to me as it was at that moment. I realized, of course, that it was up to me to develop my own scenario for making that happen. But from that day on, all my relationships, all my undertakings with people, have been about teaching."

Teaching through or about dance?

"Teaching through and about everything I could. I don't have to be a fashion designer to know that someone's underskirt is hanging three inches below their costume. And, if they don't notice that, it's my job to let them know what's going on!"

She offers up her last comment with all the fire of a social reformer and all the striving for excellence that infuses her art. "Yes Ma'am," I say, and give her a brief salute. She smiles at my theatrics.

What do you believe is the most important teaching you have to share?

"That we can love; that we *can* and *do* love, sometimes without even being aware that loving is what we're doing. I think love is the most important thing there is." Her voice is soft now, like velvet.

Love of self? Love of others? Love of God?

"Love of anything and everything," she says, and makes a sweeping gesture with her hands. On cue, the door opens and a bright-eyed toddler, her two-year-old Haitian goddaughter Rose Michele, scampers into the room. "Hello Madam," she says to Katherine, who has opened her arms wide to the child. They hug and coo. I am properly introduced and properly greeted by this sprite who is obviously the apple of Katherine's eye. After reporting on the events of her day, Rose skips out of the room with her mother in tow.

Katherine is all smiles. "You see," she says beaming, "love is the most important thing there is."

Is this the secret of your success?

"I haven't really thought much about success, but I am aware of the many positive things that have happened to me—and certainly, being able to know love has had a lot to do with any success I may have been able to achieve."

She reflects for a moment. "Yes," she says, "I think the biggest share of the credit for what I've been able to accomplish in my life should go to love."

What do you think is your greatest accomplishment?

"There have been a lot of things that were terribly important to my career, like doing *Aida* for the Metropolitan and touring with my various companies around the world. In a way, everything I did was great—even the smallest task—because I made love and the desire to enjoy whatever I was doing an integral part of my work."

Do you have any advice you would like to give to others?

"Never give up," she says firmly. "If you really believe you are supposed to do something, keep on believing in it even if others tell you differently. Nine times out of ten, your critics aren't really qualified to tell
you whether what you want to achieve is possible or not. Maybe it's just
not their role to bring what you are being called to bring to the world,
so they don't have the slightest understanding of what you are trying to
do. So don't fall prey to your critics. Learn to shut out the things that
could derail you from your goal or put you on the wrong track. If what
you want seems unattainable, study it carefully first to determine
whether this is the case. Look within yourself to find a way to make it
happen. After all, it's what inside that counts the most! Then, if you
decide to go for it, focus on those qualities of your goal that you love—
its beauty or its truth, the devotion or kindness it will bring to the
world—and this will inspire you.

"This is not to say that if you discover that your goal is dead and
buried you must sit by its grave and mourn! I don't mean that. Think
clearly about what you want to accomplish. Discern! Discern! Examine
your life carefully so you don't create something that's false for you. Don't
just sit at the table and eat what's put in front of you! Before you pick up
your spoon, look at what's on your plate! Take it in with your eyes. If you
decide to take a bite, savor the taste. And when all this examination is
done—when you know yourself, when you've learned how to see the beauty that is all around you, then love and enjoy what life has done for you.
This now is my present position."

When all is said and done, how would you like to be remembered?

She looks around her apartment, as if by assessing its contents, she
takes stock of her life. A special citation from former Mayor Guilianni
commemorating her artistic contribution to the city of New York remains
unhung in the corner of her living room. This woman, known to the
dance community as "the Matriarch of Black Dance" and to people
around the world for her scholarly and humanitarian efforts, looks back at
me and says simply, "I would like to have the words 'She Tried' engraved
on my tombstone. This is how I would like to be remembered."

She says the words softly, not as a statement but almost as a prayer.
From where I sit, her remarkable life is proof that she has done far more
than try.

To Learn More About the Life and Work of Katherine Dunham

Contact:

The Katherine Dunham Center for the Arts and Humanities
532 Katherine Dunham Place
East St. Louis, Illinois 62201
Voice: (618) 271-3367
On the Web: www.eslarp.uiuc.edu/kdunham/

Read:

- *Katherine Dunham's Journey to Accompong*, Greenwood Publishing Group
- *A Touch of Innocence*, University of Chicago Press
- *Island Possessed*, University of Chicago Press
- *Dances of Haiti*, Center for Afro-American Studies, UCLA
- *Katherine Dunham: Pioneer of Black Dance*, by Barbara O'Connor, Carolrhoda Books (for 9–12 year olds)
- *Katherine Dunham*, by Darlene Dunloe, Holloway House Publishing Company
- *Dunham Technique: A Way of Life*, by Albirda Rose, Kendall Hunt Publishing Company

View:

- *Stormy Weather, Cabin in the Sky, Star Spangled Rhythm, Casbah, Pardon My Sarong, Carnival of Rhythm,* films she danced in or choreographed
- "Divine Drumbeats: Katherine Dunham and Her People," a 1980 television special produced by PBS in New York

Eleven

Margaret J. Wheatley

O Tiger's heart wrapped in woman's hide.
—William Shakespeare, *Henry VI*

MARGARET J. WHEATLEY is recognized on five continents as one of the foremost management consultants in the world today. When she talks about unraveling organizational complexity, leaders from institutions as diverse as the U.S. Army and the Girl Scouts, Fortune 100 corporations and monasteries, listen with rapt attention. There is intelligence and power in her words; they make sense in today's market economy. There is also compassion, for she deeply understands the apprehension and helplessness many of today's leaders feel as they battle the fiscal gods that gnaw at the soul of twenty-first-century industry. With unwavering devotion to nothing less than transforming the archaic practices that govern modern commerce, she gently urges us to actively engage in conversations that restore our sense of hope, to both look within and collaborate with others to heal our professional lives.

As president of Berkana Institute, a charitable, scientific, educational, and research foundation, Meg currently travels the globe sharing her ideas on how organizations can successfully grow and sustain themselves. She began her career as a teacher and administrator in the public schools, served in the Peace Corps in Korea, then went on to earn an M.A. in communications and systems thinking from New York University and a doctorate in administration, planning, and social policy from Harvard. She has been on the faculty at the Marriott School of Management at Brigham Young University and at Cambridge College, Massachusetts; served as a fellow of the World Business Academy; and been an advisor to the Fetzer Institute's Fellows Program. She is also the mother of two teenage sons and five stepchildren, and grandmother of thirteen grandchildren.

Meg's current work is actually the outgrowth of her lifelong fascination with science and history. In 1992, her award-winning book, *Leadership and the New Science,* was published. The book outlined a groundbreaking approach to healing organizational chaos, one that evolved out of her study of quantum physics, evolutionary biology, organic chemistry, and chaos theory. Anchored in the fundamental universal principles that govern the development of all life, she sees organizations as dynamic, living systems that can be nurtured by meaning and connection. Her ideas have won her the praise and respect of colleagues, leading-edge executives, and entrepreneurs in every field of professional endeavor.

Meg's study of the new science has also led her into a deeper understanding of Spirit, an understanding that animates every aspect of her life and work. She is an ardent spiritual seeker with a profound reverence for life. Though she now practices Tibetan Buddhism, her exposure to a variety of spiritual traditions has, she feels, led her to an appreciation of the unity and order that lies just beneath the complexities of the modern world.

I first heard about Meg through a friend who praised her book with almost religious fervor. I was knee-deep in reading for this book at the time, so I passed on his recommendation. A few weeks later, over the course of one weekend, he and two other friends spoke so earnestly about Meg's ideas that, this time, I decided to pay attention. It was then that I realized that what the Powers That Be were actually telling me through my friends was that Meg would be a wonderful person to talk with for this book.

I began dialoguing with Sarah Eames, Meg's devoted assistant, the next day. As it turned out, Meg Wheatley, world traveler, would "coincidentally" be in San Diego—in my own backyard—at an international management conference in three months. Sarah set up a meeting for the end of the conference and graciously arranged for me to attend Meg's keynote address so I could, in her words, "see Meg in action." This emotional generosity characterized every contact I had with Meg and her organization.

❖ ❖ ❖ ❖ ❖

THREE MONTHS FLY by. I read Meg's books and prepare a list of questions to seed our upcoming conversation. On the morning of the keynote address, I have the thought to bring my taping gear with me on the off-chance she is free to meet me that day. I stow my equipment in the trunk of my car, drive to the hotel where the conference is being held, and make my way through its tony corridors to a large meeting room teeming with executives. I slide into an empty seat in the back of the room just as the opening speaker begins his remarks. An artist stands with her back to the audience on a corner of the stage making "pictorial notes," drawing her impressions of the speaker's message. Music plays as we take part in "games" specifically designed to demonstrate the efficacy of managing complexity with our whole brain. Everyone sits in near childlike wonder when all these creative elements are masterfully tied to the hard core realities of modern business.

A tall woman with esteemed credentials steps up to the platform and introduces Meg. She speaks of her not just as an international management consultant but as a poet and a spiritual force. A thunderous round of applause precedes her as she takes the stage, a woman of middle years who, in stature, reminds me of an oak tree; in mind and heart, a mountain stream. She walks back and forth across the stage as she talks, the hem of her long earth-colored skirt flowing behind her—running, actually, to keep up with her. She speaks slowly, deliberately, with no notes. Her words move from behind her mind as effortlessly as her breath flows in and out of her body. She talks about how, in the midst of chaos, our greatest challenge is to believe in our own goodness; how we are all afraid of change; how, when fear augers in, leaders must demonstrate patience, forgiveness, and compassion; how we must approach chaos with humility rather than blame and negation. "Would it not be helpful to know that everyone in the room here today is as confused and anxious as you are?" she asks. "Could we not ease our individual pain if we entered into the darkness of organizational life together?"

Meg recites a Gary Snyder poem that urges us to "go light," then presents an exercise which demonstrates the healing power of listening—really listening—to others. She closes her keynote with another poem by Mary Oliver. For a moment, I forget that I'm at a management conference. The room is still, almost meditative.

After a few minutes, I weave my way through the tables of serene executives to the speakers platform and introduce myself to Meg. She smiles as I extend my hand, then tells me how she tried to reach me earlier that morning to see if we could change our meeting to that afternoon. Her smile deepens as I tell her how I followed a last-minute intuition to bring along my recording gear. Our mutual surprise and gratitude at how well things worked out is the entrée into what becomes an easy connection. We arrange to meet later that day.

I grab some lunch, review my notes, then ride the elevator to the designated hotel suite and set up my recording gear. A flurry of meetings and several phone calls later, Meg joins me for our conversation—for what, unbeknownst to either of us, will become our *first* conversation. Halfway through the taping, I notice a problem with my recording equipment. I replay a section of the tape; it seems fine, so we continue on. I plan to listen to the tape on my way home. If something *is* wrong, I think to myself, perhaps Meg would be willing to meet me the next day as we had originally planned. As I leave the hotel, I pick up my phone messages and find out that my aunt has passed away. Days later, when I remember to check the tape, I discover that it is, in fact, defective. By that time, Meg has returned home to Provo, Utah.

At first, I'm horrified, then I laugh. I must approach this chaos and complexity with, as Meg counsels, humility. So I relinquish my consternation, my fear, and my pride, and e-mail Sarah to tell her what happened. "Can we work together to find a way to redo the interview?" I ask. "I will go wherever Meg is, whenever she is free." We finally decide that the best course is to do the second interview by phone six weeks later when Meg is home for Christmas.

I'm glad I've had the opportunity to be with Meg, to see her in person, as that connection helps me place myself in her presence when we talk on the phone. By the end of our conversation, I am again aware that I do not have to be with someone in order to "keep company" with them. I begin with an apology for any inconvenience this has caused her, and express my appreciation at her willingness to talk with me again. She laughs and tells me she thinks this happened because the Universe wanted her to say something she didn't cover in our first conversation. With that in mind, we begin.

Something that really intrigued me about her book is her description of the universe as an invisible web of interconnected relationships that are rich with meaning and order. Her choice of words is not unlike the language theologians use to talk about the unity of God consciousness. I ask her for her thoughts on the relationship between science and religion.

"One of the maxims I frequently use—although I don't know whether it comes from Heisenberg or Einstein—is 'We will never be able to use science to prove the existence of God because the science will change on you.' And because the experience of Consciousness is so intimate and personal, it can't be replicated or statistically measured in a laboratory environment. I'm increasingly clear in my own mind that I don't really want science to be capable of explaining the Sacred. Actually, I think the ways we access Spirit are exactly what we need to incorporate into the scientific method to gain a greater understanding of life. I think it's wonderful that the new science can explain the interconnectedness of all life, but the way I help people understand these theories is to put them in touch with their own intuition so they can feel a sense of the Sacred—the things science can't explain—within their organization and within themselves."

When she spoke at the conference, I noticed her ability to take concepts like intuition and compassion and make them must needs to an audience I thought would be impervious to such things. That she does this with ease says a lot about her skill as a speaker. It also says a lot about the receptivity of her audience. I ask her if she thinks that there are "universals" to the experience of Consciousness, enough commonalties to form the basis for a language we can all respond to despite our individualized perceptions and beliefs.

"Oh definitely. If you read the mystical literature of all the great traditions, you find similar words to describe the inexplicable experience of being 'all' yet also being 'one.' I believe Consciousness is a universal experience, but one that can only be explained through highly individual experiences."

Because we each have an intimate relationship with our God?

"Right," she says emphatically.

How would you define God?

"I think about God in terms of the feelings I have in the presence of what I consider sacred or holy. Those feelings include true happiness—joy is the right word—a feeling of expansion, a sense of mystery. Beyond that, I think I'm a pretty sloppy theologian." She laughs.

"I also have an eclectic set of beliefs that somehow fit into my perception of God: I believe there is an Intelligence or Mind at work in the universe beyond our own being that guides us. I deeply believe in karma. And I believe we each have particular gifts that we are responsible to give back to the whole. Maybe, over time, these concepts will all come together in some organized theology but, right now, this works for me. I realize some of these beliefs are contradictory, but for people like myself who love questioning, contradictions are fodder for my curiosity. Without contradictions, I think we can become rigid fundamentalists and stop questioning."

I've often thought about conflict as an impetus for growth—but never contradiction. Contradiction is more subtle, like the grain of sand inside the oyster shell, the irritation that eventually gives rise to the pearl. Meg seems to hold her contradictions lightly. She is strong and sensitive, deeply curious yet utterly at ease with not knowing. I'm interested in knowing more about her background, how she got to this point. Was she raised in a spiritual environment?

"I was raised in a Jewish-Christian home. My mother was Jewish but converted to Christianity when she married my father. I had a wonderful Jewish grandmother who was an active Zionist on the world stage. She wrote books and ran for Congress, all to help create the state of Israel. My father was English, a pagan at heart, a Shintoist in the sense that he believed all of Nature was alive and filled with Spirit.

"As a young adult, I lived in Korea for two years and was very drawn to Confucianism and Buddhism when I was there. During the '60s and '70s, I got involved with some radical theologians in the Christian tradition. Then I became a serious student of *The Course in Miracles*. Several years later, I married a Mormon and practiced that theology for a while. About four years ago, I discovered Tibetan Buddhism, which has transformed me deeply. It's now my primary spiritual practice.

"All this searching led me to understand that no one faith, no one discipline, no one job title or political party, or any box we put ourselves in, is big enough to hold all of who we are—or hold what needs to be happening in the world through each of us today. I believe we're each here to bring together, to mend, the different strands of thought in every field— spiritual and academic."

Did your study of the new science influence your thinking?

"It actually led me to new spiritual traditions, to explore Buddhism as well as theologies like Creation Spirituality and other new forms of joyful expression of what Spirit is. I saw—through the eyes of biologists and physicists in particular—that there was a deeply ordered universe, a primacy of relationships, and a great, unstoppable creativity that characterizes this universe. Each of these concepts has been well explained in the spiritual literature for millenniums.

"The horrors of the twentieth century have also influenced my thinking; they revealed a great deal to me about the indomitability of the human spirit. The Holocaust—any of the genocides in this century—have pushed the human spirit to the limit. And we have survived!"

Zainab Salbi's story of the Rwandan woman who adopted five orphans after losing her children in a church massacre is still fresh in my mind, and I share it with Meg. We talk for a while about this woman and others who, in the midst of atrocity, do not lose touch with what's important to them.

"I often tell stories like that," Meg says. "They're so important, particularly in this country where we believe people are capable of extending themselves to others or asking spiritual questions only after their primary needs for shelter, food, and security are met. I don't believe this is true. We are capable of greatness and nobility and generosity all the time—even in the midst of our greatest suffering."

In *Leadership and the New Science*, you describe a healthy organization as one that is able to adapt to the demands of the moment, is resilient and fluid, has order, partners with others, is open to various kinds of information—even information which may ultimately be disturbing—and also has a stability that comes from an ever-deepening center. I'm intrigued by how similar your description of a healthy organization is to the description of the self-actualizing individual.

"Yes it is, but I prefer the phrase 'ever-deepening identity' rather than 'self-actualization' because I think it better explains what's occuring from a spiritual perspective. What gives us power, what gives us the ability to go on in such horrific circumstances, is a deep centeredness. It doesn't matter if we're talking about an individual, an organization, or a nation. If we have a sense of that place within us where we know and trust ourselves, a place that's clear about what we stand for and what's important to our life, where there's always a feeling of peace, then we can withstand the enormous shifts taking place around us and know what action is appropriate to take. We're not reacting in the moment or feeling like a victim of circumstance.

"It would be nice if organizations as well as people had this deepening center. I have to say that, in the years since I wrote those words, organizations have less opportunity to even notice what they might like to stand for because our culture has shifted more of its attention to making money and going fast, not to thinking about centeredness. The capitalistic values we're organizing around right now make it possible to create a company whose only requirements are to return a lot of money to its shareholders and look good for the quarter. There's no thought about long-term development. The financial pressures are wreaking absolute havoc on any leader's ability to create an organization that thinks about its people."

Which may be why so many people are miserable in their jobs or leaving to create their own companies.

"Exactly. I do think that, from a higher level, what we're seeing in the world now is the end of a very destructive thought form: one that champions greed, competition, individualism, and the manipulation of the world or world resources for the advantage of the few. This is *not* how the world works! I also believe we're entering a period where we're questioning the ultimate value and meaning of this kind of behavior. People are asking themselves: 'What is this all for?' 'Why am I working longer and harder?' 'Why am I more stressed?' 'Why can't I sleep at night?' 'Why are my children falling away from me?' 'Why don't I even know my neighbors?' These concerns are starting to percolate in our consciousness. Destruction is painful, but questioning is good. We must question the old so the new can be born."

Do you think meaning arises out of pain?

"I think meaning comes from realizing that we're scrambling faster and faster for something that then reveals itself to be meaningless—like sacrificing everything in order to give your children a high standard of living, then losing your marriage or your connection to your family because you don't have the time to talk to your partner; or like realizing that no matter how hard you work for a company, they're just as likely to fire you as not. What's going on inside our largest organizations today is completely insane. I believe that meaning arises when we make time for relationships within our homes and organizations, when we develop community, when we treat others well, and when we stay in touch with our own center."

How do you create meaning in your life?

"By doing work I feel is given to me by Spirit to do, by doing work that life has given me to do, work that has a deep spiritual rootedness, that can reverse the insanity in the world. My work is about rallying people around the globe so they can recreate organizations that are sane and habitable, that make sense, that are organized around life-affirming values rather than profit.

"But having a spiritual practice nourishes me more than anything else I do. I've been meditating for many years. It keeps me grounded during the day. Now I can call forth the meditative state in meetings—just sit back for a minute, and there I am. Daily meditation, working with mantras and repetitive prayers, practicing mindfulness in every waking hour—these are the things that make it possible for me to feel peaceful in the midst of all this craziness."

She pauses for a moment, then says, "Like most human beings, even though I realize how much I gain from daily spiritual practice, there are times when I completely let it go. It's only when I begin to notice that I don't feel peaceful, that I get angry at silly things or 'lose it' more often, that I return to my daily practice. Sometimes it's hard to stay with it even when you know how wonderful it is. I once talked with some Buddhist monks about this and they told me that they experience the same thing. I think this ebb and flow is part of the spiritual journey."

You mentioned that you work with mantras and repetitive prayers. Do you have a favorite that helps you get back in touch when you feel that disconnect?

"They change depending on what I'm studying or working on. One of my consistent favorites is from *The Course in Miracles*: 'Teach only love, for that is what you are.' I have said this to myself many, many times, especially when I'm in a difficult situation with another person. Another one that I've relied on for years is 'Please God, let me see this through Your eyes.' Even though I don't necessarily believe in a God that has a human form, saying this opens me up to a whole other perspective about the situation I'm facing, a much larger perspective. I've used these thoughts when I begin to feel myself getting angry with my kids as well as in the middle of a business meeting. Each takes only a few seconds to say, and each completely shifts the dynamics of the situation for me."

There are relationships I'm tending, where seeing through Divine eyes would serve me well. Like many women, relationships forge a huge reservoir of meaning in my life. How well we mother or partner or care for another—or are cared for by others—can have a powerful hold on our self-definition. Do you find this to be true?

"Yes, but I think it goes even deeper than that. One of the insights I've gained from studying quantum physics is that nothing exists as an independent entity, devoid of relationship with something or someone else. Relationship is not necessarily with another person. We can be 'in relationship' with an idea, a tree, with God, with anything. Whatever the relationship, it calls you out of yourself and, in some way, evokes more of what's inside you."

Because it mirrors some aspect of your self?

"Because being in relationship with the other demands that you contribute a part of yourself to create something entirely new. When two energies or elements combine, they form a new perception or entity. A rose is something we see as a consequence of every other element in the universe. If there weren't sunlight, if there weren't dirt or water or evolution, the rose wouldn't exist. If you take away any one element in that relational process, you destroy the possibility that there would ever be a rose. Everything exists because of everything else in the universe. Buddhism calls this 'dependent co-arising.'"

So our relationship with everything in the universe contributes to who we are; we are what we are because everything else is what it is.

"Yes. This is one of the ways Buddhism explains the interconnectedness of all life. We really wouldn't be here except for the fact that everything else is here."

Then it follows that our relationships not only define who we are, they sustain us and are fundamental to our existence.

"Yes. Once you start thinking about this," Meg explains, "it makes perfect sense. When you contrast this understanding to the way we experience life—particularly in America where we champion rugged individualists who don't need anybody else—it's easy to see how insane our current cutthroat business practices are. None of us are truly self-sufficient. Even if you're a hermit living in a cave, you're still dependent on the elements, on the plants, and the animals."

Is it the relationship or the quality of relationship that creates meaning in our lives?

"In every relationship, we have a choice: to choose love or separation, to choose for love or to choose for hate or fear. If we get into self-protectiveness and believe others are out to harm us, we flee from them or we erect a barrier between us and them because we think this will guarantee our survival. In truth, we are all diminished by these acts."

And enhanced by how receptive and loving we are.

"Absolutely," she says.

In the weeks to come, I revisit this idea of dependent co-arising frequently. It's food for thought. *Haute cuisine*, actually. It makes me feel like I'm part of something big, that I belong to the whole world. I understand my responsibility to others more deeply: to create quality relationships with everything in my environment so that more quality, more Love, exists in the world. What evolves from these kinds of relationships is a sort of Divine Reciprocity, a giving and receiving of the best and highest of one's Self to and with others, an interrelationship that can eventually become an expression of Omnipresence, an actual manifestation of or partnership with God.

Sitting there listening to Meg on the other end of the telephone, I make a different connection: I realize that relationship must also factor in to the answers to questions like: "Who am I?" "Why am I here?" "Who can show me the way?" I ask Meg how she would answer these questions.

"About ten years ago, I was making some notes for a speech, and I found myself writing three questions on a piece of paper. The first question was 'Who are we?' The second was 'Who is God?' And the third was 'How does the universe work?' I couldn't answer them then and I can't answer them now, but over the years, they keep presenting themselves to me as the questions I need to keep reflecting on as part of my spiritual journey.

"What I do know is that each of us is an eternal being. And that our natural expression is love. Any other expression we find ourselves in is just a warp of our true identity. I believe in reincarnation, that we keep coming back until we 'wake up' to the awareness of who we really are. And that 'waking up' is enlightenment—what I view to be the purpose of life."

She pauses for a moment, then says, "One of the great things I learned from Tibetan Buddhism is that we pursue enlightenment not for ourselves, but so we can help others wake up, help others move beyond their suffering and difficulty. This value is quite different from what we have here in our culture where we think mostly in terms of 'I'm better than you are' or 'I'm going to be enlightened before you are.'"

It's that competitive thing.

"Yes. There's a great, great Buddhist practice of praying that others will wake up before you do. Boy! Does this ever change your relationship with the people who are bugging you! You begin to ask, 'What can I do that will help them?' It's a very powerful meditation."

How would you answer the question "Who can show me the way?"

"Well, once you think about being here so that others might wake up, you realize that, through the ages, there have been great ones, awakened spiritual ones, who are here to help the rest of us wake up. These great beings are available as our teachers."

Great ones from all traditions?

"Yes. I believe that at their level, their teaching is one universally rooted thought. I rely on teachers from many traditions, whether they're in form or in Consciousness."

Are they your mentors?

"Mentoring just doesn't capture it. I frame what I get from them more in terms of absolute guidance based on their experience achieving what they want all of us to achieve. They are my spiritual teachers. They can sometimes be quite harsh, tricksters who will pull the rug out from under you, but their motive is always to prod you a little, to help you grow. Once you understand this, you can tolerate their trickery."

Recently, your professional direction shifted and you've begun to focus more on conversation as a tool to help people discover what they really care about. What motivated the shift?

"I think people need more time to just think, to explore what's meaningful to them, to connect with others. It's really missing in our culture today and we're all so hungry for it! When I share my stories, something meaningful occurs for everyone involved. Closer relationships, new ideas, the courage to take action in the midst of challenge—all this arises when we sit face to face with other human beings and talk as equals. I believe that conversation is a gift we can give each other."

You once wrote, "I crave companions, not competitors, who will sail with me through this puzzling and frightening world." With whom do you sail? With whom do you share your spiritual life?

"I once wanted to be part of a spiritual community, but I actually don't need that any longer. I have certain books I work with and rely on, books I can randomly open and find helpful guidance on the page before me. And I have a few very close friends I talk with. Whenever we talk, whatever we talk about, it's natural for us to put things into a spiritual perspective. We don't all have the same spiritual framework, but that's OK. Diversity is important. It's a lot more fun to explore issues from multiple perspectives. If I stay curious and disengage from my own certainty about what I think a friend should be doing, if I don't judge her, if I hold to the goal of not needing to know what's going on, if I just keep exploring the mystery with her and let that mystery unfold, I eventually get to a place where I see that there are a lot of different ways to look at any one situation."

Has it been a challenge for you to learn how to live like this, to participate in things as they unfold, to live more "in the moment"?

"It's become less of a challenge and more of an adventure. It took a few years to feel comfortable with not knowing because our culture rewards us for what we know. It's so much more fun when I let go, when I'm willing to be surprised rather than needing to be confirmed in my preconceived ideas of what should be."

That sounds like a good definition of faith.

"That's part of it," she responds thoughtfully. "Another part is believing in Spirit—and believing that part of the surprise is that Spirit doesn't always work the way you think It should."

The truth behind her words makes us both laugh.

I really like this idea, I say, of being willing to be surprised. The sense of adventure it engenders is a good way to diffuse the symptoms of approaching chaos: the mental blurring, the teeth gnashing and nail biting, the mix master that churns in the gut. You once defined chaos as "a system standing at a crossroads between death and transformation." It's a wonderful description of what's really going on, one that also sounds a lot like what's referred to in the mystical literature as a "dark night of the soul."

"Yes, it's exactly the same thing. One is science and the other is spiritual tradition."

Have you ever had this experience and, if so, how did you make it through?

"'Dark nights of the soul' are something I'm prepared for now because I realize that they are part of the process of my being born into a whole new way of looking at something, a new way of being in the world. I can't change, I can't transform in the ways I want to if I'm not willing to walk through those dark passages. Growth and newness are only available on the other side of chaos.

"We're living in a time, both in science and in spirituality, when the old ways simply can't give us what we need to live the rest of our lives. Things change, and part of change is that our obsolete ways of doing things must fall away. Not knowing what anything means, not remembering why you're even alive or why you thought you could accomplish something or why you thought something was of value is a terrible state to be in! You lose all touch with Spirit and feel devastated and alone. It's not that you're abandoned—although you feel abandoned—it's just that you're moving into a different relationship with the Sacred. As one of my spiritual counselors, a Benedictine nun, once said to me, 'The reason you can't see God when you're feeling like this is because God is standing very close to you.'

"I still experience these dark periods about every three or four months," Meg confides, "but instead of lasting for a month, they last a few days. When one occurs, I just let it happen. I don't try to figure my way out or drink my way out or talk my way out. I just sit with it; I let it move through me. I understand it's preparing me for what will come next—and that 'next' is always more healthy and peaceful and grounded."

Is this what you referred to in your book as "the necessary heart of chaos"? Did you mean that chaos is loving and nurturing or that it's a core element of transformation?

She takes a few seconds to think about this. "I think I meant 'core,' but both interpretations are interesting. To see chaos as having a heart, as a loving process, is really foreign to our culture. It's a concept that's much more common to indigenous people who often go through rigorous initiation rites to die to the old and awaken to the new. In those instances, chaos is seen as being pivotal to the growth process. But when you're trying to control the world as we are here in the West, trying to use life for your own ends rather than participate in it, you end up thinking of chaos as your enemy.

"Chaos can release your creative power in the same way that necessity is the mother of invention. When things get extreme, when the old ways don't work, that's when you are your most inventive. If you want to grow, chaos is an indispensable part of the process. There's no way around that. As the world or your life changes, you have to give up the behaviors, habits, relationships, and ideas that no longer help you make sense of the world around you. It's an enormous letting go.

"These days, everyone is scrambling to hold on to an old form of doing business based on hierarchy and prediction that no longer works in our rapidly changing world. If we spend our time trying to shore up institutional forms that aren't right for the future, we contribute to the creation of the meaninglessness we were talking about earlier. As soon as we identify that what's going on is a necessary precursor to new growth, that it's not anyone's fault, people actually relax because they realize they no longer have to figure out how to fix what's broken. They start to get engaged with thinking about what's next or what's new. This can be very creative and exciting for everyone."

That said, is there anything in your life you would have done differently?

"Well, I think my answer is no. Actually, I love my life right now. I would have handled my divorce a little differently, in terms of my children, although it was a very honorable, loving divorce. But I'm not in a state of regret about anything, and I certainly believe that whatever situation I'm in affords me the opportunity to learn a lot, no matter how messy it is. I don't believe learning is necessarily dependent on any one particular experience though. Learning is always available. We decide what the learning is, and the learning changes as we grow and change."

What do you think is your greatest accomplishment?

"I have a deep faith—in human capacity, in life and life's processes—and I have a very deep faith in God."

What advice would you give to others?

"I don't like to give nameless, faceless advice. I do ask people to notice what attracts their attention, what's meaningful to them, and recommend they stay with that, whatever it is. I believe that's one of the ways Spirit speaks to us. What gets your attention is different from what gets mine, but I have great faith that the things that get to each of us are ours, are what we're supposed to notice. If we pay attention to them, they will greatly assist us on our journey."

When all is said and done, how would you like to be remembered?

In a heartbeat, she says, "On a good day, like today, I have no need to be remembered."

Her words explode across the telephone line like fireworks in a Fourth of July sky. All that comes out of my mouth is a resounding "Wow!" She laughs. She is as dazzled by her reply as I am. We each digest the import of her words in silence, then break the silence with laughter. My mind returns to the beginning of our conversation and her comment about how she thinks our second go-round occurred because the Universe wanted her to say something she didn't address in our first conversation. Perhaps, this was what the Universe was waiting for.

To Learn More About the Life and Work of
Margaret J. Wheatley

Contact:

The Berkana Institute
P.O. Box 1407
Provo, Utah 84603
Voice: (801) 377-2996
Fax: (801) 377-2998
On the Web: www.margaretwheatley.com
E-mail: info@berkana.org

Read:

- *Leadership and the New Science*, Berrett-Koehler Publishers, Inc.
- *A Simpler Way*, with Myron Kellner-Rogers, Berrett-Koehler Publishers, Inc.
- *Turning to One Another: Simple Conversations to Restore Hope to the Future*, Berrett-Koehler Publishers, Inc.
- *Finding Our Way: Leadership for an Uncertain Time*, Berrett-Koehler Publishers, Inc.

For a complete listing of articles by Margaret Wheatley, please visit her Web site.

- "Listening as Healing," *Shambhala Sun*, December 2001
- "Partnering with Confusion and Uncertainty," *Shambhala Sun*, November 2001
- "Restoring Hope to the Future Through Critical Education of Leaders," *Vimukt Shiksha*, a bulletin of Shikshantar—The People's Institute for Rethinking Education and Development, Udaipur, Rajasthan, India, March 2001, Spanish translation
- "Bringing Schools Back to Life: Schools as Living Systems," *Creating Successful School Systems: Voices from the University, the Field, and the Community*, Christopher-Gordon Publishers
- "Consumed by Either Fire or Fire: Journeying with T. S. Eliot," *Journal of Noetic Science*, November 1999

View:

- *Leadership and the New Science*, CRM Films, (800) 421-0833
- *Lessons from the New Workplace*, CRM Films, (800) 421-0833
- *De-Engineering the Organization*, CRM Films, (800) 421-0833
- *12 Angry Men: Teams That Don't Quit*, The Hathaway Group, (212) 679-5800
- *It's a Wonderful Life*, The Hathaway Group (212) 679-5800
- *Creating Organizations That Support Great Work*, The Berkana Institute
- *Creating Organization Futures*, The Berkana Institute

Listen:

- *Leadership and the New Science (2nd Edition)*, by Margaret J. Wheatley, Berrett-Koehler Publishers, Inc., 2 cassettes, (303) 649-2929
- *A Simpler Way*, by Margaret J. Wheatley and Myron Kellner-Rogers, Berrett-Koehler Publishers, Inc., 2 cassettes, (303) 649-2929
- *Servant Leadership and Community Leadership in the 21st Century, June 10, 1999; General Session Featuring Margaret J. Wheatley*, The Berkana Institute

Twelve
Rabbi Laura Geller

*It is only the women whose eyes have been washed clean with tears
who get the broad vision that makes them little sisters to all the world.*
—Dorothea Dix

IN 1973, LAURA GELLER sat in an old building on the campus of the Hebrew Union College in New York City, one of the all-male bastions of Jewish learning, and listened to her professor talk about the wealth of prayers that mark the life of every Jew. As one of the two women enrolled in the college, and the only female rabbinical student in her class, she was aware that she was something of an outsider. But as the lecture continued, she came to the startling realization that the prayers and texts that shaped her tradition did little to verify her personal experience and the experiences of other Jewish women. It was an insight that would shape the direction of her life and thrust her into the forefront of contemporary Judaism. As it turned out, Laura Geller became a rabbi—the third woman in the history of Reform Judaism to do so—at a time when most Jews had no conception of feminist spirituality.

Currently Senior Rabbi of Temple Emanuel in Beverly Hills, California, there is a deep sense of history about Laura, past and present, a modern day shepherdess in the tradition of her ancestors leading her flock to greener pastures. She continually asks herself how she, how all Jews, can integrate their life experience into the practice of their faith and live with greater meaning and purpose. This kind of questioning motivated her to create rituals and prayers that celebrate the totality of Jewish life, write many articles on Jewish Feminism, and serve as the co-organizer of the revolutionary conference, "Illuminating the Unwritten Scroll: Women's Spirituality and the Jewish Tradition." A respected speaker, teacher, and social activist, Laura has been honored as Woman of the Year by the California State Legislature and by the ACLU for Fostering Racial and Cultural Harmony. She has also received many other awards, including the Alan J. Kassin Award for Outstanding Professional Achievement. Her presence, and the presence of a growing number of female rabbis, has virtually altered how American Jews relate to God. The mother of two teenage children, she is likewise committed to creating a life where the blessings of work, family, and friends are equally celebrated.

Given her present standing, it's hard to fathom that this articulate and passionate woman was not aware of her calling from an early age. Born to Reform Jewish parents active in the social justice practice of *tikkum olam*— a Hebrew phrase that means "repairing the broken world"—Laura was not inherently drawn to the spiritual life. The civil rights and antiwar movements of the 1960s kindled her interest in the connection between social activism and ethics, then ethics and theology. She went on to study religion at Brown University and, after six months on a kibbutz in Israel, decided to enter rabbinical school. In 1976, she was ordained a rabbi.

I came across Laura's name in a *Los Angeles Times* article about women who were transforming Judaism just a few weeks after I began working on this book. My own experience of growing up in a Jewish family and community was colored by painful memories of "us and them," an erroneous conception of an impersonal Deity, and run-ins with a male rabbi who treated me as if I was invisible. The Judaism I read about in this article embraced diversity; it was inclusive. It was about meaning and connection to others as well as to God no matter what one's age or gender. My immediate reaction to reading about her was, "Where was *she* when I was growing up?" As it turns out, she was riding her bike and playing jacks with the kids in her Brookline, Massachusetts, neighborhood at the same time I was riding my bike and playing jacks with my pals in Detroit. When I invited her to talk with me for this book, she immediately sent me a note saying she would be "delighted to participate." My own delight grew steadily from that point on as I prepared for our conversation and when we met several months later in Los Angeles.

❖ ❖ ❖ ❖ ❖

IT'S BEEN MANY years since I've been in a synagogue, but it feels familiar as soon as I walk through the doors of Temple Emanuel. There are smells and sights and sounds that reconstitute extraordinary moments of my childhood: the wisdom-permeated silence of an empty sanctuary, the weathered fragrance of an old leather hymnal that connects me to the joy of singing to God, the constancy of the eternal light above the Torah that filled me with a sense of perpetual companionship. I stand at the entrance to the sanctuary for a while and drink it all in, then make my way to the administration wing of the Temple. Lynn, the Temple secretary, informs me that the Rabbi has called to let me know she will be late, then ushers me into Laura's office to wait for her. There are books everywhere. Scholarly tomes, feminist and Jewish literature line the walls and sit in tidy piles on the tables on either side of the couch. A large walnut desk dominates the room. I close my eyes and imagine how challenging and gratifying it must be for a woman with a childhood not unlike my own to become the first woman to lead a major metropolitan synagogue.

Lynn gives me a copy of the Temple newsletter to read. Six words on the masthead, each stacked one above the other over a stylized Star of David, immediately occupy my attention: Passionate. Activist. Visionary.

Artistic. Caring. Spiritual. They are words that will eventually, easily, come to mind whenever I think about Laura.

Fifteen minutes later, she comes through the door with an armful of books and an apology. "Carpooling problems with my son," she says as she unloads the books onto her desk. She is slender and of medium height; not quite fifty. Her short, wavy brown hair is slightly streaked with gray, and her dark eyes convey the resolve I've so often seen in the eyes of women balancing the demands of work and family. Her casual dress—slacks and a sweater and no make-up—take me by surprise. My image of "rabbi clothes" is, I realize, limited to the formal black robe worn by the male rabbis of my childhood. This juxtaposition makes me grin like a Cheshire cat.

Laura excuses herself to grab a cup of tea. When she returns, she makes final reparation for her delay. Hunkering down into the chair across from me, she gathers in her energy and gives me her undivided attention. All this makes her very approachable. I like her instantly. I open our conversation by cutting right to the chase, by asking her a question I've wanted an answer to since I was a young girl in Sunday School: Judaism is filled with descriptions of God the Father. Is this what God looks like to you?

"I've come to a place in my life where God doesn't look like any one thing but is, simply, everything. There's a text from the Psalms that says, 'I have placed God before me all the time.' To me this means that my task as a religious person is to notice God, to be aware of God in every facet and moment of my life.

"Judaism also speaks about God as one with whom we can have a relationship. In communicating about this relationship, it's natural to use the same words we use to describe our human relationships. I come from a tradition that has historically spoken about God in male terms, but that window is not the totality of who or what God is. People come in genders. God is genderless."

She smiles at me and says, "Once people know I'm a rabbi, they often approach me in public places—like the supermarket or at a party—and tell me they don't believe in God. Over the years, I've learned to say, 'Tell me about the God you don't believe in and I'll bet I don't believe in that God either!' The image of God as an old man who looks like a grandfather and sits on a cloud in the sky actually comes from inelegant translations of the Prayer Book that grew out of the lives of the male rabbis who interpreted the scriptures. It isn't that these men were mean or misogynistic; rather they only noticed what they as men were aware of. The original texts are full of feminine images and references to God.

"For example, one of the ways God is referred to in the Prayer Book is *Av harachamim. Av* means 'father' or 'source' and *rahamim* has been traditionally interpreted to mean 'mercy,' so the literal translation of *Av harachamim* is 'father of mercy.' But there is a good possibility that *rahamim* comes from the Hebrew word *rechem*, or 'womb.' So perhaps a richer and more accurate translation could be 'source of motherly love.'

"The notion of *Shechinah*, the feminine presence of God, the hovering or protecting presence that went with the Jewish people into exile, also does not appear in our Prayer Book, even though it's always been a part of the rabbinical conception of God. One of the tasks of modern Jews, and modern feminist Jews in particular, is to be aware that these images have always been a part of our tradition. In so doing, we broaden the way women *and* men can think about God, and we give them the freedom to relate to God in a way that can be more personally meaningful."

As she talks, I recall how, except for a brief grade school fascination with the Greek goddess Athena—which doesn't *really* count because, after all, she was supposedly just a mythological character—I spent the first twenty-eight years of my life never once entertaining even the remote possibility that the King of Kings could also manifest as a Queen—or as anything else for that matter. Fortunately I have since come to understand that God can and does take many forms, and that my relationship with God is not dependent on my holding any one specific image in my heart. I also know that God's heart is big enough to hold all the various parts of me.

I ask Laura if she has a personal relationship with God.

"My relationship with God is part of who I am. And I work on developing that relationship as much as I work on developing any other relationship in my life. My duty as a religious person is to align myself with the power in the universe I call God. Alignment is what relationship—any relationship—is all about. By working on myself and working with others to create a world that God wants, I've developed an active and interactive relationship with God."

How do you know what God wants?

"I understand this through the lens of my tradition, by studying Torah, by continually hearing its texts speak to me and through me. I guess I really know what God wants because, if I reduce Judaism down to one fundamental principle, it would be that all human beings are created in God's image. If I take this idea seriously, then what God wants from me is to make a world that demonstrates this belief."

She savors her tea for a moment and collects her thoughts. "My relationships with others also teach me about what God wants for me. There's something about my relationship with my father that teaches me about my relationship with God, and there's something about my relationship with God that teaches me about my relationship with my father. This is also true about my mother, my children, my husband, my friends, about everyone in my life. We need a multiplicity of images to teach us about the whole of God."

How have you personalized your approach to God?

"In Judaism, we believe we can attune our hearts and minds to the Divinity present in every moment by saying one hundred blessings a day. There is a blessing for before and after we eat, for when we wash our hands, for when we see a rainbow or a friend we haven't seen for a long time; from the sublime to the ridiculous, there's a blessing. So, before I eat an apple, I say a blessing. As I eat, I acknowledge God as the source of my apple. I also express my gratitude to everyone who made eating that apple possible. I think about those who cared for the tree on which my apple grew, those who picked it, washed it, packed it, and drove it from the field to the market. In this way God permeates even my most mundane experiences."

Did you always believe in God? Were you raised in a spiritual environment?

"I actually started to believe in God after I became a rabbi. I grew up in a thoughtful Jewish home. We went to synagogue and my parents were very involved in the education and social action committees. I became *Bat Mitzvah* and confirmed, and participated in my temple youth group. But God was a part of my life I never really thought about.

"When I went to college in the late 1960s, I got involved in the social justice movements of the times. The chaplain's office was the center of activity at Brown where I went to school, and it was staffed by two Protestant ministers who were a very powerful example to me because their politics stemmed from their religious commitments. They helped me realize how my own politics grew out of my Judaism. For the first time in my life, I began to think seriously about what it meant to be Jewish.

"Shortly thereafter, I dropped out of college for six months and went to live on a kibbutz. Living in Israel put me in touch with what it meant to me to be an American and helped me see how central Judaism was to my life. But I had no idea *why* being Jewish was important to me. When I returned to college, I took some Jewish studies classes to explore my feelings. After I graduated, I knew I wanted to continue my studies, but I still wasn't sure what I wanted to do with my life. I actually went to rabbinical school, not because I wanted to be a rabbi or because I had a clearly developed sense of God, but because I wanted to learn how to be Jewish. It was there that my spiritual life opened up. My relationship with God began to develop after I started to experience some of the losses that come with adulthood."

In one of the articles you wrote, you said that "All theology is autobiography." I find this to be a very compelling concept. It makes the practice of religion very personal; takes it out of the hallowed halls of the sanctuary or the seminary and brings God into what otherwise seems to be the most plebeian aspects of our everydayness.

"Yes it does. Most Jews speak about two Torahs: the written Torah, the Five Books of Moses; and the oral Torah, the rabbinical commentary on the written words—the *Talmud*, the *Mishna*, the *Midrash,* and so forth. But for me, the two Torahs consist of the Torah of our tradition, all of the sacred texts of Judaism, and the Torah of our lives, what our individual life experiences tell us about God and the practice of Judaism. As I listen to the Torah of my life, the Torah of my tradition deepens. And, as I study the Torah of my tradition, the Torah of my life expands. There is an interactive relationship between the two. I believe that we grow in our understanding of God as we come to understand our life stories more fully."

This reminds me of something the writer Isak Dinesen once said, that "All sorrows can be borne if you put them into a story or tell a story about them." She was investing the process of telling one's story with the power to transform their life.

"Yes. Theology is autobiography in that how we think about anything in the world is shaped by our personal stories. When I was a Hillel rabbi at the University of Southern California, I talked about this concept to a group of students one day, then told them how I had learned about God through my relationship with my father and other family members. When I finished my talk, a young woman came up to me and said, 'My father sexually abused me. I didn't learn anything about God from him.' That was important for me to hear because I saw that her anger at what happened to her did, in fact, influence the way she thought about God."

How have women's stories changed the face of Jewish tradition?

"Let me give you an example: One day, when I was a second year student at the Hebrew Union College, the rabbi who was teaching *Talmud* concluded a discussion on this practice I mentioned earlier of saying one hundred blessings a day by telling us that there was no important moment in the life of a Jew for which there is not a blessing. My first thought after hearing this was, 'Wow! What a wonderful tradition.' Suddenly, I was transported back in time, to an incident that occurred when I was thirteen. I saw myself running out of the bathroom at my parents' house looking for my mother to tell her that I had just gotten my period. When I found her, she told me that when she got her period, my grandmother slapped her on the face. I was confused, angry, and hurt at hearing this, especially because my mother could offer no explanation about why this happened. So I got on my bike and rode to my grandmother's house and asked her why she had slapped my mother. Her explanation: 'Your mother was losing blood and looked a little pale. She needed some color in her cheeks.' That was the end of the discussion. The whole experience was very painful for me."

I saw this happen to a neighbor girl. I was there when she told her mother she got her period, and I watched her recoil in horror and shame when her mother slapped her. I can still see the look on her face.

"Once I began telling this story publicly, I met other women who had been slapped or who knew someone who had been slapped. Years later, I learned that 'the menstrual slap' was an Eastern European custom designed to scare away the 'evil eye' that was assumed to be particularly attentive during such moments of transition. But sitting in class that day, the only woman in the room, listening to the rabbi talk about how all the important moments in Jewish life were commemorated with a blessing, I couldn't help but wonder what it would have been like if my mother and

I had prayed together when I got my period. What if we'd said the traditional Jewish blessing for happy occasions, 'Blessed are You God, ruling over time and space, Who has kept us in life, sustained us, and brought us to this moment'? Or what if we had said a prayer that is part of the liturgy: 'Thank you God, for making me a woman'? Or 'for making me according to your will'? or 'for making my body work properly'? My next thought was, 'Yes, there should never be a moment in the life of *any* Jew that is without a blessing!' Men *and* women must listen to the Torah of our own experience and mark the ways Divinity is present in each of our lives."

Why is Judaism changing now?

"The stamp Jewish women bring to modernity is that our experience counts. Once you say, 'I am not marginal, that Judaism is also about *me*,' the Torah of our tradition changes. The prayers and rituals women are now creating free other women—and men—to devise rituals that acknowledge God's presence in every moment of our lives, moments as varied as a child going off to college or an elderly parent moving to a nursing home."

She leans back in her chair and smiles. "Judaism is an evolving tradition. It always was and it always will be. Our lives are not the same as those of our grandparents or our parents. I believe Jewish law is an interpretation created by human beings, and therefore, it can change as Jewish life changes. In 1976, I was the third woman in America to be ordained a rabbi. Today there are over four hundred women rabbis in America. But ordination of women as rabbis is just the beginning of the journey. One of the great things about a conversation like this is that it allows me to step back and see that I really am part of a historic transformation. In two hundred years, someone will write her dissertation on what's going on today in Judaism! We are living in exciting times! Though there are those to the right of me who would disagree, it's not a problem for me to now claim the authority of my understanding of Torah, an authority based on the authenticity of my life experience as well as on the Torah of my tradition."

Did you have mentors who helped guide the development of your thinking?

"There were people who were important to me—like those two ministers at Brown, and Richard Levy, a wonderful rabbi who was my first boss. But because I was one of only a handful of women in my field, it was hard to find mentors when I started out. During my first year of rabbinical school, there were fifty men in my class. Most of them were supportive, but a few thought I was there just to find a husband or to prove women could be rabbis. School was sometimes lonely and difficult, but many of my classmates' wives were dealing with the same concerns I was—with what it meant to be a strong woman in a tradition that had not yet begun to address feminist spirituality issues. We studied Torah and approached the texts from a feminist perspective. We prayed together and we supported each other. I didn't need them to be rabbis, I just needed to be with women who were serious about their Judaism. From that point on, I've always been nurtured by a community of women.

"Today there are feminist teachers, men and women, sensitive to the issues faced by women going into the rabbinate. Female rabbinical students no longer feel isolated or wounded by the confines of a patriarchal interpretation of Judaism. I think my inner life and my professional life would have been enriched had someone been there for me in the beginning. But as more women become rabbis, I'm being mentored by my colleagues. It's a different kind of mentoring, one where we are mutually supportive rather than having someone take a particular interest in my growth and actively guide me along my path."

Given your life experiences, how would you define spirituality?

"Most definitions focus on a private relationship with God, but my understanding, one shaped by Judaism, is that community is central to the spiritual life. Jews are not the kind of mystics who go off by themselves and sit on mountain tops. While we pay attention to repairing ourselves, we also believe we have a responsibility to repair the world, to make the world a better place.

"Arthur Green, a rabbi and teacher of Jewish mysticism, once defined spirituality as 'seeking God's face, then crafting a life that can be lived in the presence of God.' It isn't just about getting into the presence of God, because we're in that presence all the time. The central question is 'How can I fashion a life where I actually live in that awareness?' Based on that response, I define what my interactions with others look like, and I get a clear picture of my responsibilities to my family and to the world at large. It's never just an internal experience, though the internal experience is important."

Do you think being able to come up with answers to these questions necessitates that we first put our inner life in order?

"I think it does. But developing an inner life is not something you do on your own. In Jewish tradition, there are two kinds of *mitzvots* or commandments: those between a person and his or her fellows and those between human beings and God. Each *mitzvah* is 'between,' is about relationship. This doesn't mean that you don't work on yourself, but ultimately, you expand beyond yourself and see your life in relation to others."

When did you feel as if you had grown up spiritually?

"Only recently actually, since I've been here at Temple Emanuel. I've come to understand what works for me and what I need for my spiritual life to grow, and I'm now better able to create that for myself. That feels 'grown up.' As it turns out, what works for me also works for a lot of other people, and that's very satisfying for me."

We are about the same age, Laura and I, and while I know my growing days are far from over, I too have begun to feel more grown than not. Maybe there's something that comes near fifty that allows one to begin to settle in to their soul life more comfortably. The elements of our autobiography that we have most labored over, that have prodded and shaped and delivered us from some of the reigning smallnesses of self, take on an anecdotal quality that somehow enables us to divest our lives of a certain degree of ego and emotion. Laura shares such a story now, about the difficulty she had weaning her son.

"Nursing Joshua had been a wonderful experience, but when he was eighteen months old, he was clearly ready to be weaned. I, however, had mixed feelings about this transition. In need of finding a way to move through this passage, I turned to the Torah for support.

"One of the best known stories in the Bible is the story of the birth of Isaac, the child born to Abraham and Sarah in their old age. In the middle of the text, it says, 'On the day Isaac was weaned, Abraham made a great feast.' Curious as to why Abraham made the feast and not Sarah, I followed the interpretation of the verse throughout the biblical literature and discovered this was, in all likelihood, connected to transferring the child from the realm of women to the realm of men. I found a similar reference in the Book of Samuel. Hannah, Samuel's mother, kept him until he was weaned then gave him to the priest. She offered a sacrifice of four bullocks and some wine and food to commemorate the event.

"Reading these verses was very encouraging. I felt I was not alone, not the only Jewish woman who had ever struggled with this transition. I took refuge in what I learned and decided to use relevant elements from my tradition and create a weaning ritual for my son.

"I held the event on a Saturday evening, the end of the Jewish Sabbath. I invited my mother and closest women friends and asked them each to bring a story that captured their own experience of weaning as mothers so that I might learn from them and benefit from their experience. We began with *Hav'dallah*, the ceremony that separates the Sabbath from the rest of the work week and brings its sweetness into the other days. In this way, the metaphor of separation, the core element of the event, was incorporated into the ritual. As we shared our stories, we embroidered small swatches of fabric that I later had made into a *yarmulke*, the skull cap Jewish men and now more and more women wear when they pray and study. We also studied biblical texts that pertained to the event. The celebration culminated with my giving Joshua a *Kiddish* cup, a symbol that he was now old enough to drink on his own. It was very moving."

Though this was a difficult experience for her at the time, Laura tells the story now, eighteen years later, with an emphasis on its spiritual import. I'm impressed with how creatively and thoughtfully she made her way through the situation.

Have you ever had a "dark night of the soul," an experience that was particularly hard to find a resolution for or that precipitated doubts or lack of faith?

"My path has not been without its twists and turns. I think that's probably true for most people. At moments of spiritual crisis, there are people I turn to. Talking with friends has always been a source of comfort for me. So has my Torah study. If I'm going through a tough time and you and I study Torah together, no matter what verse we study, something will present itself that provides me with a clue about how I can respond to the struggle before me. It never fails to happen. There is incredible power and sustenance in that."

It is Laura's deep connection to the Torah that makes this convergence of knowledge and need especially meaningful to her. "For example," she confides, "when my first husband left me, I experienced it as kind of an earthquake. I literally had the image in my mind of the temple in Jerusalem being destroyed. I drew heavily on this metaphor to come to terms with this loss. The first temple was destroyed, but it was also rebuilt. And the second temple was different than the first. I took the remnants of my marriage, of the first temple, mourned them, then put my life back together. I knew I would be able to do this because of the teachings of my tradition."

She is quiet for a moment, then says, "For me, a real crisis of faith occurred early in my career, around some tragic deaths. I struggled with this for quite a while and often asked myself how God could have let this happen. Eventually, I came to understand that God is not someone who *allows* things to happen or not happen. The real question I needed to ask was how can God help me find the strength to deal with what happens? By reframing the question, I opened myself up to other possibilities.

"My teacher, Rabbi Jonathan Omer-Man, gave me some good advice during this period. 'What difference does it make,' he said, 'if you know whether God has the power to make bad things happen or not? It's a closed door. Who cares? The question before you is: What are you going to do now? How are you going to live the rest of your life?' Life is composed of wonderful moments and tragic losses. We need the skills to negotiate both."

Do you have a favorite psalm or prayer that comforts you in hard times?

"That's changed over time. The Hebrew name of God is spelled *YHWH*. We don't know how that's pronounced and we never say the word aloud. When we speak of God, we use the word *Adonoi*, which literally means 'my Lord.' If you were to attempt to pronounce *YHWH*, it would sound a lot like breathing. So probably the real meaning of the word has something to do with breathing."

The breath, the holy breath?

"Or my breath. Or I speak God's name with each breath. Or what you breathe out, I breathe in. Breath is something that connects all living things. There's a prayer that says, '*Kol haneshama, t 'hallel ya.* With every breath, I praise God.' This is a very powerful teaching for me, a mantra of sorts. I try to be attuned to it, to have that intentionality, even when I'm not consciously paying attention to my breathing."

It's been a quarter of a century since that day in Rabbinical school when you realized that your life experience was not at home in your scripture. What surprised you most about the spiritual life since then?

"That it requires discipline. Balancing multiple roles, fitting everything in that you want to do, is difficult—especially when a spiritual life is central to your existence. My friend, Tamara Eshkenazi, a Bible professor at Hebrew Union College, helped me a lot with this. She drew support for this issue from a beautiful passage from the Book of Ecclesiastics: 'To everything there is a season and a time to every purpose under heaven.' One way she interprets this is that you don't have to do everything all at once. That was very liberating for me to hear because there are times when it's hard to do it all."

We talk about finding the balance, about what we must temporarily or permanently let go of in order to redeem the present moment. "As a busy mother, wife, and rabbi," Laura says, "it's especially hard for me to carve out time for private prayer. It's clearly something in my religious life that's missing. I do make time—at least once a week—for regular Torah study, above and beyond what I do to prepare for my weekly sermons—sometimes in a class, sometimes just with a friend. We work through the text together; we study for study's sake, to deepen our spiritual understanding. It's not about mastering information but about wrestling with the words, figuring out what they really mean and how they can transform our lives. It's remarkably sustaining, clearly a central place in which I meet God."

Given how your life has evolved, do you think your work is an assignment, something you were born to carry out?

"I think I'm very lucky that my life unfolded in this way. I couldn't imagine work that would give me greater pleasure. I wasn't 'called' in the sense that other religious people speak of. I experience my work as a gift, not an assignment."

What do you think is your greatest accomplishment?

"I'm not sure I can answer that. I love being a mother. I'm proud that I was the first woman to be a senior rabbi in a major metropolitan congregation, but I don't think about my life in terms of accomplishments. I just see opportunities to do a lot of interesting things."

What's the secret of your success?

"Maybe it's gratitude. I feel really blessed to be doing what I'm doing. My work is interesting, challenging, adventurous—and I get to make a difference in people's lives. I'm very grateful."

Do you have any advice you would like to pass on to others?

She pauses to reflect. "First, try to be a good person. Second, follow your heart. You may not be rich but you'll certainly have an interesting life."

Looking back, is there anything you would do differently?

"Though I'm now happily married, I'm divorced from the father of my children. We share joint custody and we work very cooperatively as co-parents. But because the children spend a lot of time with their father in his home, I missed out on the parts of their lives that occurred when they were with him. It's the one aspect of my life I feel sad about."

I smile at her and nod. It's a sadness I know as well.

We've come to the last question: When you leave this Earth, when all is said and done, how would you like to be remembered?

"How would I like to be remembered? As someone who believed that all human beings are created in the image of God and that I did what I could to make this belief a reality. I'd also like to be remembered by the people who are most intimate in my life as someone who really loved them. Both things are very important to me."

Her answer is a living, breathing passage from the Torah of her life.

To Learn More About the Life and Work of
Rabbi Laura Geller

Contact:
Temple Emanuel
8844 Burton Way
Beverly Hills, California 90211
Voice: (310) 288-3742
On the Web: www.templeemanuelbh.com

Read:
- "The Torah of Our Lives," *Beginning Anew: A Woman's Companion to the High Holy Days*, edited by Gail Twersky Reimer and Judith A. Kates
- "Preaching in the New Millennium," *Preaching in the New Millennium*, edited by Fredrick J. Streets, Yale University Press
- "*Haftarat Nitzavim:* Isaiah 61:10–63:9," *The Women's Haftarah Commentary*, edited by Rabbi Elyse Goldstein, Jewish Lights Publishing
- "Bringing My Whole Self to God," *Hineini in Our Lives*, Norman J. Cohen, Jewish Lights Publishing
- "Afterward: Jewish Divorce Rituals," *Divorce Is a Mitzvah*, Rabbi Perry Netter, Jewish Lights Publishing
- "Metzora: Reclaiming the Torah of Our Lives," *The Women's Torah Commentary: New Insights from Women Rabbis on the 54 Weekly Torah Portions*, edited by Rabbi Elyse Goldstein, Jewish Lights Publishing
- "Competing Values," *Broken Tablets: Restoring the Ten Commandments and Ourselves*, edited by Rabbi Rachel Mikva, Jewish Lights Publishing
- "From Equality to Transformation: The Challenge of Women's Rabbinic Leadership," *Gender and Judaism: The Transformation of Tradition*, edited by T. M. Rudavsky
- "Encountering the Divine Presence," *Four Centuries of Jewish Women's Spirituality*, edited by Ellen M. Umansky and Dianne Ashton

Thirteen
Gail Williamson

*You are searching for secret ways of belonging to God, but there is only one:
making use of whatever He offers you.*

—Jean-Pierre de Caussade

GAIL WILLIAMSON IS upbeat and approachable. Focused and direct, with a quick sense of humor that peppers her conversation, she is the perennial "girl next door." She is also the mother of eight children: two boys, her biological sons, the youngest of whom has Down syndrome; and six girls, the nieces she and her husband Tommie assumed legal guardianship for after her widowed brother passed away. The two families barely knew each other when the girls moved into the Williamson's small three-bedroom home in the San Fernando Valley. That Gail's family are Evangelical Protestants and their girls are practicing Mormons was extraneous as far as she was concerned. So was the fact that Gail was launching a career to help her son and other disabled young people become actors in an industry renowned for its "beautiful people." As formidable as it seemed, Gail intuitively knew that bringing her nieces into her home would prove to be one of the significant blessings of her life. In spite of the odds—or perhaps because of them—it has become just that.

Today, the girls and an extended family of grandparents, sons-in-law, grandchildren, and friends are all thriving in the Williamson family embrace. Before Gail became employed as the executive director of the Down Syndrome Association of Los Angeles, she was talent and industry relations coordinator at the Media Access Office, the disability resource to the entertainment industry—a job she created and initially funded through a grant from the Screen Actors Guild. She is still active in the media industry and serves as a consultant and special needs casting director to shows like *ER* and a variety of feature films.

In 1999, Gail was voted National Mother of the Year by American Mothers, Inc., the official sponsor of Mother's Day. Though she has won many other awards and regularly earns the accolades of the audiences she speaks to across the country, Gail most prizes her spiritual life. "My faith fills my soul," she told me one December afternoon. "It amplifies my strengths and allows me to do whatever I need to do to help others access their own path." There were tears of gratitude in her eyes as she spoke, not for what she has been able to accomplish, but for what God has accomplished through her.

I first heard about Gail during a visit with family and friends in Detroit. "I know a woman you should talk with for your book," my friend said as we convened around her breakfast table one morning. "She spoke at a meeting we attended recently and really brought the house down. I think she lives in L.A." The more my friend talked about Gail, the more my internal bells and whistles clanged and tweeted. I traveled two thousand miles to hear about her and there she was, practically in my own backyard. When I returned to San Diego, I sent her a letter inviting her to participate in this book and spoke to her on the phone shortly thereafter.

We agreed to meet in Los Angeles in six weeks' time. The ease and warmth of our connection was, as I would soon discover, very characteristic of Gail.

❖ ❖ ❖ ❖ ❖

I TAKE THE train to L.A. and catch a cab to the bed and breakfast where I am staying for the weekend, arriving a mere twenty minutes before my conversation with Gail is scheduled to begin. Unwilling to admit that he has no idea how to get me where I am going, my cabdriver has spent the last half hour orbiting Pasadena hoping beyond hope that my destination would somehow rise before him like a page in a pop-up book. When I finally realize what's going on, I call the bed and breakfast and have the innkeeper guide me to her doorstep. I lug my suitcase up a rose-lined walk and step inside an old Victorian home so imbued with charm that it immediately washes away my distress. My room is lovely and welcoming. I set up my taping equipment and walk back downstairs to the parlor just as Gail knocks at the front door.

She is a tall, slim woman, in her late forties with short, sandy blond hair and blue eyes. She is energetic, friendly, even playful. On first impression, she reminds me of a puppy: What you see is what you get. I offer her some tea, then we climb the stairs to my room and settle in opposite each other at a small Victorian table overlooking a rose garden. Several weeks ago, Gail sent me some background material, a few photographs of her family, and a copy of her application for "Mother of the Year." The sixty-page application included a section in which she describes her philosophy of life. It's there that we begin our conversation.

Two of the core principles you live by are, "Things are not always what they seem" and "Life isn't fair." How did these concepts become such an important part of your belief system?

"They both evolved out of my life experience. Having a child with Down syndrome was, initially, the scariest thing that had ever happened to Tommie and me. We were young, still in our twenties, when Blair was born, and totally unprepared for his diagnosis. I'd done everything 'right' during my pregnancy. It never occurred to me that he would be born anything less than perfect. It was very hard to accept at first. I felt sad and confused and, at times, very angry.

"But over the years, Blair has proven to be one of the great blessings of our lives. Because of him, we found joy in unexpected places. Our lives became brighter as we learned to balance the dark moments with a genuine appreciation of the little victories in his development. Each milestone, each step or word—even those of other children we knew—was a miracle to us. Sometimes, I feel like a kid who found a terrific gift under her Christmas tree—a gift she didn't anticipate or know anything about, a gift that opened up the whole world to her once she unwrapped it. Our sorrows have been deep, but so have our joys. So much so that when we felt called to our girls, we knew that, despite the challenges, this too would turn out to be a great blessing."

Gail wraps her fingers around her teacup and sips her tea. "This idea that things are not always what they seem has another facet to it," she says introspectively, "one that goes way beyond the notion that what seems 'bad' at first can turn out to be 'good.' Let me give you an example.

"When Blair was little, my best friend was a woman with five children. We were always together, always in each other's homes. Last year, her first grandchild was born with Down syndrome. It was then that we both realized that while God was teaching her how to help raise a child with Down syndrome by placing her in my home, He was also preparing me to raise a large family by placing me in her home. Our relationship turned out to be so much more than it seemed to be at the time."

There it is, my "Economy of God" theory: that a single experience can provide us and those who occupy the contiguous borders of our lives with a multiplicity of learning opportunities, in the present and over time. Gail and I talk about this for a moment, then I ask her about the evolution of her belief that "Life isn't fair."

"After Blair was born, many people told me that God had chosen me to have a disabled child because I had some extraordinary attribute that would enable me to accomplish something other mothers couldn't. I may have been young and confused, but I knew that God didn't sit around in heaven and single out the 'can do's' from the 'can't do's'! I think Blair has Down syndrome not because God thought I was an incredible woman—or, as others also told me, because I needed to be tested or punished—but because we live in an imperfect world. Some of us wear our shadows on the outside and some of us wear our shadows on the inside."

Her words level the playing field, particularly in a nation wedded to taut bodies and tract homes brimming with the premiums of material existence. Most of us try so hard to blot out the dark stuff—to, at least, keep it at bay. We whine; we shout, "This isn't fair!" or we hide our heads in shame or quiet desperation. But not Gail.

"If this world were perfect, if life were 'fair,'" she says, "Blair would not have been born with the extra chromosome responsible for his disabilities—or else everyone would have born with that chromosome. If life were 'fair,' my girls would not have lost both their parents when they were so young. Joy comes along, peace comes along, and we must embrace these moments. But they're not guaranteed."

Do you believe there is a Divine Order to things?

"I think there is," she says thoughtfully, "but I don't think there's a list written in some big book that says what does or doesn't come into your life. What I really think is that there are many ways you can respond to what happens to you and that it's what you choose to do that makes a difference in how things turn out. Sometimes the choice is clear. Sometimes you need to make your way through several options. Sometimes you choose a course of action that keeps you hanging out there in the wilderness longer than if you'd taken another road. I don't think there are wrong choices, just longer trips—or maybe deeper sadnesses along the way."

Do you believe in miracles?

"By all means. But I don't sit around and wait for them to happen. I pray to God, then I row towards shore." She smiles at me. There is a gleam in her eye. In spite of her height, she appears almost impish! In the next moment, our conversation takes a more serious turn.

"I know people who have prayed for years for a miracle to cure their child of a disability. Personally, I don't think that's something God is going to grant, especially when I see the difference Blair makes in the world *because* of his Down syndrome. He helps so many people. Just by being who he is, he puts people in touch with what really matters."

She looks out the window, then again at me. "Have you ever seen the Star Trek movie where Captain Kirk meets an alien who wants to erase his pain," she asks?

I shake my head no.

"There's a scene in the movie where the alien approaches Kirk and says, 'Let me help you. Let me take away your pain.' Kirk shouts back, 'No! I am a product of my pain! I won't let you take it from me!' I guess what I'm getting at here is that rather than pray for a miracle to come and take away my pain, I choose to see its value, to think of it as an opportunity to grow. I don't think I'd feel the peace I feel now if I hadn't confronted my pain."

Her last comment—the import of it—slips right by me. My mind has raced ahead of her words to an article I read that morning about the growing potential of science to eliminate certain genetic "abnormalities." I'm anxious to tell her about what I've read and to hear what she thinks about it. So I let her brave words pass. I summarize the article for her, and say, I wonder what we'd miss learning about ourselves if we didn't have people like Blair in our lives.

"Exactly my point!" she exclaims. "Isn't it interesting what we label as 'wrong' and 'right'? Several years ago, a screenwriter friend helped me with an idea I had for a *Twilight Zone* script about some scientists who travel to Earth's twin planet in search of a mineral that will prevent Earth's impending destruction. The scientists think this planet is uninhabited, but they discover it's populated by a race of people who all have Down syndrome. They get to know the people and appreciate their customs and their simple philosophy of life. They also realize that taking this substance to Earth will destroy life on the Down syndrome planet. A big debate occurs about which planet to save: Earth, with its advanced technology and 'superior minds,' or the Down syndrome planet.

"The idea evolved because I think Blair really does live on a 'twin planet,' one that has a unique culture specific to its inhabitants. Out of necessity, it's less complex and less high-tech, but there's also minimal confusion on his planet, and a heightened awareness of what's really important. Blair touches more lives than I could ever dream of touching. Yet the world was so sad when he arrived. This was the child who would hold Gail back, who would change our lives. Our lives *did* change, but not in the ways other people thought they would. You see, things are *not* always what they seem. I think miracles happen all the time. We just don't always recognize them as such."

It takes understanding—and faith—to perceive these experiences as miracles. How would you define faith?

"For me personally, faith is a belief in a Higher Power. It's also about the willingness to submit to that Power, about listening for a response, about allowing God to really speak to me. It's belief *and* action. Faith is also knowing that there's more to life than what's here on Earth, that there's a 'bigger picture.'"

By "bigger picture," do you mean more than what we can see or understand with our human mind? Or an afterlife?

"I believe in eternal life. I look forward to eternal peace and eternal rest—some days more than others." She laughs and her delight fills the room. Her repartee does not expunge her sorrow, rather it makes evident her ability to turn water into wine.

"Somewhere along the way," she continues, "I figured out that there were essentially three ways I could handle the challenges that came into my life: I could crumble. I could stay neutral, remove myself and not take ownership of the situation. Or I could rise to the occasion. Crumbling and staying neutral are human responses. Rising to the occasion is something I do through the grace of God. When I rely on His strength, I grow in ways that are far deeper than when I try to get through things on my own. If I didn't believe I could pull strength from Something besides myself, I'm not sure I could make it through the day. Yet I enjoy each day immensely specifically because of my faith.

"My faith also gives me greater confidence in myself and in others. And because of my faith, I know God will be there for me no matter what, even when I'm angry."

Gail tells me about an incident that illustrates her point. It happened many years ago, when she got very angry about something a child said to her older son about Blair being retarded. "All the pain of 'Why me? Why my child? Why both my children?' poured out of me," she says. "I felt extremely free to yell and scream at God throughout this experience because I knew I would still be loved and supported when my pain subsided."

What does your God—a God you can yell and scream at, if need be—look like to you?

"Though I don't have a specific image in my mind, I do have a definite conception of God: To me, God is warmth, comfort, guidance, and peace. He is also about relationship—about my relationship to Him as well as my relationship to others. He is perfect and, though He loves me unconditionally as I am, He wants me to grow and develop myself as His child."

How did you come to this understanding?

"When I was a very young child, I went to church occasionally with my mom or with the kids in my neighborhood. When I was eight, I walked by myself to the church down the street every Sunday for a whole year. I was very shy then, particularly in new situations, so it was quite unusual for me to do something like this on my own. It was almost as if God went looking for me rather than I went looking for Him. That year, I earned a white Bible with my name engraved on it for regular church attendance and for memorizing certain scriptures. But after that, I didn't go to church for six years.

"Then, when I was fourteen, I went with my little sister to another church in our neighborhood, and it was there that I first learned that God loved me just as I was. These were the words I was waiting to hear. They brought wholeness to me and were incredibly freeing because I always thought I had to be perfect before anyone—even God—would love me. When I accepted the gift of His son, understood that Jesus gave his life for my salvation, it felt like a huge weight had been lifted from my shoulders."

She tells me how her beliefs deepened over the years because she made a conscious choice to nurture her spiritual growth. "As a young mother, I was a missionary for Youth for Christ Campus Life Clubs. One of the things they teach is that we're all born with a vacuum in our souls, a 'God-shaped void' that we need to fill in order to be balanced human beings. Some people try to fill that void with money and possessions, some try to fill it with their children, others try to fill it with drugs or alcohol. I've learned that the only thing I can fill it with that keeps me in balance is God, is faith in God."

Tell me about your spiritual practices. What do you do to fill that void?

"Prayer is the most important thing in my life. To 'pray without ceasing' brings me great comfort. I pray all the time, even when I'm doing the most ordinary things. I pray for my children as I fold their clothes. Sometimes, I even refuse their help with the folding just so I can use that time to pray for them.

"Everything brings me to prayer. When my brother was dying, I asked him how I could help him, and he told me to plant a garden. Gardens were always a happy place for us when we were growing up, so I planted a rose bush for each of his children in our back yard. Now, when I tend the roses, I pray for each of the girls."

Gail says these last words quietly. Tears spill from her eyes. Her willingness to allow me to see this side of her honors me. I pass her a tissue and she wipes her eyes.

"Attending church is also important to me. So is my participation in Bible study and prayer groups. I love to worship with others; I love the group experience. And service is a big part of our spiritual lives. Tommie and I met as high school students when we worked as counselors at Vacation Bible School. That was the beginning of our ministry together."

You and Tommie and your sons are Protestant. Your brother's children, your girls, are Mormon. Is it difficult having two different religions under one roof?

"When the girls came to live with us, the only things they brought with them were their clothes and their faith. We couldn't take that away from them; it would have been far too damaging. At first, everyone thought the religious issue would be a problem. I've yet to meet a Mormon *or* an Evangelical who doesn't roll their eyes when I tell them what we're doing!

"The girls were worried that we might try to evangelicalize them. We understood their concerns and assured them this would not happen. Ours would be a home, we said, where we would celebrate the similarities of our beliefs. Our family would be like an orchestra where they play the piano and we play the violin, but we all have the same Maestro, God. Because we had certain expectations for their continued spiritual growth, we also told them that if we—as people who knew 'music'—felt they were having trouble with their 'playing,' we wouldn't hesitate to send them to their 'teachers,' the home teachers the LDS church had assigned to them, or to their Bishop for further instruction.

"Because we didn't want to risk having anyone approach the girls and try to evangelicalize them, Tommie and I stopped holding Bible studies in our home. I also spoke to leaders in their church and asked them for their support. I made it very clear that if anyone tried to undermine our role as parents, we would take the girls out of their church. I needed the assurance that we could all work together for the girl's benefit."

Gail Williamson, you are a tough cookie!

She sidesteps my praise. "There are still days when I don't get to church because I'm making sure everyone else is out the door on time, but that's OK. My faith is there, and in a few years I can go back to participating in all the activities I used to. These are important years for the girls. I want them to be as firmly rooted in their faith as I am in mine."

You're acting like a mother rather than an Evangelical.

"Exactly. Because that's what I was called to be. I have to help them find their path, not my path for them."

And being a mother transcends . . .

". . . species!" she says fervently. "Look at all the animals that care for the abandoned babies of other species. It's pretty amazing, when you think about it!"

Her commitment to do right by these girls reminds me of something her minister said in a letter of recommendation he wrote for her application for Mother of the Year: "Gail is able to remain present in all situations," he said, "and not withdraw or be sidetracked, no matter how stressful or painful the task." I want to know how she manages to do this, particularly given the potential for distraction eight children can generate.

She laughs aloud at my comment. "Well, when I was a child, I had an uncle who was a quadriplegic. In those days, quadriplegics were put away in homes where they lived out the rest of their lives, but my little bitty Aunt Alyce took my uncle everywhere and did everything with him. They went to the theater, to the Grand Canyon, everywhere. He had to eat at a certain time, eliminate and sleep at a certain time, but meeting these obligations gave them both immense freedom. Watching them taught me that accepting responsibility breeds freedom—and joy. When you confront your responsibilities head on, you don't spin your wheels; you don't waste time and energy in worry or denial.

"Because I accepted the obligations Blair brought, I was able to genuinely enjoy the first steps of a friend's child, even though I had to wait four years for Blair to do the same thing. Because we stepped in and took the girls when they needed us, we didn't have to worry about what might happen down the road that could make picking up the pieces of their lives more difficult for everyone."

So accepting responsibility keeps you on track?

"Not exactly. I accept the responsibility necessary to stay on track because I desire the freedom that comes to me when I do this."

Her answer is so clear, so honest, that it catches me off guard.

"It's like this," she says, by way of explanation. "I enjoy river rafting. When I'm in the white water and the going is rough, I have to use every ounce of strength and concentration to meet the challenge. But once I make it through the rough spots, I sit back and enjoy a calm and wonderful ride. I see all the things I didn't notice when I was working so hard to get through the turbulence. Before I know it, the next patch of white water approaches. There's a bit of an adrenaline flow. I could pull out and be done with it, but I know that going down the next rapid will bring with it another period of incredible calm. I love the calm so I'm willing to endure the storm. The joy on the other side of the challenge feeds my soul."

She faces the darkness head on, trades the notorious ties that bind— the denial, the worry, the resentment, and the whole panoply of Seven Deadly Sins—for joy. And it serves her well. I can see it in her eyes.

Her minister also said that Gail sees everyone, including herself, as a mixture of gifts and skills as well as disabilities and weaknesses, and that the latter doesn't sabotage her joy or energy. Her joy and energy are obvious. I ask her how she manages to keep her head above the other stuff.

"I think it's because I consciously choose to celebrate and promote people's talents and skills. Blair will always be retarded. I can't change that. But I can adjust my expectations of him according to what he can do and rejoice when he does what he needs to do to get through his day. Everyone comes as a full package. You have to accept the whole person. I don't fill my life with pain over something I can't change. Life may not be fair, but I've still got to find a way to live it."

I pour us each another cup of tea and we crack open a box of English biscuits as she tells me about the mentors who have inspired and supported her.

"I've been fortunate to have a lot of wonderful people in my life. My parents gave me a solid code of moral ethics with very traditional, all-American values. My father had a strong sense of national pride, of 'the American Way.' We had a flagpole in our front yard and all his kids knew how to fold a flag. He also taught my sister and I to do whatever he or any other man could do—fix a car, dig a garden, build any number of things.

There was no gender bias at our house. My mother taught me to laugh, taught me the importance of humor. She is also a very inclusive person. Her station wagon was always loaded down with neighborhood children. Wherever we went, everybody on the block went along for the ride.

"My Grandmi, my mother's mother, and the women of her generation of our family were all very adventurous and progressive; they were women who were way ahead of their time. I have pictures of my Aunt Alyce and Aunt Bessie at the Great Wall of China, riding camels in India, and my favorite, the two of them on a Harley—Alyce driving and Bessie flashing a peace sign. They were incredible women who taught me a great deal.

"My younger sister is also an important mentor. We appreciate our similarities as well as our differences and we're always there to support each other. The men and women at my church teach me about my faith by how they live their lives. My pastor is a gifted teacher and has probably encouraged my spiritual growth more than anyone. And my husband Tommie, well, it's hard to tell sometimes where one of us leaves off and the other begins. We've been best friends since high school. Our shared spiritual belief is the core of our relationship. That alignment has given us each a tremendous amount of strength."

What surprised you most about the spiritual life?

"The comfort," she says immediately. "That God is a real comfort to me. The peace in my soul is amazing, especially when I consider that my world is not a peaceful or comfortable one."

Do you believe you have an "assignment," some task you were born to carry out?

"I think we all have an assignment: to discover what we can offer one another. Maybe it's a skill or talent we were born with, or maybe it has to do with what we become as a result of the choices we make in our lives. Because of Blair's disability and his interest in acting, I have a desire to provide him and others like him with positive role models, to help people with disabilities and their families live more fulfilled lives. That's what I *do*, but I think my actual 'assignment' is related more to sharing how far I've come because of my faith. What I do is simply the vehicle to allow that sharing to come forth."

If you had your life to live over again, would you do anything differently?

"Not a thing," she says emphatically. "Sure, there are days when things happen that I'm not too happy about. But if I changed any one thing in my life, it would affect everything else, and I don't want to unleash a domino effect."

What do you think is your greatest accomplishment? And what do you think is the secret of your success?

"I'd answer both of these questions in exactly the same way: my relationship with God. It's the root of the tree. Everything—everything— branches out from that."

Do you have any advice you would like to pass on to others?

"That it's very important to listen—to other people, to your family, and to what's going on inside of you. I think listening is as important as searching. When I stop talking and allow myself to be quiet, when I pay attention to what's going on inside and outside of me, I learn so much."

She looks out the window at the rose garden, then says, "My other little bit of advice is to embrace the moments of grace that come into your life. This became especially clear to me after an experience I had with my girls' mother." Gail smiles then tells me the story.

"Though my brother and I shared the same father, he lived with his mother when we were growing up and only came to our house every other Sunday of our childhood. After we were grown, he moved to Northern California. Tommie and I live with our two boys in the Los Angeles area, so we didn't see him and his family very often—really no more than a few hours once a year. In fact, of his six daughters, I only knew the three oldest girls. When we took them into our home, it was as if they were complete strangers.

"Despite all of this, when I look back on our lives, I see that there were times when God was preparing me for what would come. As an example, when Ali, our youngest girl, was a baby, we visited my brother's family. After we arrived, I went into the bedroom to spend time with Carol, his wife. She had ALS and things were at the point where she had no muscular control and couldn't hold the baby without help. She asked me to put Ali in her arms and wrap my arms around the two of them and rock them back and forth. She wanted the experience of holding and rocking her baby.

"I didn't know then that Ali and her sisters would come to live with us eight years later. All I knew at that moment was that rocking babies was something we mothers do. Now, when I look back on that day, I think of it as the moment when the cradle was passed."

Gail has been crying softly as she tells me this story. I give her a moment to regroup, then ask her how she would like to be remembered.

"There's a wonderful Bible verse that says 'well done, good and faithful servant.' That about says it for me. I want to know that the people I care about most in the world can move on without me because I have done my job in a way that's made a positive impact on them."

Then she adds, "Maybe that's the calling, the assignment, we all have."

We are quiet for a minute. I ask if there's anything else she would like to talk about and she shakes her head no. Then she laughs.

"Wow! This was just like a good therapy session!" she says. "I examined my life, I cried, and I'll leave here feeling good about myself!"

A grin explodes across my face. Whatta girl!

To Learn More About the Life and Work of
Gail Williamson

Contact:

The Down Syndrome Association of Los Angeles
315 Arden Avenue, Suite 25
Glendale, California 91203
Voice: (818) 242-7871
Fax: (818) 242-7819
On the Web: www.DSALA.org
E-mail: Gail@DSALA.org

Read:

- "DSALA Connections Newsletter," available at www.DSALA.org
- "They're Her All-Star Kids," *Family Circle Magazine,* July 13, 1999
- "Who Is Gail Williamson?" *Ability Magazine,* 1999
- "So You Want to Be an Actor?" *News & Views, National Down Syndrome Society,* July 1997
- "Working in Business," *Association for Theater and Accessibility (ATA) Newsletter,* June, 1997
- "A Star Is Born," *Exceptional Parents Magazine,* June 1992
- "A Flag Flying Fourth," *Exceptional Parents Magazine,* July 1990

Fourteen

Sri Daya Mata

How could I resist my nature,
That lives for oneness with God?
—Mechtild of Magdeburg

ON A BALMY day in 1920, Paramahansa Yogananda, one of the most highly regarded spiritual figures of the twentieth century, sat in a secluded spot on the grounds of his school for boys in Ranchi, India, grateful to reap the benefits of a few minutes of meditation. To his surprise, a panorama of Western faces—Americans all—passed before his inner sight. He intuitively understood that the experience was a sign, an interior presentiment that he would soon go to America. The following day, he was invited to speak at a conference in Boston, Massachusetts. That August, he set sail for America, poised to bring India's ancient practice of Yoga meditation to the modern Western world. Two years later, an eight-year-old girl named Faye Wright learned about India in school and that day told her mother, "When I grow up, I will never marry. I will go to India." Though she eventually made several trips to India, initially India came to her. In 1931, she heard Yogananda speak at a lecture in her hometown of Salt Lake City, Utah, and was instantaneously drawn to his message. A year later, Faye became his first American monastic disciple and was given the Sanskrit name Daya Mata, "Mother of Compassion."

Daya Mata spent more than twenty years with Yogananda, receiving his personal instruction and assisting him in the spiritual and humanitarian work of Self-Realization Fellowship (SRF), the organization he founded to spread his Kriya Yoga teachings. Yogananda passed away in 1952, and in 1955, Daya Mata became the third president of Self-Realization Fellowship. She has since guided its work—overseeing the operation of its temples, retreats, and meditation centers; its publishing activities; a worldwide prayer circle; and international lecture tours—and served as "Spiritual Mother" to its thousands of members and friends around the globe. Among Yogananda's followers, she is often lovingly referred to as "Ma," and formally addressed as Sri Daya Mata. The Sanskrit word *Sri* is a title of respect and means "holy" or "revered."

What is most remarkable about her is not that she is one of the first women in modern times to lead a worldwide religious movement, or how rapidly the work spread under her direction, but that she remains immersed in a deep love for God that permeates every aspect and moment of her life. When you are with her, it is difficult to remain unmoved by the devotional undercurrent of her inner communion. Her writings and her conversation, though always practical, are based not on philosophical constructs, but on personal experience. "My words come from here," she told me, pointing to her heart. That was quite apparent. Throughout our conversation, and for many days thereafter, I felt embraced.

I first heard Sri Daya Mata speak in December of 1976. I was living in Los Angeles then, the home of SRF's international headquarters, and a newcomer to meditation. A member of the Fellowship invited me to attend a Christmas *satsanga*, an informal talk she was giving that day at the Biltmore Hotel. I drove downtown and walked through the hotel corridors amidst a steady flow of the happiest faces I had ever seen. I walked to the ballroom and stood in the back for a moment to get my sea legs. Men and women of all ages and races strode by me. Eyes danced, smiles radiated with what seemed to me to be the true spirit of Christmas. A simple upholstered chair sat center stage, and a large photograph of Yogananda wreathed Indian-style in a garland of red and white roses stood to the right of the chair. An usher approached me and led me with a gentle upturn of his hand to one of the few remaining seats in the hall. Though I had no idea why, I felt like a child about to open a gift I had waited all my life to receive.

In a short while, a gentleman in a dark blue suit and yellow ascot walked on stage. He welcomed us as one would greet their favored relatives and introduced a group of young SRF monks who sang Christmas carols. Then Sri Daya Mata walked on stage. She was in her early sixties at the time, silver-haired and radiant. She wore a simple, ochre-colored sari and shawl that slipped off her shoulders each time she waved to the crowd. Everyone stood at the sight of her. People called out to her as she walked across the stage, "We love you, Ma!" "I love you too!" she replied with a laugh. She settled into the chair, motioned for us to sit down, and began to talk. She spoke about her Christmases with Yogananda, about the universal truths that underlie all religions, about the importance of daily meditation and of loving God. We meditated together, then she walked through the crowd greeting those she could touch with her hands or her eyes. I knew she could not possibly have known everyone in the room, yet the unconditional love she had for each of us was unmistakable—even to a spiritual novice like myself. I arrived home later that day and told my daughters, "I've spent the afternoon with an angel." There were no other words to describe the experience.

Years later, when this book began to take shape, I determined to invite Sri Daya Mata to participate. Given her demanding schedule, it took well over a year to arrange a meeting. When we finally met, twenty-three years had passed, almost to the day, since I saw her at the Biltmore Hotel.

❖ ❖ ❖ ❖ ❖

TO AVOID THE Southern California freeways, I ride the train to Los Angeles, a relatively peaceful two-hour excursion from my home in San Diego. Lauren Landress, a member of the Fellowship's Public Affairs Department, meets me at the station. She has served as my contact with Sri Daya Mata these many months and has graciously offered to drive me to our meeting at Self-Realization Fellowship headquarters, a venerable white building on the outskirts of Pasadena known affectionately to SRF members as the "Mother Center." Lauren negotiates the gritty streets of downtown L.A. with skill, then edges up a narrow road that traverses the tranquil hilltop neighborhood that is home to the Fellowship. The closer we get to our destination, the more serene I become.

At the top of the hill, we turn onto a private drive and make our way to a modest parking area bordered on one side by a verdant oriental meditation garden. We walk the circular drive to the main building, past sunlit palms Yogananda planted seventy-five years before. Birds are singing. A warm breeze rustles the stalks of the bird-of-paradise plants that stand as sentries near the front door. A deep peace permeates the grounds. I turn and catch a glimpse of the city below. From this vantage point, even Los Angeles has an ethereal glow. If Daya Mata is an angel, then this must surely be heaven.

Lauren excuses herself to let Daya Mata's secretary know I have arrived. I take a seat in the lobby across from a life-size painting of Yogananda that stands in greeting of all who visit his headquarters. Artifacts from around the world, gifts from his many friends and admirers, tastefully adorn the room. Photographs of a young Daya Mata and of Rajarsi Janakananda, the second president of Self-Realization Fellowship, hang opposite Yogananda's portrait. Though it is almost fifty years since his passing, Yogananda remains the guiding force behind his society. "He is a living, sustaining presence," Daya Mata will tell me, "in the hearts of SRF's devoted members in the same way that other world teachers live on in those who keep them near."

Thirty minutes later, Lauren and a senior nun of the Order escort me to the third floor study. Daya Mata sits in a chair at the end of the room, wearing her traditional ochre garb. Daylight streams across her face from the windows behind her and lights her silver hair, almost like a corona around her head. Her eyes are remarkable, like liquid suns. I cannot, to this day, say what color they are, for each time I look into them I see only splendor, a molten flow of multicolored light. Though she is now in her mid-eighties, she has the vitality and presence of a much younger woman. I greet her with the traditional Indian *pronam*, palms gently together at the heart, and bow my head slightly. She welcomes me warmly, then directs me to the chair nearest her. Lauren and several nuns who assist Daya Mata sit nearby. I dig out my notes, check with Daya Mata as to her readiness, then ask my first question.

All the great religious traditions agree that the external world and our individual consciousness are manifestations of an underlying Divine Reality. How would you describe this Reality? What do you call it?

"That Divine Reality I call God. How would I describe God? God is infinite and eternal. He is infinite Love, Wisdom, Bliss. The Divine can also be approached as the idealization of our most cherished human relationships. Paramahansa Yogananda taught me to pray, 'Heavenly Father, Mother, Friend, Beloved God,' because God—who is One—takes on all of these aspects in relating to us."

How do you experience God? Is your God personal or transcendent?

"My God is both personal and impersonal. By this I mean that though in His infinite nature He is formless and all-pervading, I have come to have a relationship with God that is so close, so sweet, so profound and blissful, that it is deeply personal.

"God can also manifest in form—in great ones like Jesus, Buddha, and Krishna," she says. "When I first came to live here at our international headquarters, Paramahansa Yogananda gave me a book about the life of Buddha and suggested I read it. What a great soul! He gave up everything—wealth, family, fame—to seek God. When I finished reading that book, Paramahansaji gave me another about Bhagavan Krishna, the Yogi Christ of India. In the story of his life, I saw how God was so joyous and loving. Then Paramahansaji gave me a book about Divine Mother, that aspect of God that has been worshipped for centuries in India. My heart was captured! That concept appealed strongly to me because the Mother is all compassion, all love, ever ready to forgive Her children.

"Though the Divine can be approached in many ways, I personally relate to God as essentially beyond form. I don't want to limit God to a form. To me, God is Love. I'm not speaking of a physical or personal love, but of the Love that created all of us and everything in this universe, the unconditional Love, the infinite Power that transcends everything in this finite world. When you know that Love through personal experience, It's something that's with you constantly. You have only to turn your mind within to feel It. It's not just a thought or mental process. It's an experience, a joy that wells up in your heart. I could not live without that inner communion. It's more precious to me than life or breath."

Do you talk with God?

"Oh, all the time." She chuckles, as if to say, but of course! "Throughout the many years I've been a part of this work, my relationship with God has been unbroken. I believe very much in what the saints called practicing the presence of God—in keeping the thought of God always in the background of my mind no matter what I'm doing. When you love someone very deeply, you go about your day with the constant thought of them in your mind. This is my relationship with God. I find it easy to sit quietly and carry on a mental conversation with Him, to just think, 'I love you, Lord. I love you.' When we call to God like this, how sweetly He fills our souls."

She is silent for a moment, long enough for me to realize that she is not just describing how she talks with God, but that she is actually telling God she loves Him. The ardor and affection in her voice rouses my own heart to new frontiers of spiritual longing. I sigh, then look at her and smile.

Given the depth of your relationship with God, why do you think some people find it difficult to believe in God?

"I think it has to do with how they were brought up. I was raised in a religious family where God was part of our environment. Before we went to bed, my brother, sister, and I would kneel at our mother's knee and say our prayers; and whenever we visited our grandparents' homes we prayed together as a family. Prayer, communing with God, became a part of my life. This kind of nurturing of children, helping them develop a relationship with God, is rare today, and that pains me very much."

She looks away for a moment, as if she is recalling something grievous. "It's so sad," she says. "Millions of people in the world don't think of God. Yet even the atheist will inadvertently say, 'Oh my God!' when going through a terrible experience. This is the unconscious cry of the soul calling out to the One who created us."

You've been a nun for more than seventy years; you made a conscious choice to seek God, and your lifestyle supports that choice. Why should those of us who are not monastics cultivate a relationship with God?

Without a moment's hesitation she responds, "Because God is the answer to all life's questions, the solution to all our problems. We *need* Him; we *need* His love. I see the torment people go through, how they hurt and are hurt by each other when they don't have Him in their lives. God alone loves us unconditionally. Even when we turn away from Him or ignore Him, He silently waits for us."

How can we develop an intimate relationship with God?

"Sometimes people say to me, 'I asked God to love me, but I did not get a response.' That's not the way to bring Him into our lives. We should tell God we love Him, or ask Him to help us love Him. Start that way. Love must begin with us. Then it will come back to us. Just pray to Him, 'Where You have placed me, there You must come.' Bring God into your life wherever you are and take Him with you wherever you go. It takes effort to do this. There's no question about that. Seeking God doesn't mean your life will become a bed of roses. There are challenges along the way. But we need to make that effort, we need to make time to commune with God and with our soul, to have times of quiet, of stillness.

"The Bible says, 'Be still and know that I am God.'" This, she tells me, is actually a reference to meditation. "When you are still within and without, you begin to feel His sweetness bubbling up within you. This is the way to feel His presence."

Listening to you, I feel a responsibility to bring God more into my life, as if the more I cultivate this relationship, the better I will become.

She nods her head. "I believe we have a responsibility *and* a choice. God gave us free will, to choose Him or not, to do good or to go against good. How we use our free will determines what comes into our lives. We sow the seeds, then reap the seeds we've sown. That's the principle of karma. We cannot blame God for what happens to us. Rather we need to turn toward Him. Then we learn how to escape from pain and suffering."

There is conviction in her voice—and promise. She is crystal clear and emphatic, yet immeasurably kind. I want to know about the origin of her beliefs, what religious traditions she draws from.

"Self-Realization Fellowship follows original Christianity as taught in the Judeo-Christian scriptures and original Yoga as taught in the *Bhagavad Gita* and *The Yoga Sutras of Patanjali*. The Ten Commandments teach, 'Thou shalt not steal. Thou shalt not lie. Thou shalt not covet.' and so forth. The *yamas* and *niyamas* of Yoga teach the same things: non-stealing, truthfulness, non-covetousness. Truth is universal. All religions embrace the same basic principles, and all lead toward the same goal—union with God."

What kind of spiritual practices do you engage in?

"The first thing I do when I rise in the morning is sit for a period of meditation and practice the techniques taught to me by Paramahansa Yogananda for interiorizing the consciousness and absorbing the heart and mind in God. After my meditation, I go to my altar and pray for all those who have asked for prayers. Before I go into my study, I read from one of Paramahansaji's books. I take his thoughts deeply into my mind and say, 'Lord, let me follow these words this day.' As I begin my duties, I once again pray, 'Lord, whatever decisions I make today, let them be based upon Your wishes.' Then I go to work. I face whatever comes, good and bad. And I love it! I would be unhappy if I weren't serving. For me, part of loving God is finding a way to give constructive service. Then, before retiring, I again have a period of meditation, of communion with Him."

You said you pray each day and ask that your decisions be based on God's wishes. How do you know what God wants you to do?

"The more you meditate and contact God, the more you get in tune with your divine duties and God's will. I've found that doing God's will always leads to your greatest happiness. Meditation helps you find your way; it helps you make the right decisions. Without it, it's hard to discriminate between what you want to do and what God wants you to do."

This has gradually become my own experience with meditation—though, in my case, God's will is more often done through me, in spite of me—or without my knowing. Daya Mata has made a conscious commitment to not act without internal sanction. There is an allegiance within her, a fidelity, that redefines, for me, the whole notion of partnership.

"When you make it your goal to seek God first and attune yourself with Him," she declares, "you are divinely led to what you can do for others."

How did you get to this place of such surety? What convinced you this was the case?

"The Bible says, 'Seek ye first the kingdom of God . . . and all these things shall be added unto you.' When I first came into the ashram, I took those words from the scriptures and gave one hundred percent of myself to proving they were true. How else would I know for certain whether something does or doesn't work unless I proved it for myself? When I made that effort, I found the answers I was seeking."

But of course, I think to myself, as she says this. It's like proving a scientific theory. Later, on the train ride home, her words circle round my head like seraphim—until it occurs to me that what Daya Mata actually proved to herself was not "just" that the kingdom of God is the consummate source of supply and demand but that it is *accessible*. This insight does three things within me, almost simultaneously: It causes a formidable blip on the internal screen of my consciousness, as her accomplishment is quite beyond my ability to cognize. It elicits a voracious desire to have a deeper relationship with God. Then finally, it fills me with peace as I rest in the possibility that awaits anyone who makes the effort she has made.

This experience is, however, four hours into my future. In the present moment, I ask Daya Mata about something I'd been thinking about that morning.

Earlier you spoke about finding a constructive way to serve. Serving others is something women are naturally drawn to. Yet sometimes, in the joy or self-validation serving brings, we neglect our own needs or we feel guilty or selfish if we do something for ourselves. Can you speak about this?

"Ultimately, anything God wants you to do does not mean neglect of self; it fosters the development or expansion of your true Self, your soul. You cannot remove the mote from someone else's eye until you know how to remove it from your own. Sometimes you need to be 'spiritually selfish'—to take time for yourself, to nourish your soul. I've found that life is a balance of nurturing myself in meditation, then giving of myself in joyous service to others."

Is this the goal of your spiritual practice?

"My goal is complete absorption in God. That's all I want. That's all I've ever wanted. Whatever Divine Mother does with me, however I can serve Her, I'm content. I have no personal aims. I'm not looking for fame or glory. My ideal is to be like a kitten that is happy wherever the mother cat places it, whether on a beautiful cushion in a palace or down in the basement on top of a coal bin. The kitten doesn't mind where it is because it's always with its mother."

Her voice softens and she utters the words not as a metaphor, but as a prayer. I do not want to talk, to disturb the silence that has wrapped my heart in unruffled calm. After a moment, her words about being raised in a religious environment rise to the surface of my mind and form my next question: Did you have any experiences as a child that influenced your spiritual development?

"When I was about nine years old, I lost a dear little cousin. I remember seeing him lying in his casket; he was so still. His body was there, but the boy I used to play with was gone. That shook me. I began to wonder, 'After this life is over, what then? Is this the end?' My spiritual search really began then. I wanted to know what God was; I wanted to love Him.

"When I was a little older, I was sitting quietly one day on my bed— I've always had the notion that stillness is part of seeking God—and suddenly I saw a beautiful light appear within my forehead at the point often referred to as the spiritual eye, between and a little above the two physical eyes. I thought, 'What is this light?' I was fascinated by it. It gave me such a sense of calmness and inspired me to continue seeking. I found that if I sat very still, I would become aware of God's presence; I would have certain experiences, accompanied by great peace and bliss. I didn't know until much later, until Paramahansa Yogananda explained it to me, that what I was experiencing had been described and taught for centuries in the scriptures of Yoga.

"About that time, I also began to visit many churches looking for spiritual nourishment—not just intellectual answers, but something I could take within and live by. I heard many people talk about God, but I never met anyone who actually *knew* God, and this was the burning desire of my heart. By the time I reached high school I knew I would not be happy in the world and decided I'd either be a nurse, as my mother was, or become a nun. I even sent away for some literature about joining a convent."

When did you meet Yogananda?

"He came into my life in 1931, when I was seventeen. From the moment I first laid eyes on him, I knew I had found what my heart was seeking. Here was someone who truly knew God, and I vowed in my heart that I would follow him."

Can you tell me about that meeting?

"My mother heard that a great teacher, a swami from India, was giving a series of public lectures in Salt Lake where we lived, and she invited my brother, sister, and me to go with her. I didn't want to go at first, but Mother said, 'They say he is a remarkable teacher and that he brings the teachings of the *Bhagavad Gita* to life.' I'd read the *Gita* two years before, and though I didn't understand it completely, I loved the book. So I agreed to go.

"My sister and I walked to the hotel where the classes were held and arrived a little late. Paramahansaji had already begun to speak, so we stood at the entrance of the lecture hall and listened to him. He was talking about love for God and the spiritual potential of will power. I was transfixed. Never before had I heard anyone speak about God as he did. I knew intuitively that he knew God, that he was speaking from his own direct experience. A great force came over me, and at that moment, before I had even met him or understood what his teachings were about, I made a vow: 'Him I shall follow.' I didn't have any idea how I would do that or when; I only knew that this was what I would do with my life.

"We went daily to his public lectures and later attended the classes he gave for those who wanted to pursue his teachings. One night, he taught the audience a devotional song of love for the Divine: 'Door of my heart, open wide I keep for Thee. Wilt Thou come, wilt Thou come? Just for once, come to me?' He told us that if we really called out to God with devotion and determination, God would respond. Later that night, I got out of bed and went into the sitting room and mentally sang that song over and over again. I sat in the dark sobbing, calling out to God, 'I want only You, my Lord. I want only You.' After several hours, a great peace came over me and I knew He had heard my prayer. I didn't know how it would be answered; I only knew I would be able to dedicate my life to God."

When did you decide to become a nun?

"About a week later, Paramahansaji's secretary, Miss Marquardt, telephoned my mother to ask if I would be interested in helping her out in her office at the hotel. Fortunately for me, I had taken shorthand and English in high school. Mother knew I would be glad to help and agreed to let me do so, and I began to do little assignments for her.

"One day, Miss Marquardt asked me if I would show Paramahansaji how to get to the meeting room she had reserved for him to conduct some personal interviews. I knew my way around the building, but I was very much in awe of him, and so shy. I thought, 'How can I say anything to him?' We walked down the hall, and before I knew what I was doing, I blurted out, 'Sir, I want so much to come to your ashram and give my life to God.' He looked at me very piercingly and said, 'And you will. And you will.' I was overwhelmed by his reply, and thought, 'How kind he is.' But I never said another word to him about it.

"Soon after that Mother invited him for dinner. He seldom accepted invitations, but he came to our home. After the meal, my sister and I went into the kitchen to wash the dishes. When we left the room, he spoke to Mother about my wish to join the ashram. 'She has never mentioned it since,' he said. 'Has she lost interest?'

"'On the contrary,' Mother said. 'Her heart is breaking. Her nature is to only ask for something once. She thinks that since you haven't said anything more about it to her, that you don't want her to come, that you've decided against it.'

"'Oh, that's it!' he said. 'Do you and her father give her your permission?' My parents agreed. I still have the letter they wrote to him," she says wistfully. The sentiment behind her words is so tender it melts my heart.

"Mother called me out of the kitchen and Paramahansaji told me the news. 'Your parents have given their consent for you to come to Mount Washington, and I too want you to come.' I was ecstatic! My sister and I started jumping up and down, dancing for joy."

She lifts her gaze and looks back seventy years to the young girl she once was. "Oh, those were happy days!" she exclaims. My eyes unexpectedly fill with tears.

"Paramahansaji stayed in Salt Lake for two more weeks giving classes. He took the train, and I drove with another of his disciples to Los Angeles in the little green Ford they had at that time. Mount Washington has been my home—my blessed home—ever since."

I smile at her, for her. She is so utterly content, so at home within herself. This teaching is her life, it has become who she is. But in 1931 when she first heard Yogananda speak, awareness of Eastern spirituality was not what it is today. I'm curious as to how she knew this was the right path for her.

"Paramahansaji had what I wanted; he loved God as I had always longed to love Him. He did not just talk or write about God, he was steeped in love for God and lived it in every aspect of his life. I saw it in the way he treated others, in his deep understanding and compassion—and in the expression on his face whenever I would come upon him unannounced and find him quietly communing with God. In the more than twenty years I was with him, I never once entered his presence when I did not see him engrossed in the bliss and love of God."

She moves from the realm of her own experience to share counsel given to her by Yogananda on this issue: "Paramahansaji used to advise that in the beginning of one's spiritual search, it's wise to compare various paths and teachers. But once you find teachings you feel attuned to, that you know will bring you to God, you should stay with that path. And this is what I did."

Yogananda passed away in 1952. Is it different for you now that he's no longer alive?

"I resolved long ago that he would never be only a dream or a memory to me. He is as real to me now as he ever was; I feel no separation. He once told me, 'When I am gone, you will know me more than when I was here.' I have found this to be true not just for me, but for anyone who sincerely follows his teachings, for anyone who strives to remain close to him in thought and action. Great saints do not need a physical body in order to bless and guide those who are attuned to them. Paramahansa Yogananda's presence is strong for those who keep him in their hearts."

Once you met Yogananda and accepted him as your guru, he guided your spiritual journey. Was there anyone else—a mentor, perhaps—who influenced your life?

"Before I came into the ashram, my mother was my mentor. I adored her. She was everything a mother could be. Paramahansaji used to call her 'The Great Mother.' Everyone came to her with their problems because she had such compassion and kindness. It was she who first nurtured my relationship with God.

"In my early years in the ashram, and whenever Paramahansaji was traveling, Sister Gyanamata was my mentor. She was one of his earliest disciples—a very saintly example of wisdom and humility from whom I received much inspiration."

Daya Mata writes freely in her books about some of the "dark nights" she's faced, and how her faith has sustained her during difficult times. I ask her now about these experiences.

"I don't think anyone lives their life without going through periods of suffering. I've had mine, though I have never had that struggle, an inner dark night of the soul, in relation to my spiritual life. I've never, at any moment, been tested to the point of wanting to leave the spiritual path. That does not enter into my consciousness. Whatever comes, I fight through it because I know God will help me. The one thing I could not bear would be to feel a separation from Him. That would be intolerable for me. The search for God, love for God, is my life.

"I found that the way to overcome suffering is to go back to the Source of all comfort and strength. Look into your own soul, into the reflection of God within you. Call God by any name you choose but call on Him, rely more on Him. Look to Him for the perfection you seek in the external things of the world, and in your relationships with others. People cannot give us the perfect love and support we crave. How can we expect from others what we ourselves cannot give, what only God can give?"

The world is changing so rapidly now. To put our faith in external things, transitory things, seems almost illogical.

"Yes, we are entering an age where having an inner life will be important in order to cope with all the external change. I think this is why we now see so many people hungering for spirituality. Change is not something to be frightened of though. Change is a part of growth."

What role do you think women will play in all this, in what some now call a "spiritual renaissance"?

"Women have come into their own in many ways, and their compassionate influence is needed. But Paramahansaji taught that men and women are equals. Woman did not inherit half a soul from man; she is whole within herself. Man is also whole within himself. Both are reflections of God, both express His nature in different ways. In woman, God made feeling more predominant; in man, He made reason uppermost. This doesn't mean that woman shouldn't develop her intellect or that man shouldn't become more gentle or sensitive. Men and women are meant to be helpmates, working together as divine friends, as divine companions, to help each other become more balanced within themselves. This is part of the divine purpose of marriage, of every relationship between man and woman. Neither should try to control or dominate the other."

Daya Mata tells me about a conversation she had many years ago with the famous conductor Leopold Stokowski that illustrates, what was for them, an ideal example of this internal marriage of masculine and feminine qualities.

"Mr. Stokowski was a student of Paramahansa Yogananda and he would visit Mount Washington sometimes when he was in Los Angeles. Once we were talking about the teachings and he said, 'You know, I have such admiration for Paramahansaji. He combines in perfect balance the qualities of a man and of a woman. That is what I want to develop in myself.' I thought how true that is. When one draws close to God, one reflects all of His qualities. There is a blending of compassion and wisdom, feeling and reason. It's one of the things that draws us to great souls for it represents the balance each of us is meant to achieve."

I heard a story about Sri Daya Mata in this regard, one that reflects her own internal balance. She was at a social gathering, perhaps a banquet honoring a visiting Indian dignitary, talking with a woman of some renown, listening to her, present to her as if the two of them were the only people in the world. During their conversation, Daya Mata received a phone call that required her immediate attention. She excused herself to take the call, and negotiated the business at hand with the skill and demeanor of a CEO of an international organization that, indeed, she is. She then returned to her companion and, once again, began to minister all the motherly compassion the woman seemed to need. What stood out to the person who told me this story—and to me when I heard it—was that in each situation, Daya Mata effortlessly and expertly acted from that aspect of her nature that best met the demands of the moment.

More than two hours have passed since we began our conversation and Daya Mata is as present to me as I imagine she was to the woman in that story, as I trust she is to others. All too soon, our time together will end and her assistants will deftly squire her out the door. She will look back at me over her shoulder and say, with a gleam in her eye, "Now, if you have any more questions, dear, don't hesitate to ask." The glee in her voice makes me smile. The example of her kindness stirs me to greater kindness.

That good-bye is still an hour away. I ask her now if she has any advice she'd like to share with others?

"Find a spiritual path that brings God close to you, that you feel in tune with, and then remain steadfast on that path. Daily meditation, deep communion with God, is also important, even more important than prayer, because it helps you draw close to God. Having a personal relationship with Him doesn't mean you have to give up everything. But it does mean you must take more control over what you do with your life. So keep it simple. Cut out things that waste time. Analyze yourself and your habits and decide what you want to change. Ask yourself what you can do to bring more happiness into your own life and the lives of others—especially your children."

Daya Mata's childhood developed in her a deep regard for family life. "I'm so grateful," she says earnestly, "for the loving care my mother gave all four of her children. I remember too, how my father used to take us fishing each summer in the canyons around Salt Lake. He made us each a fishing pole with a string—but no hook!—and we sat at the edge of the pond and dangled the line in the water. It was very simple but those were marvelous times. There is so much joy in being together as a family. We need to get back to that, to reclaim our family life again."

She lifts a hand to her heart and says, "There has been such a forsaking of children today. It's a tragedy. Children aren't turtles that go off into the water and swim away once they're born! They have to be nurtured. It's the job of both parents to do that; neither parent should sacrifice their children for their career.

"Parents don't need to spend all their time with their children but I do think they need to talk with them, give them love and understanding, and do things together. Tell them little stories about being truthful, about sharing and being unselfish. And bring God into the discussion. Help them feel like they can come to you, that they don't have to hide anything from you. If your own experience of family life was not a good one, then take some classes and learn how to be a good parent. It's that important," she says adamantly.

Yogananda personally prepared her to guide the work of his society after his passing, and under her direction, his teachings have spread to more than fifty countries around the world. Given all she has achieved, I ask her what she thinks is her greatest accomplishment.

She looks down at her hands resting quietly in her lap and says, "Oh, I don't think I've accomplished very much. I've just endeavored to serve Paramahansaji's work. The work is going well; we've managed to spread his spiritual message throughout the world. I wish I could do more."

Out of the corner of my eye, I catch the expression on the face of a young nun sitting near me, an admixture of amazement and gratitude at what Daya Mata has done to preserve and spread the teachings they both love. I turn to her and ask if she has any thoughts about what Daya Mata just said.

Respectfully, reverentially, she looks at Daya Mata and declares, "Ma, the example of your life has transformed thousands of lives."

"But I don't think of myself in that way," Daya Mata replies. "I hope I touch the lives of others. I have a deep love for people. But I'm happy just loving God. Maybe that sounds simplistic, but it's what really matters to me." The sincerity and humility in her voice are palpable.

I hesitate for a moment. It seems unnecessary to ask my last question—how she would like to be remembered—given what she just said.

"Anything else?" she asks. I just shake my head.

"We've covered a lot. I hope I've managed to answer your questions."

She smiles and rises from her chair. We all stand in deference to her. Though I have kept this conversation on track for three hours, I am now speechless. She takes a few moments with each of us. When my turn comes, I manage some words of thanks. Then she is gone.

But she stays with me still.

To Learn More About the Life and Work of
Sri Daya Mata

Contact:
Self-Realization Fellowship
3880 San Rafael Avenue
Los Angeles, California 90065
Voice: (323) 225-2471
Fax: (323) 225-5088
On the Web: www.yogananda-srf.org

Read:
A complete catalog of publications and audio and video cassettes, including works in English, Spanish, French, German, Italian, Portuguese, Dutch, Japanese, Indian dialects, and other languages is available from Self-Realization Fellowship upon request.
* *Autobiography of a Yogi*, Paramahansa Yogananda
* *Only Love: Living the Spiritual Life in a Changing World*
* *Finding the Joy Within You: Personal Counsel for God-Centered Living*
* *Enter the Quiet Heart: Creating a Loving Relationship with God*
* *A World in Transition: Finding Spiritual Security in Times of Change*, Paramahansa Yogananda, Daya Mata and the monks and nuns of Self-Realization Fellowship
* *How to Change Others*
* *The Skilled Profession of Child-Rearing*
* *Overcoming Character Liabilities*
* *Intuition: Soul Guidance for Life's Lessons*
* *Self-Realization* magazine

View:
* *Him I Shall Follow*
* *Security in a World of Change*
* *Living in the Love of God*

Listen:

- *My Spirit Shall Live On: The Final Days of Paramahansa Yogananda*
- *Moral Courage: Effecting Positive Change Through Our Moral and Spiritual Choices*
- *Free Yourself from Tension*
- *Karma Yoga*
- *God First*
- *Understanding the Soul's Need for God*
- *Let Us Be Thankful*
- *Anchoring Your Life in God*
- *Is Meditation on God Compatible with Modern Life?*
- *A Heart Aflame*
- *Living a God-Centered Life*

EPILOGUE

Come, come, whoever you are—wanderer, worshipper, lover of leaving—it doesn't matter. Ours is not a caravan of despair. Come even if you have broken your vow a thousand times. Come, come yet again, come.

—Rumi

When I was six years old I wrote the following poem:

I wish I were a lion,
The king of all the beasts.
I'd have a great big party
And invite everyone to the feast.

Not a terribly profound little ditty, I grant you, but one that unleashed a host of dazzling possibilities in the heart of this first grader. It was exciting to be inspired, to venture beyond the confines of my reading primer. But it was sublime to create something, to give an idea, a feeling, life. When Mrs. Matimoe asked me to read my poem to the rest of the class, well—I was on top of the world.

Today, as I busied myself with loose ends relating to the completion of this book, this little verse leapt out from behind some long untenanted chamber of my mind, and I was aware that the years had conferred it with new meaning. I understood that, like the women featured in these pages, the more we cultivate our relationship with Spirit, the more lion-hearted we become. We exhibit a greater willingness to reign over our inner beasts. We push the edge of our envelopes. We refuse to take "no" for an answer. We stand and walk in our truth. We honor our vulnerability. We make mistakes again and again, but we pick ourselves up and rejoice in what we are learning. We cultivate love. As our relationship with Spirit deepens, we

239

want to share our hard-won expansion of consciousness with others, invite everyone to the "feast." Ultimately, if we play our cards right, we become "kings"—authentic human beings, spiritual beings, beings of love and wisdom, strength and joy.

In Sweet Company has been my way of inviting you to my feast, some of the remarkable moments of clarity and exaltation that are turning this little lamb into a lion. I am so very glad you could come to my party.

ACKNOWLEDGMENTS

This book has literally been loved into the world, not just by me but by all those who have supported my efforts and who visibly and invisibly gathered round me in anticipation of its coming. Hardly a day went by when someone did not call or e-mail or stop me on the street and say, "How's the book going, Margaret?" This support buoyed my spirits and nourished me in the very solitary moments that, against all odds, brought this book into being. I am immeasurably grateful for every kindness that has come to me in this regard.

I wish to thank Alma Flor Ada, Lauren Artress, Sri Daya Mata, Olympia Dukakis, Katherine Dunham, Riane Eisler, Laura Geller, Le Ly Hayslip, Grandmother Twylah Hurd, Nitsch, Miriam Polster, Sister Helen Prejean, Zainab Salbi, Margaret Wheatley, and Gail Williamson—women who welcomed me into their lives as a stranger then opened their hearts to me as a friend. Who you are has helped make me more of whom I have always longed to be.

To your support persons who survived my endless pestering with grace—F. Isabel Campoy, Sarah Eames, Bonnie Kramen, Lauren Landress and the monks and nuns of Self-Realization Fellowship, Sister Margaret Maggio, Dawn Montcrief, Bob and Lee Nitsch , Erving Polster, and Madeline Preston—I extend my heartfelt appreciation for the example of your kindness and your professionalism.

To Denise Hornbeak, Dr. John Harrison, and Dr. David Olsen, confederates who keep me in motion as I lumbered to create new neural pathways in my brain, I offer my admiration and gratitude. Your skill as clinicians is surpassed only by the elegant quality of your hearts.

I am indebted to Lucinda Lawton, who painstakingly transcribed the audio tapes of these conversations into written form; to Paula Goldbeck, Caroline Hobson, and Kim Moreno, who initially read this manuscript and gave me their inspired and resourceful feedback; and to Diana Ong for her beautiful image on the book cover. My deepest thanks to Sheryl Fullerton, my editor at Jossey-Bass, who recognized this book for what it is and what it could be and ushered it into the embrace of more hearts than even I could imagine.

For their faith in me and their willingness to put their resources where their heart is, I wish to thank Walter Cruttenden, Jo Ann and Dick Goodrich, and Sherry Sweet. Your gifts honored me and taught me much about the joy of receiving.

Many thanks to Vivian Mueller, the first person to believe in this book, and to my trusty Posse—Janene Drilling, Doug Glener, Carla Green, Andrew Greenfield, Sue Herner, Rowena and John Jackson, Peter La Barbara, Jeffrey Quillin, Silvia Reyes, Edie and Paul Sanchez, Juanita Scott, Diane Shepard, Steffie and Jimmy Zack, and Margot Watkins and the indomitable women of the Gift Shop—great souls who supported me in ways too numerous to mention and gave me counsel and the best of themselves whenever I needed an infusion of clarity and goodness.

I wish also to thank my daughters, Julie Gidion-Smith and Janey Gidion, whose practical advice, unique brilliance, and faith in me fills my heart. And to my husband, Jonathan, who made it possible for me to do this work in more ways than I can ever name, I offer my deepest gratitude. Thank you.

To all of you who will find the way to your best selves in these pages, I am grateful for what you will become through your own efforts and I rejoice in your homecoming.

PERMISSIONS

I would like to acknowledge and thank the following photographers for allowing me to use their work: Brian Folk for the photograph of Le Ly Hayslip, Tony Maddox for the photograph of Gail Williamson, Robin Rosenzweig for the photograph of Riane Eisler, Edie Sanchez for the photograph of Katherine Dunham, Samantha Schoeller for the photograph of Zainab Salbi, Self-Realization Fellowship for the photograph of Sri Daya Mata, and Julie Gidion-Smith for the photograph of Margaret Wolff and grandsons.

Permission to use the photographs of Alma Flor Ada, Lauren Artress, Olympia Dukakis, Laura Geller, Grandmother Twylah Hurd Nitsch, Sister Helen Prejean, and Margaret Wheatley were given by them for use in this book. Permission to use the photograph of Miriam Polster was given by Erving Polster.

I also want to pay tribute to all the writers and thinkers whose words and ideas were mentioned in these pages. Your thoughts added greatly to the clarity and power of these conversations.

Every effort was made to contact the copyright holders to obtain permission to use the quotes in this book. If any work has been inadvertently used without permission, I extend my apology. Please contact me so that due credit can be given to you in future editions of this book.

The following quotations all fall within the realm of fair use: William Blake from *Blake: Complete Writings;* Jean-Pierre de Caussade from *Abandonment to Divine Providence;* Empedocks's last treatise as quoted in *Roman de la Rose;* Dorothea Dix from *Heart's Work: Civil War Heroine and Champion of the Mentally Ill, Dorothea Dix;* Kahlil Gibran from *The Prophet;* Henry Wadsworth Longfellow from *Resignations;* Rumi from an inscription on his tomb; William Shakespeare from *Henry VI;* Alfred, Lord Tennyson from *In Memorium A.H.H.;* Mark Twain from *Joan of Arc;* and the Bible.

ABOUT THE AUTHOR

Margaret Wolff, M.A., is a journalist, storyteller, and trainer. She has degrees in art therapy, psychosynthesis, and leadership and human behavior. Her twenty-five-year career includes writing for numerous national and international publications, facilitating over five hundred workshops and retreats, and speaking at conferences throughout the United States. She is a principle trainer, a cofounder of the Anjali Foundation, and on the faculty at University of San Diego, Leadership and Education Sciences Program. Her work provides models, skills, and inspiration that help others connect to their innate wisdom and integrate their most deeply held values into their daily lives.

Margaret lives in Southern California with her husband, Jonathan. Her daughters, son-in-law, and two grandsons all live within an arm's reach.

INDEX

Index

Index

Index

Index

right brain, 75
Runes, 80

sacred, 23–25, 68–69, 71, 74, 84, 99, 111,
   116, 120, 163, 173–174, 182, 193
salvation, 98, 210
satsang, 60
science, 68, 115, 170, 173, 175–176, 182, 208
scripture, 200
second-hand religion, 73
self-actualization, 176
Self-Realization Fellowship, 220, 222, 226
selflessness, 54
Seneca, 20–23, 30, 32
service, 26, 36, 61, 70, 78, 211, 226–227
shadow, 79–80
silence, 8, 11, 23, 52, 54, 58, 60, 84, 112,
   184, 189, 228
sister, 1–5, 7–8, 10, 12, 57, 210, 213–214,
   224, 229–231
social justice, 3, 9, 15, 188, 192
Sophia, 71
soul, 15, 25, 29, 41, 47, 52–54, 56, 62, 68–69,
   71, 73, 78–82, 95, 100, 127, 130, 138,
   148, 154, 159, 170, 182, 197–198, 204,
   213–214, 223–225, 227, 232
soul assignment, 81–82
Spirit, 4, 6, 23, 36, 44, 52, 54, 56, 58, 61,
   68–69, 71, 74–76, 78–79, 82, 100, 125,
   139, 149, 163, 170, 175, 177, 182, 184,
   221, 228
spiritual eye, 228
spiritual practice, 47, 55–56, 58, 75, 80,
   110–111, 127, 164, 175, 177, 227
spirituality, 6, 15, 38–40, 58, 60, 71, 88–89,
   95, 97–99, 107, 110–111, 138–139, 157,
   158, 164, 175, 182, 188, 196, 230, 232
stability, 24, 176
Starbird, Margaret, 90
stillness, 14, 60, 225, 228
Stokowski, Leopold, 233
Stone, Merlin, 88, 93, 100
story/stories, 11–13, 17, 28, 30, 43–44, 46,
   51–52, 59, 62–63, 74, 79, 87, 90–91,
   96, 99–100, 106–107, 111, 115, 119,
   121, 123–124, 131, 136–138, 140,
   142–145, 175, 181, 193–194, 197–198,
   215–216, 223, 233–234
strength, 14, 42, 118, 124, 144–145, 199,
   209, 213–214, 232

study, 20, 37, 44, 46, 154, 158, 167, 170,
   175, 188, 193, 198, 200, 211, 222, 226
success, 5, 17, 48, 63, 101, 118, 166, 200, 215
suffering, 4–5, 9, 12–16, 61, 112, 114,
   128–129, 142–143, 176, 180, 225, 232
surrender, 7
Swami Paramananda, 94–95

Talmud, 193–194
terrarium existence, 6
therapy, 36, 40, 44–45, 86, 91, 100, 156, 216
Tibetan Buddhism, 170, 175, 180
tikkum olam, 188
Torah, 189, 192–193, 195–198, 200–201
transformation, 10, 74, 87, 89, 96, 99, 117,
   182–183, 195
trust, 6, 9, 12–13, 46, 56, 82–83, 95, 141, 176,
   233
truth, 14, 24–29, 92, 127, 167, 179, 182, 226

unconscious, 71, 224
unity, 15, 23–27, 68, 170, 173
user, 31

Vedanta, 87, 92
Vibral Core, 23–24
victim, 61, 128, 143, 176
vulnerability, 89, 100, 136

war, 86, 106, 122, 128, 136, 140–141, 144,
   146, 155, 158, 188
Watsu, 58–59
wholeness, 26, 28–29, 68, 74–75, 77, 82, 210
will power, 100, 229
wisdom, 16, 20, 24, 30, 40–41, 46, 71–72,
   96, 105, 189, 223, 231, 233
women, 2–3, 5, 8, 13, 35, 40–42, 45–46, 53,
   55, 60, 70, 72–73, 75, 80–81, 86–88,
   90–92, 95–100, 106–107, 109, 111, 115,
   116, 122–123, 127, 135–138, 141–149,
   153, 155–156, 178, 187–188, 190–191,
   194–198, 214, 220–221, 227, 232
Wordsworth, William, 43

YHWH, 199
yoga, 98, 220, 226, 228
Yoga Sutras of Patanjali, 226
Yogananda, Paramahansa, 60, 219–223, 226,
   228, 230–231, 233–234

Zen, 8

In Sweet Company Retreats, Workshops, and Keynotes

There is a renaissance going on, a grassroots spiritual revolution spearheaded by women of all ages, faiths, and backrounds—women who are gathering in coffeehouses and conference rooms to share their stories, to explore their options, and to give and receive support.

Margaret Wolff's programs provide models, skills, and inspiration that help women respond to their innate wisdom and integrate their most deeply held values into their lives, no matter what their spiritual tradition. Personal reflection, interactive exercises, storytelling, and excerpts from *In Sweet Company* are used as stepping-stones to self-exploration.

Programs include

Women in Spirit: The Emerging Face of Women's Spirituality A new vision of power—one that champions diversity, collaboration, and connection—has emerged. Trace the roots of this movement, historically and within your own life, and discover direction for the future.

Listening to Your Inner Voice There is a still, small voice, an internal guide, an intuitive knowing within you that can align you with an inner wellspring beyond logic, beyond "shoulds," beyond strategizing. Connect to that unfailing source of decision making and transform the anxiety of not knowing into self-trust.

Spirit at Work: Making Your Work and Your Life Be About What You Value Most Take stock of your knowledge, skills, achievements, resources, and dreams, and reframe the direction of your work and life in ways that feed your soul.

Women as Peacemakers Move beyond the compelling images of global wounding and experience what the mystics of all religions tell us: we are wedded to each other—undeniably bound—as the varied expressions of a singular and loving consciousness. Nurture your inner peacemaker and explore options for global peacemaking.

To schedule a program or speaking engagement, learn where Margaret Wolff is speaking, or sign up for the *In Sweet Company Newsletter*, visit www.insweetcompany.com.

WHAT OTHERS ARE SAYING

"I laughed, I cried, I was silent, I cheered. Most of all, I loved."

"I had the intense experience that I had finally found someone who could speak to what I have been experiencing for my entire life."

"Margaret Wolff's eloquence was a highlight of our program."